NTC's *Basic* JAPANESE

LEVEL 2

NTC's *Basic* JAPANESE

LYNN WILLIAMS

National Textbook Company
a division of NTC/CONTEMPORARY PUBLISHING GROUP
Lincolnwood, Illinois USA

All cover photos courtesy of Japan National Tourist Organization.

CONTENTS

INTRODUCTION

NTC's Basic Japanese is the product of years of experience presenting the Japanese language in classrooms around the world and aims at responding to the widely felt need for a truly communicative Japanese textbook series. The resulting textbooks thus provide a variety of lively, stimulating, communicative activities that will help students acquire a firm foundation in Japanese and motivate them to continue their study of the language.

Level 2 consolidates previously learned structures and works to extend students' discussion, listening and questioning skills. Five Topics are covered: Shopping; My Town; Eating and Drinking; Leisure, Sports and Hobbies; and Travel. Each of the Topics is further divided into specific Units, which provide considerable lesson plan flexibility for teachers, depending on the amount of class time at their disposal. The textbook has been designed to be completed within one year, though the sample practice material and extension activities provided will enable teachers to extend the course beyond a year if needed.

Level 2 moves students away from tightly structured practice into more independent use of what they have learned. It extends the process of real discussion and conversation, allowing students to take part in open-ended situations in which they are making a genuine contribution, and through which their real opinions, within the limits of their present knowledge of vocabulary and structures, can be expressed. All aspects of the lesson material, including grammar, vocabulary, cultural information, and reading and writing activities, are designed for a communicative teaching environment.

Teachers and students alike will find this textbook both accessible and convenient to use. All Topics are presented in such a way that students may easily review and practice material on their own. The textbook also aims at accommodating a variety of learning styles and approaches, thus enabling students to work through material at their own pace, with ample opportunity for review and mastery. The exercises in the course also contribute to the goal of relative autonomy and can be completed by students with little assistance from an instructor. They are also designed to uncover any problems students may be having, so they can then ask for help on these points.

Detailed explanatory notes on grammar and usage enable this text to be used as a self-study book, when that approach is necessary.

Teachers will notice that certain grammatical items are introduced only partially. This technique helps students develop an intuitive knowledge of usage, before they go more deeply into the complexities of a particular structure or pattern. The author has done her best to avoid jargon or linguistic labels, since students grasp grammatical structures more easily and quickly without the use of such language. At the same time, those seeking to attain a more academic level can easily substitute more advanced grammatical labels, where necessary.

Units move at a pace designed to insure that students make real progress in communication. In addition, numerous extension activities vary routines, as well as provide material for review and reinforcement.

Activities and exercises encourage *individual* work and augment the role plays and group work. Regardless of their length, activities provide students with the opportunity to communicate normally without long preparation.

While great care has been taken to insure that all the basics normally covered are dealt with in this course, each unit also provides a rich variety of materials and activities to amplify the basics and to allow teachers and their students the flexibility to suit their own time, pace, and classroom situation. At first glance, some activities may appear too simple. Nonetheless, in practice, they have proven to reinforce with considerable effectiveness the areas they were designed to review. Teachers will also be delighted to learn that the textbook allows for a variety of individual teaching styles. The wide range of activities provided in each Topic encourages teachers to personalize material by means of their own methods and approaches.

Hiragana, introduced in *Level 1*, is continually reviewed in *Level 2*, while Katakana is gradually introduced. The option is given of teaching Katakana from a chart or in groups of syllables, in order to avoid confusion over characters that are similar in shape. Numerous review items, along with checkpoints, are given to help students master the syllabaries gradually, completely, and enthusiastically.

The language taught throughout the course is generally colloquial and in daily use. However, you may find that better and more popular ways exist to express certain ideas. Nevertheless, given the controlled grammar and vocabulary in the course, the author has chosen to stress the more practical and manageable structures. At the end of the course, students will have a solid base for practical communication and will have been equipped to take on more complex colloquial forms and more extended grammar. Also, after completing *Level 2*, students should be able to write and read Katakana as well as Hiragana. Students are expected to read and understand passages written in both syllabaries; however, all passages presented in Kana are also given in Roomaji for self-correction. Review exercises are offered in Roomaji for the sake of efficiency, and more Kanji is presented for interest.

A vocabulary checklist appears at the end of the book, in addition to Hiragana and Katakana tables, puzzle solutions, and other reference items.

FURTHER READING

Benedek, Dezso and Junko Majima. *EasyKana*. Knoxville: The HyperGlot Software Company. (A software program for Hiragana and Katakana practice.)

Benedek, Dezso and Junko Majima. *KanjiMaster*. Knoxville: The HyperGlot Software Company. (A software program for Kanji practice.)

De Mente, Boye. *Discovering Cultural Japan*. Lincolnwood, IL: Passport Books. (A travel companion that explains key Japanese cultural traits – and how to best enjoy Japan.)

De Mente, Boye. *Everything Japanese*. Lincolnwood, IL: Passport Books. (A comprehensive A to Z Encyclopedic overview of all things Japanese.)

Kaneda, Fujihiko. *Easy Hiragana*. Lincolnwood, IL: Passport Books. (A comprehensive worktext for practicing Hiragana.)

Kataoka, Hiroko C. and Tetsuya Kusumoto. *Japanese Cultural Encounters*. Lincolnwood, IL: Passport Books. (More than 50 cultural situations are presented in a problem solving format.)

Lampkin, Rita and Osamu Hoshino. *Easy Kana Workbook*. Lincolnwood, IL: Passport Books. (Provides Hiragana and Katakana practice along with Japanese sentence building.)

Schwarz, Edward A. and Reiko Ezawa. *Everyday Japanese*. Lincolnwood, IL: Passport Books. (Book and audiocassette language program with many cultural notes and illustrated vocabulary.)

Walsh, Len. *Read Japanese Today*. Tokyo: Tuttle Books. (Explains Kanji origins, meanings, readings, and examples of usage.)

Welch, Theodore F. and Hiroki Kato. *Japan Today!* Lincolnwood, IL: Passport Books. (A concise A to Z compendium covering all aspects of Japanese culture, society, and customs. Also includes an audiocassette.)

Wells, Tina and Aoi Yokouchi. *Easy Katakana*. Lincolnwood, IL: Passport Books. (A comprehensive worktext for practicing Katakana.)

Introduction

ACHIEVEMENTS

By the end of this topic, you will be able to:
- ask for things you want in shops;
- ask prices and understand prices given to you;
- know the names of some kinds of shops;
- write some *katakana* syllables.

かいもの   *Kaimono*   **Shopping**

Shopping in Japan is exciting. Shops are open every day, keep long hours, and the variety of goods available is mind-boggling. Although many tourists believe Japan is expensive, that is not necessarily so. There are many magnificent, exclusive, expensive shops but there are also thousands upon thousands of cheaper department stores, supermarkets and small family-owned businesses competing for trade. Many tourists are taken to the exclusive shopping areas like the Ginza in Tokyo and never have the opportunity to wander in the less fashionable areas, going away with a false impression of Japan's prices.

It also, of course, depends on what you want to buy. If you are on a slender budget and want to buy souvenirs to take home, Japan is a marvelous place. There are countless souvenir objects selling from a few cents upwards, that to foreigners are interesting, different and cute, such as chopsticks, special foods from particular areas of the country, handmade papers, interesting crafts, blessings and amulets from temples and shrines, and unusual things like bamboo ear cleaners! There are myriad souvenirs in every temple, shrine and town and an incredible number of keyring shops!

It is not only visitors who buy the souvenirs. When Japanese people go away for a break to another part of the country, they see it as a duty to return with gifts for all their friends who have not been so privileged. They take lots of photos too, to be able to share their holiday with those less fortunate, to give them a little bit of the experience they themselves have enjoyed. This is particularly true if they go overseas, but is important within Japan, too.

いらっしゃいませ   *Irasshaimase*   **Welcome**

Shops open about ten o'clock in the morning and close about seven o'clock at night or later for six days a week, including Saturday and Sunday, and are usually closed on one weekday. Often the shops in one area will choose the same day to close.

One of the things enjoyed by visitors is to stand outside a department store to watch the opening of the store for the day. In many department stores, before the outside shutters are raised, the staff line up behind the manager in order of seniority and as the shutters are raised they chorus **Irasshaimase** to the first customers. This means "welcome" and it is important to the morale of the store that they get good spending customers as their first customers to set the good fortune for the day. In some stores staff line up at the end of the day too, to say goodbye to the last customers.

Every time you enter even the smallest shop you will be greeted by *Irasshaimase*. The doormen say it literally thousands of times a day in big stores. As you leave they say **"Maido arigatoo gozaimashita"** – literally "Thank you for every time," meaning "Thank you for shopping here." This is an encouragement for you to return and shop there again.

Special shopping areas

In Tokyo there are lots of specialty areas for shopping. For example, if you want electrical goods, you go to **Akihabara**. Many of the shops there are discount shops, but the main value of the area is that it has such a vast range of all things electrical. It is one of the few places in Japan where you can bargain. Because Japanese people on the whole like to have the most up-to-date appliances, last year's models can often be bought very cheaply. In general though, prices are in line with prices elsewhere, and the shops have very little leeway for discounting because of price controls.

Shinjuku is the area of Tokyo for cheap watches, calculators, and cameras.

Harajuku is the place most teenagers enjoy because of its boutiques and interesting toy and souvenir ships. On Sundays, the streets of Harajuku, closed to traffic from one pm, are thronged with young people listening and dancing to pop music, showing off their prowess on skateboards and rollerskates, parading their latest fashions, having their fortunes told, and buying from the street vendors as well as the shops. It is a lively, fun place to be on other days, too. The Oriental Bazaar there has a tremendous range of reasonably priced souvenirs of all kinds. For many visitors Harajuku is a one-stop shopping and sightseeing place, as there are several beautiful temples and shrines there too, notably the Meiji shrine with its peaceful park (*Meiji jinguu*).

There are also interesting second-hand shops there that sell wedding and other kimonos, *koinobori* carp streamers, festival banners (and western style clothes) at a fraction of their original cost. You may not want to buy wedding kimonos but it's interesting to look at these magnificently woven examples of traditional Japanese clothing.

デパート   **DEPAATO**   **Department stores**
Japan has some of the world's largest department stores, with record numbers of customers daily. In Japan, the most expensive floor is always the ground floor (which the Japanese call the first floor). Often there is a bargain sale floor or part of a floor at the top of the building where discounted goods from all departments are sold. Twice a year department stores have huge sales in all departments.

Vending machines
Automatic vending machines are a feature of Japan, too. They sell a large range of both hot and cold drinks, alcoholic beverages, and food. In addition, machines sell things like toothbrushes, small towels and shampoo, cigarettes, books and magazines, batteries, toys, and even bags of rice.

Currency
Japanese currency is the yen (**en** in Japanese), the symbol of which is ¥. There are bank notes (**satsu**) of 10,000, 5,000, and 1,000 yen and coins of 500, 100, 50, 10, 5 and 1 yen.

The one-yen coins are made of aluminum and are light and virtually useless. The five-yen is however very special. It is made of brass, has a hole in the middle and is traditionally the good luck coin for relationships. The ten-yen coin is brass. The fifty-yen coin also has a hole in the middle, but like the hundred-yen coin is silver in color as is the five-hundred yen coin.

The most useful coins for vending machines and telephones are the 100-yen and the ten-yen, though many of the vending machines, particularly in stations, give change from notes as well as coins.

Audio store in Shinjuku (top left)
Shopping on Sundays (right)
Marui department store (left)

Dancing in Harajuku (top left)
A TV sales promotion (lower left)
Calling customers to an appliance store in Akihabara (top right)
Elevator hostess welcoming customers (lower right)

Unit 1

これ は いくら です か
kore wa ikura desu ka
How much is this?

NEW WORDS

いらっしゃいませ	*irasshaimase*	welcome
みせ の ひと	*mise no hito*	store clerk
おきゃくさん	*okyakusan*	customer
みせ	*mise*	shop, store
ひゃく	*hyaku*	one hundred
にひゃく	*nihyaku*	two hundred
さんびゃく	*sanbyaku*	three hundred
よんひゃく	*yonhyaku*	four hundred
ごひゃく	*gohyaku*	five hundred
ろっぴゃく	*roppyaku*	six hundred
ななひゃく	*nanahyaku*	seven hundred
はっぴゃく	*happyaku*	eight hundred
きゅうひゃく	*kyuuhyaku*	nine hundred
せん	*sen*	one thousand
にせん	*nisen*	two thousand
さんぜん	*sanzen*	three thousand
よんせん	*yonsen*	four thousand
ごせん	*gosen*	five thousand
ろくせん	*rokusen*	six thousand
ななせん	*nanasen*	seven thousand
はっせん	*hassen*	eight thousand
きゅうせん	*kyuusen*	nine thousand
まん	*man*	ten thousand
いちまん	*ichiman*	ten thousand
みせて	*misete*	show
おつり	*Otsuri*	change
とけい	*tokei*	watch/clock
まいど ありがとう	*maido arigatoo*	Thank you for shopping
ございました	*gozaimashita*	here
えん	*en*	yen
ドル	*DORU*	dollar
セント	*SENTO*	cents
それ では ありません	*sore dewa arimasen*	not that one

Interest

てんいん	*ten'in*	(another word for "store clerk")

A customer is shopping in a department store.

み　stands for みせ　の　ひと (*mise no hito*)
お　stands for おきゃくさん (*Okyakusan*)

み　いらっしゃいませ。

お　おはよう　ございます。それ　を　みせて　ください。

み　これ　です　か。

お　それ　では　ありません。
　　それ　を　ください。

み　ああ　そう　…どうぞ。いい　とけい　です　ね。

お　はい、いくら　です　か。

み　ななせん　えん　です。

お　いい　です。これ　を　ください。

み　ありがとう。ななせん　えん　です。
　　おつり　は　さんぜん　えん　です。どうぞ。

お　ありがとう。

み　まいど　ありがとう　ございました。

M:　*Irasshaimase.*
O:　*Ohayoo gozaimasu. Sore o misete kudasai.*
M:　*Kore desu ka.*
O:　*Sore dewa arimasen. Sore o kudasai.*
M:　*Aa soo . . . doozo. Ii tokei desu ne.*
O:　*Hai, ikura desu ka.*
M:　*Nanasen en desu.*
O:　*Ii desu. Kore o kudasai.*
(The customer hands the clerk a 10,000-yen note)
M:　*Arigatoo. Nanasen en desu. Otsuri wa sanzen en desu. Doozo.*
(The change is counted out from large denominations down to small and put on a saucer in front of the customer, who does not attempt to check it, trusting that it will always be correct.)
O:　*Arigatoo.*
M:　*Maido arigatoo gozaimashita.*

Check your understanding of the conversation.

M: Welcome.
O: Good morning. Please show me that.
M: This?
O: No, not that. That one, please.
M: Oh . . . here you are. It's a good watch, isn't it?
O: Yes, how much is it?
M: Seven thousand yen.
O: That's good. I'll take it.
M: Thank you. That's seven thousand yen. The change is three thousand yen. Here you are.
O: Thank you.
M: Thanks for shopping here.

百
千
万

Kanji numbers (for interest only)

In shopping situations you will mostly see amounts written in Arabic numbers (1, 2, 3 etc). However, some shops, restaurants, and some of the more exclusive shops selling things like kimono, state their prices in *kanji*. So recognizing the *kanji* can be fun and sometimes useful, too.

一	二	三	四	五	六	七	八	九	十
1	**2**	**3**	**4**	**5**	**6**	**7**	**8**	**9**	**10**

百	千	万
100	**1,000**	**10,000**

Here are some numbers written in *kanji*:

27	二十七		150	百五十
84	八十四		235	二百三十五
467	四百六十七		8,297	八千二百九十七
595	五百九十五		9,100	九千百

For interest, see if you can work out how to write some numbers in *kanji*.
   Work out what the following numbers are.

十七   二十五   四百八十一
   七百三十六   九十二

円

Answers: 17, 25, 481,
   736, 92
Here is the kanji for *en*: 円

STUDY

- **Kore o kudasai** "Please may I have this?" / "Please give me this." This expression may of course be used for anything you want – foods, drinks, and articles you want to buy. It is usually possible to point to things if you don't know the Japanese name.

   Later you will learn a more precise way to ask for food items, but using *JUUSU o kudasai* or *HANBAAGAA o kudasai* you are able to ask for food and drink in coffee bars and restaurants. If you want more than one, use your fingers to show how many until you learn the specific counting patterns!

- Review the numbers to one hundred and learn the numbers up to ten thousand, taking particular note of the following:
  sanbyaku, *roppyaku*, *happyaku*, *sanzen*, *hassen*.

- (Extension) Counting in groups of ten thousand takes quite a lot of practice if you are used to thousands and millions. Cars and other expensive items that you may see for sale in Japan will be priced in this way, so it is good to gradually accustom yourself to hearing and understanding these larger numbers.

  Two million in Japanese is two hundred *man* – *nihyakuman* (two hundred times ten thousand). The quick way to work it out is to count back four places from the end of the number; e.g., 23456 – count back four places from the end and you will find that you are talking about *ni man* (two times ten thousand), *sanzen* (three thousand), *yonhyaku* (four hundred), and *gojuuroku* (fifty six).

  Practice giving each other numbers to work out in Japanese up to ten thousand. If you practice them thoroughly, you will find that you are very quickly at ease with shopping amounts and can hear and understand even if the numbers are spoken quickly.

Counting out change

- Here are some priced articles. How would you read the prices in Japanese?

カメラ	ペン
KAMERA	*PEN*
¥5,900	$3.50
かばん	ノート
kaban	*NOOTO*
¥2,300	$1.20
はな	ふでばこ
hana	*fudebako*
¥500	$5.60
とけい	はこ
tokei	*hako*
¥4,900	$2.75
ほん	ざっし
hon	*zasshi*
¥1,400	0.80¢

Using the priced articles, how much would you spend if you bought
1   a camera and a bunch of flowers?
2   a pen and a notebook?
3   a pencil case and a pen?
4   a bag and a book?
5   a watch and a box?
6   a magazine and a notebook?
7   a pen, a camera, and a notebook?

1 yen

5 yen

10 yen

50 yen

100 yen

500 yen

8   a box, a book, and a magazine?
9   a watch, a bunch of flowers, and a magazine?
10 a pencil case, a camera, and a watch?
Check your mathematical ability with your partner and compare your Japanese answers.

● Practice giving change Japanese style from the larger denominations down to the smaller ones. For many people this takes a bit of getting used to!

In your own country it may be perfectly acceptable to check your change in front of the sales clerk. In Japan it is bad manners to do so, implying lack of trust in the clerk.

ACTIVITIES

● Practice the conversation with a partner, substituting another object of your choice. Don't forget your *ojigi* (bow) if you are the store clerk.

● Practice giving the following numbers in Japanese:
250   374   690   723   815   2,340   3,500   4,000   5,600   6,720   10,000

Use the cards you made when learning the numbers to one hundred if you still have them or make a pack of 30 cards numbered zero to nine. In groups of three, take turns putting down cards side by side. The first one will be a single number read, for example, "3." The second card may be put down ahead or behind this number and will be read, for example, "39" or "93," depending on its position.

A third card is then put down ahead or behind the two already down and is read "439" or "934." Each person reads out quickly in Japanese the new number made. The other two listen carefully, and a record is kept of the number of correct readings by each participant.

When the pack is exhausted, turn over the pile, shuffle and re-deal.

- Play the same game with four participants and use **man** (ten thousands) as well.

- Set up a shop in the classroom with items priced in yen or dollars and cents. (Use the price cards on p. 14.) This may be done with real objects; e.g., the contents of your school bag, picture cards of objects, or the vocabulary cards of objects that you have used previously.

    In twos or small groups practice shopping, paying particular attention to giving amounts in Japanese accurately, working out the change and handing it over Japanese style.

- Have a contest to see how many of you can hear and write down correctly ten numbers, using hundreds and thousands.

- In pairs, work through the following situation and be prepared to do it in front of the class.

    Imagine you are being interviewed for a store clerk position. Say good morning, introduce yourself politely, give your age and nationality in response to his/her questions.

    The interviewer, despite electronic cash registers, wants to find out if you really know Japanese numbers and role plays a customer with you to test your ability to make the correct greetings and shopping conversation. He/she asks for the price of a pen (250 yen), a pencil case (400 yen), a packet of paper (300 yen), and decides to buy the packet of paper. He/she hands over a 1,000-yen note, and you give back the change. He/she watches to see if you know not only the vocabulary but the way such a transaction is done in Japan. Did you do it well enough to get the job?

- In pairs, role play giving change from a 5,000-yen note for the following amounts spent:

    a 250 yen   b 400 yen   c 650 yen   d 825 yen   e 1,250 yen
    f 2,360 yen   g 3,500 yen , h 3,990 yen   i 4,635 yen   j 4,782 yen
    Example: 200 yen spent
    Student 1:   *Ikura desu ka.*
    Student 2:   *Nihyaku en desu.*
    Student 1:   *Gosen en satsu kara Otsuri wa ikura desu ka.*

Student 2:   *Otsuri wa yonsenhappyaku en desu.*
(Counts out change) *Sen en, nisen en, sanzen en, yonsen en, gohyaku en, roppyaku en, nanahyaku en, happyaku en, doozo.*

- Use the photocopiable bingo cards on p. 13 for numbers beyond 1,000. If you photocopy the page and then laminate each copy, they last well. Students cross off the called numbers with non-permanent marker pens, and wipe the sheets clean after the game. Cut up the sheets into strips either across or down, and leave one master sheet.

- Use the photocopiable price cards on p. 14 for bingo or other listening tests, or for putting beside objects in a shopping role play. For bingo or listening tests, photocopy, laminate, and cut the sheet into strips for students, who mark off called numbers with a non-permanent marker pen.

Writing practice

Hiragana is now quite familiar to you. With every lesson your confidence in reading and writing it will grow, and one day you'll wonder why it ever looked difficult or strange.

    Katakana is your next writing challenge. The first step is being able to see that there are differences between syllables, because in the *katakana* chart there are many that at first do look very similar. If you keep practicing, however, they sort themselves out quite quickly.

- Pick out the syllables that are the same/different from the following lists.
  アアアアアアアイアアアア
  フフフフクフフフフフフフフ
  ママママママムママママママ
  セセセセセセセセセセセサセセ
  シツシシシシシシシシシシシ
  ラララララララララテララララ
  ンンンンソンンンンンンンン
  ソソソソソソシソソソソソ
  ルルルルルルレルルルルルル

- Match the *roomaji* to the *katakana* for the following country names.
  OOSUTORARIA   *AMERIKA*   *IGIRISU*   *KANADA*
  アメリカ   オーストラリア イギリス カナダ

Bingo Sheet

1,000	2,400	3,500	4,600	5,700	6,800
7,900	8,100	9,050	1,250	2,370	3,480
4,590	5,220	6,335	7,485	8,921	9,230
1,250	2,125	3,240	2,680	4,560	6,920
8,241	3,736	8,922	3,489	6,541	1,376
9,287	1,323	4,564	5,490	1,960	2,500
3,488	7,647	9,999	4,444	1,234	4,567
7,890	8,907	9,123	1,357	5,790	7,913
1,289	1,376	1,487	1,598	1,609	1,718
2,123	2,234	2,345	2,456	2,567	2,678
3,434	3,468	4,656	3,576	3,678	3,789
4,545	4,578	5,767	4,678	4,789	4,812

Prices Sheet

¥50	¥100	¥1,000	¥2,600
¥75	¥250	¥2,000	¥3,500
¥65	¥380	¥3,000	¥4,000
¥45	¥457	¥8,000	¥5,000
¥35	¥938	¥2,500	¥6,500
¥25	¥624	¥6,750	¥2,380
¥18	¥810	¥8,225	¥5,500
¥27	¥175	¥9,170	¥1,690

みみかき   *mimikaki*

The traditional *mimikaki* is an ear cleaner, made from a narrow stick of bamboo about 20 cm (8 inches) long. One end is curved for scooping wax, and attached to the other end is a small fluffy pompom, mainly intended for soothing itchy ears.

Although barbers provide ear-cleaning services using *mimikaki*, traditionally wives and mothers hold the job of cleaning and dewaxing their families' ears. The mother sits on the floor and the person whose ears are being cleaned lies with his or her head in the mother's lap – a time of closeness and relaxation for children and adults alike.

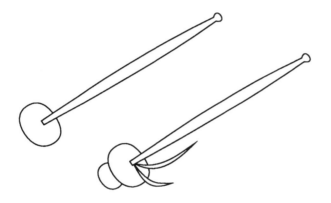

Unit 2

なに を かいました か
nani o kaimashita ka
What did you buy?

NEW WORDS

けさ	*kesa*	this morning
やすい	*yasui*	cheap
かいもの	*kaimono*	shopping
デパート	*DEPAATO*	department store
から	*kara*	from
まで	*made*	until/as far as/up to
Review		
やきゅう	*yakyuu*	baseball
ひとり　で	*hitori de*	by myself
かいます	*kaimasu*	buy
あかい	*akai*	red
あおい	*aoi*	blue
また	*mata*	again
そして	*soshite*	and then
Interest		
バーゲン　セール	*BAAGEN SEERU*	bargain sale

Read the conversation aloud with a partner. Try to read with an intelligent understanding of the text! Or use it as a listening comprehension exercise as two people read and the class listens. The readers may ask the class questions to test their understanding. As always, look at the new vocabulary list before you begin.

Sue is asking Tom about his day.

S: けさ　どこ　に　いきました　か。

T: けさ　バス　で　まち　に　いきました。

S: なに　を　しました　か。

T: かいもの　を　しました。そして　としょかん　に　いきました。

S: なに　を　かいました　か。

T: あたらしい　かばん　を　かいました。

S: なに　いろ　です　か。

T: あかい　の　です。

S: いくら　でした　か。

T: にせんごひゃく　えん　でした。

S: やすい　です　ね。かばん　を　みせて　ください。
どこ　で　かいました　か。

T: デパート　で　かいました。バーゲン　セール　が　ありました。

S: そう　です　か。あした　また　バーゲン　セール　が　あります
か。

T: はい、あります。あなた　も　やすい　かばん　を　かいます　か。

S: あおい　かばん　が　ありました　か。

T: はい、ありました。せんきゅうひゃく　えん　から　さんぜん　えん
まで　でした。

S: では、あした　わたし　は　あおい　かばん　を　かいます。
デパート　は　なんじ　から　なんじ　まで　です　か。

T: じゅうじ　から　しちじ　まで　です。

S: よじ　はん　に　まち　まで　いきます。
いっしょ　に　いきましょう　か。

T: いいえ、いきません。わたし　は　やきゅう　の　れんしゅう　を
します。

S: では、ひとり　で　いきます。じゃ　また。

S: *Kesa doko ni ikimashita ka.*
T: *Kesa BASU de machi ni ikimashita.*
S: *Nani o shimashita ka.*
T: *Kaimono o shimashita. Soshite toshokan ni ikimashita.*
S: *Nani o kaimashita ka.*
T: *Atarashii kaban o kaimashita.*
S: *Nani iro desu ka.*
T: *Akai no desu.*
S: *Ikura deshita ka.*
T: *Nisengohyaku en deshita.*
S: *Yasui desu ne. Kaban o misete kudasai. Doko de kaimashita ka.*
T: *DEPAATO de kaimashita. BAAGEN SEERU ga arimashita.*
S: *Soo desu ka. Ashita mata BAAGEN SEERU ga arimasu ka.*
T: *Hai, arimasu. Anata mo yasui kaban o kaimasu ka.*
S: *Aoi kaban ga arimashita ka.*
T: *Hai, arimashita. Senkyuuhyaku en kara sanzen en made deshita.*
S: *Dewa, ashita watashi wa aoi kaban o kaimasu.*
DEPAATO wa nanji kara nanji made desu ka.
T: *Juuji kara shichiji made desu.*

S: *Yoji han ni machi made ikimasu. Issho ni ikimashoo ka.*
T: *Iie, ikimasen. Watashi wa yakyuu no renshuu o shimasu.*
S: *Dewa, hitori de ikimasu. Ja mata.*

Check your understanding of the conversation.
S: Where did you go this morning?
T: I went to town by bus this morning.
S: What did you do?
T: I did some shopping, and then I went to the library.
S: What did you buy?
T: I bought a new bag.
S: What color?
T: Red.
S: How much was it?
T: Two thousand five hundred yen.
S: That's cheap, isn't it? Please show me. Where did you buy it?
T: At the department store. There was a bargain sale on.
S: Is that so? Is there a sale again tomorrow?
T: Yes, there is. Are you going to buy a cheap bag too?
S: Were there blue bags?
T: Yes, there were. They were from 1,900 yen to 3,000 yen.
S: Tomorrow I'll buy a blue bag then. What time will the store be open?
T: It's open from ten o'clock until seven.
S: I'll go to town at half past four. Shall we go together?
T: No, I won't go. I have baseball practice.
S: Well then I'll go alone. See you.

STUDY

Compare prices of 100 grams of meat with those in your own country

• **Akai no wa** "a red one" is short for *akai kaban* "a red bag."

• **Kara . . . made. Kara** "from" and **made** "until" are very useful for explaining things more accurately. With time words they can be used as in the conversation, for the times when shops will be open from and until and for saying that you will be at a certain place from a certain time. They can also be used for distances and travel, and giving a range of prices, ages, etc.

　　Examples: (1) *NYUU YOOKU kara WASHINTON made ikimashita.* "I went from New York to Washington." If you use *made* instead of *ni* to say "to Washington," the assumption is that you are going as far as Los Angeles and no further. It is used a great deal in Japanese conversation where English speakers would be more inclined to use "to," if you are going that far and no further.

　　(2) *Senkyuuhyakuen kara sanzen en made.* "From 1,900 yen to 3,000 yen."

　　(3) *Nihon no kootoogakkoo wa juugosai kara juuhassai made desu.* "Japanese high schools go from fifteen years old to eighteen years old."

　　(4) *BAAGEN SEERU wa getsuyoobi kara suiyoobi made desu.* "The sale is on from Monday to Wednesday."

• **Kaimono o shimasu/kaimono ni ikimasu.** The difference between these two sentences is that in the first you are saying "I will do shopping" and in the second "I will go to shop." Therefore, you use the one that is most appropriate for the context.

- **hitori de**. You learned *hitori* when counting numbers of people: *hitori* "one person" **hitori de** "by myself"
  futari "two people" **futari de** "two people only/by themselves"
  Remember, if you are talking about three or more people, you just count on in the ordinary way, putting **nin** on the end: *sannin, yonin, gonin, rokunin, nananin, hachinin, kyuunin, juunin* . . . Watch the spelling of *yonin*. (It's like *yoji* "four o'clock." The "n" of *yon* has been taken off for the sound's sake.)

  The *kanji* to write one person, two people, three people, etc., uses the numbers you looked at earlier and the *kanji* for person.

一人　二人　三人　四人　五人　六人　七人　八人　九人　十人

Check your understanding

1 わたし は がっこう で はちじ はん から さんじ はん まで べんきょうします。
2 ぎんこう は じゅうじ から さんじ まで です。
3 デパート は しちじ まで です。
4 きのう サンフランシスコ から シカゴ まで いきました。
5 らいしゅう ともだち は ホノルル から きます。

ぎんこう	*ginkoo*	bank
サンフランシスコ	*SANFURANSHISUKO*	San Francisco
シカゴ	*SHIKAGO*	Chicago
ホノルル	*HONORURU*	Honolulu

1 *Watashi wa gakkoo de hachiji han kara sanji han made benkyoo shimasu.*
2 *Ginkoo wa juuji kara sanji made desu.*
3 *DEPAATO wa shichiji made desu.*
4 *Kinoo SANFURANSHISUKO kara SHIKAGO made ikimashita.*
5 *Raishuu tomodachi wa HONORURU kara kimasu.*

ACTIVITIES

- Write a conversation using the one in this unit as a guide and adding in extra comments. Try to make it about one minute long to read through.

- Have it checked for accuracy, then practice it with a friend.

- When you feel confident, let the class watch and question them afterwards on the facts.

Shopping carts often have seats for children

Writing practice

- Learn the syllable **SE** セ

- Learn **RU** ル

- Learn to make the long sound (double vowels) using the bar.

- Write **SEERU** セール

- Identify *SE* and *RU* in the lines below:
  カマルフシセヌセカキセルチルルルセセコノロリカ
  ヤカキクヒセスムセシフユルレテチリルウメックヌ

Unit 3

どこ で かいました か
doko de kaimashita ka
Where did you buy it?

NEW WORDS

はは　の　ひ	*haha no hi*	Mother's Day
はなや	*hanaya*	flower shop
さかな	*sakana*	fish
さかなや	*sakanaya*	fish market
にく	*niku*	meat
にくや	*nikuya*	butcher/butcher's shop
スーパー（マーケット）	*SUUPAA (MAAKETTO)*	supermarket
やさい	*yasai*	vegetables
やおや	*yaoya*	greengrocer/vegetable shop
くだもの	*kudamono*	fruit
くだものや	*kudamonoya*	fruit stand
くつ	*kutsu*	shoes
くつや	*kutsuya*	shoe store

It's Mother's Day in Japan (the second Sunday in May). Every flower shop and stall is full of red carnations. Red in Japan is the color of happiness. Two sisters get home after shopping and to their surprise both have bought the same thing. In the *genkan* Sachiko takes off her shoes and calls out. Michiko answers from inside the house.

さ　ただいま。

み　おかえりなさい。あした は はは の ひ です。あかい はな を かいました。

さ　わたし も はな を かいました。

み　あなた の はな は どこ で かいました か。

さ　はなや で かいました。あなた は。

み　デパート の はなや で かいました。

さ　いくら でした か。

み　ごひゃく えん でした。あなた の は。

さ　ごひゃく えん でした。いま はな が たくさん あります ね。

み　はは は はな が すき です から だいじょうぶ です。

S: *Tadaima.*
M: (calls out from inside the house): *Okaerinasai. Ashita wa haha no hi desu. Akai hana o kaimashita.*
    (Sachiko enters with her gift.)
S: *Watashi mo hana o kaimashita.*
M: *Anata no hana wa doko de kaimashita ka.*
S: *Hanaya de kaimashita. Anata wa?*
M: *DEPAATO no hanaya de kaimashita.*
S: *Ikura deshita ka.*
M: *Gohyaku en deshita. Anata no wa?*
S: *Gohyaku en deshita. Ima hana ga takusan arimasu ne.*
M: *Haha wa hana ga suki desu kara daijoobu desu.*

Mother's Day carnations outside a department store

Check your understanding of the conversation.
S: I'm home.
M: Welcome back/I'm pleased you're home.
    Tomorrow is Mother's Day. I've bought red flowers.
S: I've bought flowers, too.
M: Where did you buy your flowers?
S: At the flower shop. How about you?
M: I bought them at the department store flower shop.
S: How much were they?
M: Five hundred yen. And yours?
S: Five hundred yen. Now we have a lot of flowers, don't we?
M: Mom loves flowers, so it's OK.

STUDY

• Notice that in most cases the name of a type of shop is made by adding **ya** to the items sold. Note too that the proprietor is also called by the same word; e.g., **hanaya** but **san** is added – **hanaya san**. If someone you know owns a shop, you are now able to describe his job; e.g., *Wakisaka san wa hanayasan desu.* "Mr Wakisaka is a florist." (Don't forget *the san* or you will be saying "Mr Wakisaka is a flower shop!")

There are exceptions though, as in **yaoya**, so don't take it for granted that you can always make the name of the shop out of the name of the items sold.

- **Anata no wa**? "What about yours?" The full sentence would have been *Anata no hana wa*? but as you learned previously, it is possible to leave out the noun to avoid sounding too repetitive.

ACTIVITIES

- How would you tell someone the following in Japanese? "Yesterday I met Ana Brown's father. I went to the shoe shop. The shoe shop owner was Mr Brown. He's very tall. He has black hair. He's very handsome. I liked him a lot. There were lots of shoes. They were beautiful. I bought black ones. They were three thousand yen."

- Read the following passage aloud, or use it for listening comprehension. After you have read it yourself, go through with a friend to check that you both understand.

きょう まち で かいもの を しました。いもうと の たんじょ
うび は あした です。いもうと と いっしょ に いきました。

みどり	あした あなた の たんじょうび です から きょう あなた の プレゼント を かいます。とけい が あります か。
いもうと	はい、とけい が あります が 「Swatch」 の とけい が すき です。 わたし の ともだち は 「Swatch」 の とけい が す き です。
み	そう です か。じゃ、デパート で バーゲン セール が あります。「Swatch」 の とけい が あります。いきまし ょう。
い	バーゲン セール が きらい です。バーゲン セール の とけい が きらい です。
み	そう です か。じゃ、バーゲン セール の とけい が きらい です から とけい を かいません。ほん が すき です か。
い	ほん が きらい です。
み	ええ と、がっこう の かばん を かいましょう か。
い	がっこう が きらい です。がっこう の かばん が きらい です。
み	じゃ、プレゼント は かいません。

プレゼント   *PUREZENTO*   present

Kyoo machi de kaimono o shimashita. Imooto no tanjoobi wa ashita desu. Imooto to issho ni ikimashita.

Midori: *Ashita anata no tanjoobi desu kara kyoo anata no PUREZENTO o kaimasu. Tokei ga arimasu ka.*

Imooto: *Hai, tokei ga arimasu ga "Swatch" no tokei ga suki desu. Watashi no tomodachi wa "Swatch" no tokei ga suki desu.*

Midori: *Soo desu ka. Ja, DEPAATO de BAAGEN SEERU ga arimasu. "Swatch" no tokei ga arimasu. Ikimashoo.*

Imooto: *BAAGEN SEERU ga kirai desu. BAAGEN SEERU no tokei ga kirai desu.*

Midori: *Soo desu ka. Ja, BAAGEN SEERU no tokei ga kirai desu kara tokei o kaimasen. Hon ga suki desu ka.*

Imooto: *Hon ga kirai desu.*

Midori: *Ee to, gakkoo no kaban o kaimashoo ka.*

Imooto: *Gakkoo ga kirai desu. Gakkoo no kaban ga kirai desu.*

Midori: *Ja, PUREZENTO wa kaimasen!*

- **Listening and speaking**. In groups of about five people play a version of "I went to market and bought . . ."

    The game starts with one person saying "I went to town. At the flower shop I bought (red flowers)." The second person repeats all that was said by the first person and adds a sentence: *Machi ni ikimashita. Hanaya de akai hana o kaimashita. Sakanaya de sakana o kaimashita.* Around the group each person repeats what has gone before and adds on a sentence. See how many sentences you can add before someone forgets the sequence.

    (When you run out of specific shops, just say what you bought or did not buy. Remember that you can meet people and do things as well as shopping so you should have plenty of options for something to add. If you are all so good at remembering that you need more material, add in times and how you travelled home, what you did when you arrived home, etc.)

- Write ten sentences telling what you bought in particular shops on particular days; e.g., *Getsuyoobi ni hanaya de hana o kaimashita.* Mark each other's work in pencil. If you disagree, ask the teacher to check it for you.

- **For review.** Play an "around-the-class" story-building game in which each person adds either a phrase or a sentence. The sentences must make sense.

    Suggestion for theme: Imagine that you are telling the story of what one person does in the course of a week. Use all the verbs you know to talk about their basic daily activities, like getting up and eating, going shopping at various stores, and add in specific activities for particular times of particular days.

- Write a story in *hiragana* either about your own life or that of an imaginary person. Choose whether to write about action in the present, past or future, or a mixture.

Kimono are very expensive

Writing practice

- Learn **SU**   ス

- Learn **HA**   ハ

- From **HA** you can make **PA**   パ

- Write *SUUPAA*   スーパー

- Identify the following syllables.
  セ　セ　セ　ス　ス　パ　ス　パ

- Read the following aloud to yourself.
  ル　ル　ル　ル　セ　ス　セ　セ　スー　スー

- Which of the following lines contain syllables that you know? Identify *HA*, *SU*, *SE* and the bar used to double the sound.
  1　カサタナハマヤライキシチニヒミユ
  2　イキシチニヒミユリウクスツヌムヨ
  3　エクケセテネヘメワレオコソトノホ
  4　オコソトノホモヲロエケセテネヘス
  5　セクスツヌフムヨハイキシチハマヤ
  6　コセツニマルムチカスヲフマースー

- For interest only, here are two *kanji* associated with food:
  肉　*niku*
  魚　*sakana*

Unit 4

たいへん たかかった です
taihen takakatta desu
It was very expensive

NEW WORDS

オートバイ	*OOTOBAI*	motorbike
がくせい	*gakusei*	student
だいがく	*daigaku*	university
だいがくせい	*daigakusei*	university student
ふるい	*furui*	old
はやい	*hayai*	fast/early
たいへん	*taihen*	very
せんげつ	*sengetsu*	last month
こんげつ	*kongetsu*	this month
らいげつ	*raigetsu*	next month
あたらしかった	*atarashikatta*	was new
たかかった	*takakatta*	was expensive
やすかった	*yasukatta*	was cheap
やすい	*yasui*	cheap
かいしゃいん	*kaishain*	office/company employee
おかね	*Okane*	money
でも	*demo*	but
Interest		
バイク	*BAIKU*	motorbike

Review words for members of a family.

Tsutomu's older brother has bought a new motorbike. Tsutomu is discussing it with his friend Masake.

つ　きのう あに は あたらしい オートバイ を かいました。たいへん きれい です。

ま　どこ で かいました か。

つ　まち で かいました。

ま　なに いろ です か。

つ　あかい かわさき の オートバイ です。

ま　いい です ね。いくら でした か。

つ　いちまん えん でした。

ま　いちまん えん。やすかった です ね。あたらしい です か。

つ　あたらしくない です。ふるい です が いい オートバイ です。

ま　はやい　です　か。

つ　ええ、たいへん　はやい　です。

ま　せんげつ　あに　は　あたらしい　オートバイ　を　かいました。あたらしかった　です。たいへん　たかかった　です。

つ　でも　あなた　の　おにいさん　は　かいしゃいん　です。あに　は　だいがくせい　です。おかね　が　ありません。

ま　そう　です　ね。がくせい　は　いつも　おかね　が　ありません　ね。

T:　*Kinoo ani wa atarashii OOTOBAI o kaimashita.*
　　Taihen kirei desu.
M:　*Doko de kaimashita ka.*
T:　*Machi de kaimashita.*
M:　*Nani iro desu ka.*
T:　*Akai Kawasaki no OOTOBAI desu.*
M:　*Ii desu ne. Ikura deshita ka.*
T:　*Ichiman en deshita.*
M:　*Ichiman en? Yasukatta desu ne. Atarashii desu ka.*
　　(He snorts disbelievingly.)
T:　*Atarashikunai desu. Furui desu ga ii OOTOBAI desu.*
M:　*Hayai desu ka.*
T:　*Ee, taihen hayai desu.*
M:　*Sengetsu ani wa atarashii OOTOBAI o kaimashita.*
　　Atarashikatta desu. Taihen takakatta desu.
T:　*Demo anata no oniisan wa kaishain desu.*
　　Ani wa daigakusei desu. Okane ga arimasen.
M:　*Soo desu ne. Gakusei wa itsumo okane ga arimasen ne.*

Check your understanding of the conversation.
T:　My older brother bought a new motorbike yesterday. It's really beautiful.
M:　Where did he buy it?
T:　He bought it in town.
M:　What color is it?
T:　It's a red Kawasaki.
M:　That's great. How much was it?
T:　Ten thousand yen.
M:　Ten thousand yen? That was cheap, wasn't it? Is it new?
T:　It's not new. It's old, but it's a good bike.
M:　Is it fast?
T:　Yeah, it's really fast.
M:　My older brother bought a new bike last month. It was new. It was very expensive.
T:　But your older brother is a company employee. My brother is a university student. He doesn't have any money.
M:　That's right. Students never have any money, do they?

STUDY TIPS

Although this topic is principally concerned with shopping, in learning a language we must be careful to use all that we have learned as often as possible. We are continually building on to what we know. It would be simple just to learn shopping material in isolation but in doing so you might find that other material slips out of your memory and takes more effort to retrieve.

In this book it has been assumed that you have already learned good study habits – that you keep note of new vocabulary without being reminded, you keep going over old work so that you don't forget it, and you make note of questions that come into your mind to ask your teacher about. In other words, you should take responsibility yourself for maintaining steady progress, so there is no need for your teacher or your conscience to nag you!

Having done all this, you will derive immense satisfaction from your learning, because little by little things fall into place.

STUDY

- **Sengetsu, kongetsu, raigetsu** only have a particle after them if the time is being stressed *Sengetsu wa* . . . "talking about last month . . ." or if you want to say "last month, too":
  Sengetsu mo ikimashita. "I went last month, **too**."
  Usually no particle follows:
  Sengetsu nihon ni ikimashita. "Last month I went to Japan."
  Kongetsu ane wa tsukimasu. "This month my older sister arrives."
  Raigetsu otooto no tanjoobi desu. "Next month is my little brother's birthday."
  Kongetsu OOTOBAI o kaimasu. "This month I'll buy a motorbike."

- To join two sentences with "but" use **ga** between them.

- Learn how to use the past and past negative of adjectives, and review some sentence patterns at the same time.
  In Japanese an ending must be added to the original adjective where in English we say "was" plus adjective or "was not"; e.g., was red/was not big.
  You are already familiar with the method for making the negative of adjectives in Japanese: take off the *i* and add *kunai*. To make the past, "was . . ." take off the *i* and add *katta*. And for the past negative "was not . . ." take off the *i* and add *kunakatta*. After all adjectives add **desu** for politeness. The *desu* **never** changes.

- Adjectives are placed before the nouns they describe, as in English; e.g., (1) *akai kuruma desu* "a red car," or (2) used with *desu*; e.g., *Kuruma wa akai desu.* "The car is red."
  When you use the negative or past negative you can only use the second pattern. Never try to say *akakunai kuruma* – "a not red car" would sound funny in English and sounds even more peculiar in Japanese! The

· correct pattern is:

Kuruma wa (to say what you are talking about) *akakunai desu*. "The car is not red."

Kuruma wa akakatta desu. "The car was red."

Kuruma wa akakunakatta desu. "The car was not red."

   Work through all the adjectives you know in the following way to review them and to learn the process thoroughly.

ookii desu "is big"   *ookikunai desu* "is not big"

ookikatta desu "was big"   *ookikunakatta desu* "was not big"

   Make sentences together using both patterns. Next put those sentences from pattern 2 into the past and past negative forms.

ちいさい	chiisai	small
あかい	akai	red
あおい	aoi	blue
くろい	kuroi	black
しろい	shiroi	white
おもしろい	omoshiroi	interesting/entertaining
ひろい	hiroi	spacious/wide
せまい	semai	narrow/cramped
ながい	nagai	long
みじかい	mijikai	short
ひくい	hikui	low/short in height
たかい	takai	high/expensive/tall
あたらしい	atarashii	new/fresh
ふるい	furui	old
はやい	hayai	fast/early
やすい	yasui	cheap
あつい	atsui	hot
さむい	samui	cold
すずしい	suzushii	cool
あたたかい	atatakai	warm
わるい	warui	bad
いい　よい	ii/yoi	good

● いい/よい *ii/yoi* good

   This is the only tricky one to remember in this list. **Ii** is only used in the present. If you want to say "is not good" you must use the **yoi** form and say **yokunai**. The **yoi** form is probably used because the sound is smoother.

   "was good" **yokatta**

   "was not good" **yokunakatta**. Learn it carefully.

● Review the twenty-two adjectives and then cover the English to test yourself from the *hiragana* or from the *ROOMAji* and vice versa.

● Together compose sentences using all the different adjectives you know in all their forms. Try to make some sentences that include times, days, and dates. Use the following pattern first.

Pattern 1:

[Topic (*wa*), time (*ni*), place (*de*), adjective, object (*o*), verb]

e.g.: *Watashi wa getsuyoobi ni gakkoo de aoi hon o mimashita.*

  "I saw the blue book at school on Monday."

Pattern 2:

[Topic (*wa*), adjective in one of its tenses, *desu*]

e.g.: *Getsuyoobi wa atsukatta desu.*

  "Monday was hot."

Pattern 3:

[Topic (*wa*), adjective *desu*, but (*ga*), adjective *desu*]

e.g.: *Hon wa furui desu ga omoshiroi desu.*

  "The book is old but it's interesting."

  Eiga wa atarashikunai desu ga omoshiroi desu.

  "The film is not new but it's entertaining."

  Jitensha wa atarashikunai desu ga hayai desu.

  "The bicycle is not new but it's fast."

Pattern 4:

[Topic (*wa*), focus on a particular thing (*ga*), adjective *desu ga*, time word, opposite adjective, *desu*]

Sengetsu wa ane no kami no ke ga nagakatta desu ga ima mijikai desu.

"Last month my older sister's hair was long, but now it is short."

- With a partner work out sentences to particular patterns. Read them to others and get them to translate what you have said.

ACTIVITIES

- Mime the adjectives (in teams or individually) and guess which adjective is being mimed.

  To express: "is not . . ." cross your arms over your face before you begin. For "was" point over your shoulder. For "was not" cross arms behind your back. The faster you can do these the more fun they are to play.

  Maybe you can extend this into mimes of whole sentences and stories, to be answered in Japanese, of course!

Fruit is often sold singly

- Make up a role play in groups of four in which one person is the shop-keeper and one person is buying things encouraged by a friend. Walk away from the shop discussing the purchase. At home tell the fourth person what you bought and how much it cost, in response to his/her questions and comments.

Check your understanding

How would you say:
1   Henry's car was old.
2   My bicycle is not new, but it is fast.
3   The tree is very, very old.
4   My older sister is not tall.
5   Your mother's hair is not red.
6   My room was blue, but now it is white.
7   My old house was cramped, but the new house is spacious.
8   Yesterday was cold, but today is hot.
9   My birthday party was good.
10 The park was not big.

Writing practice

- Learn **O**   オ

- Learn **TO**   ト

- Review **HA**   ハ
  And learn **BA**   バ

- Learn *I* イ

イ イ Write *OOTOBAI* オートバイ

- Learn **TE** テ

  And **DE** デ
Write *DEPAATO* デパート

- Read the following sentences aloud or silently. Read them several times for practice. Then write what they mean in English.
  1 わたし の オートバイ は はやい です。
  2 きょう デパート で セール が あります。
  3 スーパー に いきました。
  4 わたし の なまえ は スー です。
  5 おにいさん は オートバイ が あります。
  6 トースト を たべました。
  7 はは は スーパー で やさい を かいました。
  8 ちち は オートバイ が すき じゃない です。
  9 セール は あした です。

- Look for words you know in these lines of syllables.
  1 ムヌクキシチマミツテセールイマラミマ
  2 ンレツテヒスーパーカキシチーキーハマ
  3 コオートバイヒミユヨムルワハマスオー
  4 セールスーパークスミユレヘセールトテ

Unit 5

なにか ほしい もの が ありますか
nanika hoshii mono ga arimasu ka
Is there anything you'd like?

NEW WORDS

いって まいります	*itte mairimasu*	I'm going out
いって いらっしゃい	*itte irasshai*	OK/See you
ほしい	*hoshii*	want (adjective)
ごろ	*goro*	about (a particular time)
パン	*PAN*	bread
かって ください	*katte kudasai*	please buy
ええ と	*ee to*	(hesitation noise) let me think . . .

Interest

なにか	*nanika*	something/anything
もの	*mono*	thing
ほしい もの	*hoshii mono*	wanted things/things you want
アスピリン	*ASUPIRIN*	aspirin

Today is Thursday. Judy's mother returned home from the hospital a few days ago after having an operation on her leg. She is finding it painful to walk.

ジュディ おかあさん、けさ かいもの に いきます。わたし と いきます か。

おかあさん ええ と、わたし の あし が たいへん いたい です から いきません が……

ジ なにか ほしい もの が あります か。

お ええ と、アスピリン と にく と パン が ほしい です。

ジ にくや で にく を かいましょう か、スーパー で にく を かいましょう か。

お にくや で にく を かって ください。でも、パン と アスピリン を スーパー で かって ください。おかね が あります か。

ジ ええ、だいじょうぶ です。

お なんじ に かえります か。

ジ   じゅうにじ　ごろ　かえります。いって　まいります。

お   いって　いらっしゃい。

JUDI: *Okaasan, kesa kaimono ni ikimasu. Watashi to ikimasu ka.*
Okaasan: *Ee to, watashi no ashi ga taihen itai desu kara ikimasen ga . . .*
J: *Nanika hoshii mono ga arimasu ka.*
O: *Ee to, ASUPIRIN to niku to PAN ga hoshii desu.*
J: *Nikuya de niku o kaimashoo ka, SUUPAA de niku o kaimashoo ka.*
O: *Nikuya de niku o katte kudasai. Demo PAN to ASUPIRIN o SUUPAA de katte kudasai. Okane ga arimasu ka.*
J: *Ee daijoobu desu.*
O: *Nanji ni kaerimasu ka.*
J: *Juuniji goro kaerimasu. Itte mairimasu.*
O: *Itte irasshai.*

Check your understanding of the conversation.
Judy: Mom, I'm going to go shopping this morning.
           Will you come with me?
Mother: Um, my leg is painful, so I won't (go) but . . .
J: Is there anything you want?
M: Let me think . . . I want aspirin, meat and bread.
J: Shall I buy the meat at the butcher's or at the supermarket?
M: Buy the meat at the butcher's and the aspirin and bread at the super-market, please. Do you have any money?
J: Yes, it's OK.
M: What time will you come home?
J: About twelve o'clock. Bye (I'm going now).
M: Bye (Go and come home safely).

STUDY

- **_Nanika hoshii mono ga arimasu ka_**. "Is there anything you want/would like?" is a useful phrase to know. **_Nanika_** means "something" and never has a particle after it.

  You have met **_mono_** before in a phrase saying "lots of things": **_takusan no mono_**. *Mono* means "things." *Tabemono* are "things to eat": food, *nomimono* "things to drink": drink(s).

  In the phrase we are discussing, *hoshii mono* literally means "wanted things." Don't worry too much about the structure at the moment if that seems difficult, just learn it as a phrase.

  Nani ga hoshii desu ka. "What do you want?/What would you like?" is simpler to learn but is not quite so polite.

- **_Hoshii_** means "want/wanted thing." It is an adjective and is used for **things** not actions you want. It always takes the particle **_ga_** except in negatives.

I want a car.	*Kuruma ga hoshii desu.*
I want new shoes.	*Atarashii kutsu ga hoshii desu.*
I don't want a car.	*Kuruma wa hoshikunai desu.*
I don't want new shoes.	*Atarashii kutsu wa hoshikunai desu.*

It can only be used with articles – concrete things that you want. It cannot be used to say that you want to **buy** something or **do** something. That has to be done with a new verb form which is introduced later. Look at these examples:

Neko ga hoshii desu. "I want a cat." Not, I want to "buy" a cat or "get" a cat, "borrow" a cat or "steal" a cat. You are only expressing a desire to have a cat.

Ringo ga hoshii desu. "I want an apple." You want one, not necessarily to eat, cook, paint, or look at – you just want one.

Hoshii is an adjective. *Itai desu* that you learned in the health topic is also an adjective. Although *itai* and *hoshii* don't sound like other adjectives that you know, they are adjectives and should be learned carefully:

Kuruma ga hoshii desu.	I want a car.
Kuruma wa hoshikunai desu.	I don't want a car.
Kuruma ga hoshikatta desu.	I wanted a car/a car was the wanted thing.
Kuruma wa hoshikunakatta desu.	I did not want a car/a car was not a wanted thing.

itai desu	it hurts/is sore/aches
itakunai desu	it doesn't hurt
itakatta desu	it (did) hurt
itakunakatta desu	it did not hurt

- **Goro** means "about." It can only be used in relation to a specific time: "about three o'clock." "about five thirty," etc. **It cannot be used for distance or lengths** of time; e.g., "about three hours" or "about five miles."

- **Demo** "but" is usually used at the beginning of a sentence. *Demo, SUUPAA de PAN o katte kudasai* "But please buy bread at the supermarket."

  In English you are usually taught not to begin a sentence with "but." In Japanese conversation it is quite common to use *demo* at the beginning of a sentence.

- **Itte mairimasu** and **itte irasshai** are another pair of common, very polite expressions to learn. When going out it is automatic to say *itte mairimasu,* (literally "I'm going out and coming back") and anyone who is in the house will reply, *itte irasshai.*

- *Kutsu ga hoshikunai desu.*
  If you are focusing on the shoes, or some item, use **ga** in the negative, too. It will probably be new information; e.g., you introduce the idea of not wanting shoes into the conversation – no one has mentioned it before. The **ga** focuses attention on the **item**, which is the subject of the sentence.

  If the subject has already been mentioned, use **wa** with the negative to show that your emphasis is on the fact that you **don't want** the item.

Compare:
Kuruma ga hoshikunai desu.
The car I don't want./I don't want a car.
Kuruma wa hoshikunai desu.
I don't want a car.
(The emphasis is on not wanting it.)

ACTIVITY

- Around the class game. One person asks *Nanika hoshii mono ga arimasu ka*, and taking turns around the class, each person responds with *Watashi wa . . . ga hoshii desu*, or, if you want the same thing as the person before you, *Watashi mo . . . ga hoshii desu*.

  Extension: each person must say that she/he doesn't want the article mentioned by the previous person by saying: . . . . . . *wa hoshikunai desu*. Then say what they want, with: *Watashi wa . . . . . . ga hoshii desu*. (Remember, in the negative you always use *wa* if you are emphasizing "don't want.")

Check your understanding

Match up the sentences:

1	I wanted a red car.	a	*Manga ga hoshii desu.*
2	Bevan wants a magazine.	b	*Otoosan no shinbun wa hoshikunai desu.*
3	I don't want Dad's newspaper.	c	*Nani ga hoshikatta desu ka.*
4	My younger sister wants a cat.	d	*Inu wa hoshikunai desu.*
5	What did you want?	e	*Imooto wa neko ga hoshii desu.*
6	I didn't want money!	f	*Akai kuruma ga hoshikatta desu.*
7	Do you want the book?	g	*SUKOTTO kun wa atarashii PEN ga hoshii desu.*
8	I don't want a dog.	h	*Hon ga hoshii desu ka.*
9	Scott wants a new pen.	i	*BEBAN kun wa zasshi ga hoshii desu.*
10	I want a comic book.	j	*Okane wa hoshikunakatta desu.*

Don't forget that want and need are two different things! With *hoshii* you are not saying you **need** something, only that you want something.

Writing practice

- Learn the syllable **A**   ア

- Learn **FU** (**HU**)   フ

  From *FU* you can make **PU**   プ

- Learn **RI**   リ

- Learn **N**   ン

- Write *PUURU*   プール   *PAN*   パン

- Find the following words in the sentences below. (Not all words will be used.)

1 *DEPAATO*	デパート	9 *BASUKETTOBOORU*	バスケットボール
2 *BAAGEN SEERU*	バーゲン セール	10 *HOKKEE*	ホッケー
3 *BASU*	バス	11 *GITAA*	ギター
4 *TENISU*	テニス	12 *PIANO*	ピアノ
5 *TAKUSHII*	タクシー	13 *HANBAAGAA*	ハンバーガー
6 *SUUPAA*	スーパー	14 *SANDOITCHI*	サンドイッチ
7 *SAKKAA*	サッカー	15 *HOTTODOGGU*	ホットドッグ
8 *FUTTOBOORU*	フットボール	16 *BAREEBOORU*	バレーボール

a リサ さん は テニス が すき です。
b おかあさん は バーゲン セール が すき です。
c フィリップ さん は いつも ハンバーガー を たべます。
d ジム さん は ピアノ を れんしゅう します。
e きょう デパート に いきます。
f ホッケー が すき です か。
g ふゆ は サッカー を します。
h どようび に フットボール を します。
i ホットドッグ が きらい です。
j バス で かえりました。

a *RISA san wa TENISU ga suki desu.*
b *Okaasan wa BAAGEN SEERU ga suki desu.*
c *FIRIPPU san wa itsumo HANBAAGAA o tabemasu.*
d *JIMU san wa PIANO o renshuu shimasu.*
e *Kyoo DEPAATO ni ikimasu.*
f *HOKKEE ga suki desu ka.*
g *Fuyu wa SAKKAA o shimasu.*
h *Doyoobi ni FUTTOBOORU o shimasu.*
i *HOTTODOGGU ga kirai desu.*
j *BASU de kaerimashita.*

- Having done the practice above see how many of the words below (or parts of words) you can recognize without looking back:
  バス ホッケー バスケットボール テニス サッカー ギター
  ピアノ ホットドッグ パーティー デパート タクシー
  フットボール バレーボール

Unit 6

たかい です ね
takai desu ne
It's expensive, isn't it?

NEW WORDS

だめ	*dame*	no good (qualitative noun)
Review		
はやい	*hayai*	fast (adjective)
おもしろい	*omoshiroi*	interesting/fun (adjective)
たいへん	*taihen*	very
この	*kono*	this
その	*sono*	that
あの	*ano*	that over there
どの	*dono*	which
Interest		
じてんしゃや	*jitenshaya*	bicycle shop

Junji lives in New York now with his parents. He goes window shopping with his Italian friend, Mario. Because Junji doesn't speak Italian and he doesn't speak much English yet, he is glad to have found a friend like Mario who has been learning Japanese.

マリオ　　まち に いきましょう か。

じゅんじ　おかね が ありません。あなた は。

マ　　　　わたし も おかね が ありません が みせ の まど を みましょう か。

じ　　　　おもしろい でしょう。あたらしい じてんしゃ が ほしい です。じてんしゃや に いきましょう。

マ　　　　わたし も あたらしい じてんしゃ が ほしい です。いきましょう。

じ　　　　それ は いい じてんしゃ です ね。

マ　　　　はい、でも たかい です ね。どれ が すき です か。

じ　　　　その あおい の は...でも よんひゃく ドル です。たいへん たかい です ね。

マ　　　　そう です ね。でも きれい です。

じ　　　　はい、たいへん きれい です。はやい でしょう。

マ　　　　わたし も その あおい じてんしゃ が すき です。だめ です。おかね が ありません。かえりましょう。

Mario: *Machi ni ikimashoo ka.*
Junji: *Okane ga arimasen. Anata wa?*
M: *Watashi mo okane ga arimasen ga mise no mado o mimashoo ka.*
J: *Omoshiroi deshoo. Atarashii jitensha ga hoshii desu. Jitenshaya ni ikimashoo.*
M: *Watashi mo atarashii jitensha ga hoshii desu.*
         Ikimashoo.

(Later looking in the bicycle shop window.)
J: *Sore wa ii jitensha desu ne.*
M: *Hai, demo takai desu ne. Dore ga suki desu ka.*
J: *Sono aoi no wa . . . demo yonhyaku DORU desu. Taihen takai desu ne.*
M: *Soo desu ne. Demo kirei desu.*
J: *Hai, taihen kirei desu. Hayai deshoo.*
M: *Watashi mo sono aoi jitensha ga suki desu.*
         Dame desu. Okane ga arimasen. Kaerimashoo!

Check your understanding of the conversation.
M: Shall we go to town?
J: I don't have any money. What about you?
M: I don't either, but shall we look in the shop windows?
         (Go window shopping)
J: That would probably be fun. I want a new bike. Let's go to the bike shop.
M: I want a new bike, too. Let's go.
J: Those are good bikes, aren't they?
M: Yes, but they are expensive, aren't they? Which do you like?
J: That blue one, but it's four hundred dollars. Very expensive, isn't it?
M: I agree. But it is a beauty.
J: Yes, it's a beauty. It's probably fast.
M: I like the blue bike, too. It's no good. I don't have any money. Let's go home!

STUDY

- **. . . no mise**
  (Jitensha) no mise is an alternative way of describing a (bicycle) shop.

- **Dame** is another Qualitative Noun. So mentally put it into that file in your mind.

- **Takai desu ne/yasui desu ne** are useful phrases to learn.
  Remember that the negative of *takai* – *takakunai* (meaning "not expensive") allows you to say that something is not actually cheap but is not really expensive. Don't forget to use negatives in your role plays.

- **Deshoo** was introduced in the weather unit and is very useful as a way to express uncertainty or to ask someone's opinion. In English we use several different ways of expressing similar ideas; e.g.,

Do you think it will rain?   *Ame deshoo ka.*
Perhaps it will be hot.   *Atsui deshoo.*
Do you think it will be interesting?   *Omoshiroi deshoo ka.*
I think it may be expensive.   *Takai deshoo.*
I don't think it will be expensive.   *Takakunai deshoo.*
I think it was/may have been expensive.   *Takakatta deshoo.*
I don't think it was expensive/It probably wasn't expensive.
Takakunakatta deshoo.

- If you add **ne** to the end of similar phrases – *takai deshoo ne* – you include the opinion of the person to whom you are speaking so that it becomes "I think it may be expensive, don't you?" As this is something the Japanese like to do as often as possible, it makes your conversations sound more natural. Remember too that the Japanese don't like to be too definite in statements they make. It is part of their politeness to sound slightly uncertain and to give others the right to an opinion even on non-controversial topics.

- Look at the following examples:
Ikura deshoo ka.	How much do you think it will cost?
Takai deshoo ne.	I think it will be expensive, don't you?
	It'll probably be expensive, won't it?
Omoshiroi deshoo.	It'll probably be interesting.
	Perhaps it will be interesting.
	I think it will be interesting.
Hayai deshoo ka.	I wonder if it's fast?
	Do you think it will be fast?
Hayai deshoo ne.	It's probably fast, isn't it?

You can use *deshoo* in this way with adjectives and nouns. (But not with verbs. Later in your study of Japanese you will learn the correct way to do that. Be content to use it only with adjectives and nouns for the present.)

Using *deshoo* with nouns. Look at the following examples:
Maybe you need to pay an entry fee to a show, and your friend asks *Ikura deshoo ka.* "How much do you think it will be?" You answer: *Ni DORU deshoo.* "It'll probably be two dollars."
It's late at night and you hear a noise and say:
Nan deshoo ka. "What do you think it is?" Someone reassures you with:
Neko deshoo. "It's probably a cat."

Nani o kaimashoo ka.
What shall I buy?

- **Dore** "which." It means "which one" out of several things. The sentence pattern is *Dore ga hoshii desu ka*. "Which one do you want?/Which one would you like?"

- **Kono, sono, ano, dono** – "this," "that," "that over there," and "which." These look very similar to the *kore, sore, are, dore* family that you learned previously but they are used in a different way. The **no** ending of each of them may be used as a reminder that these words all go in front of **nouns:**
  kono kasa   "this umbrella" (close to speaker)
  ano hito   that person over there (away from both people)
  dono kaban   which bag
  There is never a particle between these words and the noun.

Check your understanding

1   *Kono kaban wa watashi no desu.*
2   *Kore wa watashi no kaban desu.*
3   *Sono inu wa ookii desu.*
4   *Sore wa ookii inu desu.*
5   *Ano hito wa BURAUN sensei desu.*
6   *Are wa watashi no jitensha desu.*

You will have noticed that there is a different emphasis in the sentence depending on whether you say "**that** is a big bag" or "**that bag** is big."

If you use *kono, sono, ano,* you **must** have a noun right after it so it is like a package. You are talking about the bag and defining which one you are talking about by saying "this" or "that" bag.

Sono kaban wa ii desu.	That bag is good.
Kono kaban o kudasai.	Please, may I have this bag?

Any particles will be after the noun.

If you use *sore*, you must follow it immediately with **wa, ga** or **o** particles because you are choosing to pick that out as the topic or the object of your sentence:

Kore wa kaban desu.	This (thing here) is a bag.
Kore o kudasai.	This (thing here) please/Give me/ Please, may I have this?
Sore ga suki desu.	I like that (thing there).

Remember the **re** on the end of this group reminds you that it is "heRE" or "theRE."

You cannot use *are* when talking about a person. It would be rather impolite to say "That thing over there is James"!

ACTIVITIES

- Make up a role play with two others in which you go out shoping:
  a   Suggest going out and by what means of transportation.
  b   Suggest which shops you'll go to.
  c   Look at various articles in shops and comment on them; e.g.,
       kono/sono/ano kaban wa kirei desu ne/takai desu ne/yasui desu ne.
  d   Decide to buy something. Ask how much it is. Comment on the price.
  e   If you have enough money, buy it.
  f   Suggest what you could do next or what day and time you will meet
       again.
  g   Say you're sorry but you have to leave, and say goodbye.

- Choose a story title from the following and write five or six sentences in
  hiragana on that topic:
  1   Noises in the night. (*kikimasu* means "hear" as well as "listen")
  2   A TV show.
  3   Your day in the mountains.
  4   A day at school.
      When you have finished, share them with each other by reading them
  to your group or allowing others to read them, or by putting them on the
  wall. If you prefer, don't put your name on the copy of your work that you
  offer.

- Write ten sentences using *deshoo*, writing the English equivalent that you
  intend beneath. With a partner check your two pieces of work. If there are
  any you disagree about, consult your teacher.

- Brainstorm what you remember about shops/shopping in Japan from the
  cultural notes in this unit.

Fortune telling (left)
Stall in park (right)

SOME STUDY TIPS

Students sometimes ask "Do we have to learn the cultural background notes?" To learn a language without knowing a little of the culture would be quite boring and would not improve your understanding of the country or its people, traditions, and customs. Without some knowledge of the culture, you would never be able to be really proficient in speaking or writing the language. The likelihood of misunderstanding and intolerance is greatly reduced if you know, not just the words and grammar, but why people react in certain ways or use certain expressions. The greater our understanding of the culture, the greater the chance that in our contact with other nations we will achieve harmony.

On a less philosophical level, the information gives you background to understand stories and conversation in greater depth. If names of places or festivals or facts occur in passages or in conversation, you don't get confused or spend ages looking them up, wondering what they mean. You may not remember all the details, but if you recognize the word, it really helps.

You may like to discuss this further among yourselves. Do you agree or disagree? Why?

ACROSS

4 opposite of expensive
5 bicycle
7 eight thousand
8 shopping
10 after that
13 this month
14 The most famous shopping street in Tokyo
18 a time keeper
19 three thousand
21 I don't want it
25 two people
27 six hundred
30 new, fresh
31 *sanbyaku* plus *yonhyaku*
33 this morning
34 Someone says this to you as you leave the house
36 expensive
37 welcome (in a shop)
39 The vegetables will always be fresh there
40 What you get back from a shopkeeper if you gave too much

DOWN

1 After high school I plan to go to . . .
2 If something is over 90 years old, it is . . .
3 fruit
6 that
9 *masu* form of the verb "show"
11 next month
12 by myself
15 where you buy flowers
16 I've got a cold; please get me medicine from the . . .
17 twice four hundred
20 nine hundred
22 I'm going out now
23 customer/guest
24 and then
26 Interesting, amusing
28 three hundred
29 until
32 from
35 that (thing over there)
38 Japanese currency

CROSSWORD (TOPIC TEN REVIEW)
Try this crossword. Write in *ROOMAji*.

Vocabulary checklist (Topic Ten)

Introduction

えん	*en*	yen
かいもの	*kaimono*	shopping
いらっしゃいませ	*irasshaimase*	welcome
Interest		
めいじ　じんぐう	*Meiji jinguu*	Meiji shrine
さつ	*satsu*	banknotes
ぎんざ	*Ginza*	Famous street in Tokyo
あきはばら	*Akihabara*	District of Tokyo
しんじゅく	*Shinjuku*	District of Tokyo
はらじゅく	*Harajuku*	District of Tokyo

Unit 1

みせ の ひと	mise no hito	store clerk
おきゃくさん	Okyakusan	customer
みせ	mise	shop
ひゃく	hyaku	one hundred
にひゃく	nihyaku	two hundred
さんびゃく	sanbyaku	three hundred
よんひゃく	yonhyaku	four hundred
ごひゃく	gohyaku	five hundred
ろっぴゃく	roppyaku	six hundred
ななひゃく	nanahyaku	seven hundred
はっぴゃく	happyaku	eight hundred
きゅうひゃく	kyuuhyaku	nine hundred
せん	sen	thousand
にせん	nisen	two thousand
さんぜん	sanzen	three thousand
よんせん	yonsen	four thousand
ごせん	gosen	five thousand
ろくせん	rokusen	six thousand
ななせん	nanasen	seven thousand
はっせん	hassen	eight thousand
きゅうせん	kyuusen	nine thousand
まん	man	ten thousand (counter)
いちまん	ichiman	ten thousand
にまん	niman	twenty thousand, etc.
みせます／みせる	misemasu (miseru)	show
みせて ください	misete kudasai	please show me
おつり	Otsuri	change
とけい	tokei	watch/clock
ドル	DORU	dollar
セント	SENTO	cents
カメラ	KAMERA	camera
まいど ありがとう 　ございました	maido arigatoo 　gozaimashita	thank you for shopping 　here
それ では ありません	sore dewa arimasen	not that one
Interest		
てんいん	ten'in	store clerk

Unit 2

けさ	kesa	this morning
やすい	yasui	cheap
デパート	DEPAATO	department store
から	kara	from
まで	made	up to/until/as far as
Interest		
バーゲン セール	BAGGEN SEERU	bargain sale

Unit 3

ははのひ	haha no hi	Mother's Day
はな（や）	hana (ya)	flower (shop)
さかな（や）	sakana (ya)	fish (shop)
にく（や）	niku (ya)	meat (butcher)
スーパー （マーケット）	SUUPAA (MAAKETTO)	supermarket
やさい	yasai	vegetables

やおや	yaoya	greengrocer
くだもの（や）	kudamono (ya)	fruit (stand)
くつ（や）	kutsu (ya)	shoe (shop)
それから	sorekara	after that/then/so

Unit 4

オートバイ	OOTOBAI	motorbike
がくせい	gakusei	senior student
だいがく	daigaku	university
だいがくせい	daigakusei	university student
ふるい	furui	old
はやい	hayai	fast/early
たいへん	taihen	very, very
でも	demo	but (beginning of sentence)
せんげつ	sengetsu	last month
こんげつ	kongetsu	this month
らいげつ	raigetsu	next month
あたらしい	atarashii	new/fresh
かいしゃいん	kaishain	company employee
おかね	Okane	money
が	ga	but
Interest		
バイク	BAIKU	motorbike

Unit 5

いって　まいります	itte mairimasu	I'm going out
いって　いらっしゃい	itte irasshai	come back safely, etc.
ほしい	hoshii	want (adjective)
ごろ	goro	about (a time)
パン	PAN	bread
かって　ください	katte kudasai	please buy
ええ　と	ee to	hesitation noise
Interest		
なにか	nanika	something/anything
もの	mono	thing
ほしい　もの	hoshii mono	wanted thing
アスピリン	ASUPIRIN	aspirin

Unit 6

だめな	dame (na)	no good (Qualitative Noun)
おもしろい	omoshiroi	interesting
じてんしゃや	jitenshaya	bicycle shop
でしょう	deshoo	probably
ね	ne	isn't it?
どれ	dore	which out of more than two things
たかい	takai	high/tall/expensive
この	kono	this
その	sono	that
あの	ano	that over there
どの	dono	which

TOPIC ELEVEN
my town

Introduction

ACHIEVEMENTS

By the end of this topic, you will be able to:
- make clearer, and more, requests;
- ask for directions;
- give and understand directions;
- tell someone about your town;
- tell the time in greater detail;
- join sentences with the *te* form;
- give more exact positions of things and places;
- say when activities begin.

You will also learn more *katakana* syllables.

Japanese cities and towns

The majority of large Japanese cities have been built on the coastal plains. Particularly on Honshu, the largest island, the cities sprawl in a neverending stream across the only flat land that Japan has, on valuable, previously fertile agricultural land. They have grown up where years ago there were small farming villages. Even now in the center of large towns you may come across small fields of rice or market-gardening vegetable plots.

The cities are busy, noisy places like cities anywhere, alive and bright day and night, with huge neon signs, bustling traffic and hurrying pedestrians. One of the most remarkable things about Japanese cities is the sheer volume of traffic. Every day two million people pass through Shinjuku station in Tokyo during the rush hour. For foreigners it is an amazing experience to be caught up in that throng, to see everywhere around you a solid mass of black-haired people. The uniformity of the crowd is surprising initially, if you come from a society where there are many hair colors. (Japanese people comment a lot on hair and eyes of other nationalities and often want to touch blond hair and have their photos taken alongside foreigners they may have only fleetingly met.) Businessmen dress very conservatively and uniformly in Japan. There is quite a strict code of dress for all workers in fact, and that, combined with the mass of dark-colored school uniforms, gives a somber color to the crowd as it swarms into stations during peak periods.

Crowds of shoppers in Shibuya

Trains are clean, efficient and punctual

Getting around

Trains and buses are very punctual. They have to be to keep the traffic flow moving smoothly. There are even people employed to push passengers into the trains to make sure that each train takes as many people as possible during the busiest times. These people are called **oshiya** – literally, "pushers" – often university students doing it as a part-time job. They wear neat uniforms and white gloves and look very gentlemanly for their rather bizarre job!

On trains and buses, whether standing or sitting, many people read or sleep, knowing instinctively where to wake up and get off! During the last ten years the number who regularly read has increased dramatically. This is perhaps due to increases in traveling time as people commute further to their work, and maybe partly because of the example set. The majority of Japanese like to fit in, to do and have the same as others. Reading on trains means time for yourself in an otherwise very busy schedule, and keeping yourself to yourself as politeness demands. It has also become "the thing to do."

Popular novels in Japan are designed to fit easily in pockets and briefcases, and the station bookstalls have hundreds of titles to suit every taste, plus magazines, comic books, and newspapers to supply the commuters' needs. Students may often be seen doing their homework for school or cram school, too.

Buses and trains in Japan are cheap, reliable, and very easy to use. Japanese people are extremely kind to visitors, too. You only have to stand looking puzzled or reach for a map to have someone or several people immediately offer to help, all eager to try out their English and to be seen communicating with you. (If you are trying to use your Japanese, it can actually be frustrating, as people are so anxious to try their English!)

Road signs (left)
Street signs (right)

Streets are usually very narrow. Pedestrians keep inside the white lines where there is no space for footpaths

Street signs in major centers are usually written in *roomaji* as well as *kanji* and *kana*, which is helpful to visitors. Signs at railway and bus stations are also in both, but signs on the road are in *kanji*. Outside the major centers it is necessary to know *hiragana* and the names of the towns you want to visit in *kanji* if you are driving.

Amenities and leisure

Japan's large population of 122 million means that local councils have to provide a lot of services. However, they have the advantage of many long-established services and a reasonable income from fees and taxes.

Municipal services like libraries and parks, sports centers and community education centers are very well used, as people strive to keep fit and to advance their job prospects.

Because homes are small, students spend more time studying in libraries than many other nationalities who have greater privacy and better opportunities for study at home.

Visitors to Japan often comment on the cleanliness of streets and public places, the attention to detail in weeding and sweeping up leaves in parks and temple grounds, and the army of workers constantly cleaning the public vehicles. In Japan many more people are employed to look after the cleanliness of cities and the safety of others than in most countries. There are many jobs, performed by people who would otherwise be unemployed, that are of real benefit to society. This is one reason why unemployment in Japan is so low, even though the job market is very competitive.

There are people employed to make sure that traffic coming out of a parking lot is not a danger to pedestrians, to watch traffic around road works and signal danger by the blowing of whistles, and to help commercial traffic to back and turn. All these people have neat uniforms and have a significant role to play in helping the smooth running of daily life. Best of all, they have self-respect and take pride in their jobs no matter what they are, because they are usefully employed.

Parks and other public amenities are well used as people take the opportunity to use their very limited leisure time. Some commentators on Japan say that Japanese students, and adults too, don't know what holidays or leisure time are, and certainly never have "free time." Even so-called leisure time is tightly scheduled, often by the school, company, or parents.

Shopping is a consuming interest for the Japanese. They have a high standard of living and can afford consumer items, but besides this, shopping and window-shopping are social outlets. If you can't entertain at home, don't have a lot of maintenance to do on your home and garden, and live in or near a city, you go out with your friends and enjoy the amenities of town life – the restaurants, theaters, concerts, art galleries, museums, shops, and other entertainment. Just walking around together is a major part of socializing. This is particularly true of Japanese young people.

Golf clubs, fishing, martial arts, sports and other clubs like *ikebana* flower arranging and *bonsai* tree culture occupy many people, too.

Others choose to visit instead the temples and shrines. These are havens of peace in busy towns and manage to achieve an atmosphere of tranquility even when surrounded by the town's bustle – a good place to go to sit quietly to talk or to have a rest from walking the hard pavements.

Because shops are open seven days a week from about ten in the morning until seven or eight o'clock at night, the cities are busy all the time. Shops and offices have different days when they close, so there is always a vast number of people who have their time off on weekdays, as well as the people who are using the amenities in their lunch breaks and after work.

This man's job is to clean chewing gum off the pavement outside a department store (top right)
Weekends in the park (left)
Playing the Japanese harp (*koto*) (lower right)

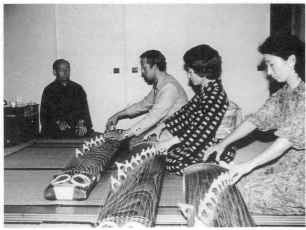

Japanese religion is a daily practice for many people and does not have a particular day each week for its observance. So religion does not affect the commercial week, except for major festival times.

Patterns of living for most people are tightly structured. Children know that they have to work hard at school and there is not much leisure time. It is the same for adults too, as they struggle for advancement in their jobs. Life in the towns is busy, and everyone can find activities to suit their own needs.

Bonsai trees are suited to the space available in city dwellings

On weekends many people visit shrines and temples, like this one at Asakusa in Tokyo

Unit 1

きて、みて ください
kite, mite kudasai
Please come and watch

NEW WORDS

はじまります	*hajimarimasu*	start/begin
ゲーム	*GEEMU*	game
おばあさん	*Obaasan*	grandmother
たいせつ	*taisetsu*	important
もちろん	*mochiron*	of course
あと　で	*ato de*	afterwards/after
まえ	*mae*	before/in front
ふん / ぶん	*fun/pun*	minutes
じゅうごふん	*juugofun*	fifteen minutes
バスてい	*BASUtei*	bus stop

Anna has an important tennis match today.

アナ	おかあさん　きょう　は　たいせつ　です。きょう　は　まち　の　こうえん　で　テニス　を　します。ゲーム　は　たいせつ　です。きて、みて　ください。
おかあさん	なんじ　に　します　か。
ア	にじ　はん　に　テニス　の　ゲーム　は　はじまります。
お	ええ　と、にじ　に　おばあさん　の　うち　に　いきます　が…
ア	きて　ください。ゲーム　は　たいへん　たいせつ　です。あと　で　おばあさん　の　うち　に　いって　ください。
お	じゃ、ゲーム　に　いきます。
ア	ありがとう　ございます。にじ　じゅうごふん　に　きて　ください。
お	はい。おもしろい　でしょう　か。
ア	もちろん。わたし　は　いい　テニス　を　します。あと　で　わたし　も　おばあさん　の　うち　に　いきます。

ANA: *Okaasan, kyoo wa taisetsu desu.*
            Kyoo wa machi no kooen de TENISU o shimasu.
            GEEMU wa taisetsu desu.
            Kite, mite kudasai.

Okaasan: *Nanji ni shimasu ka.*
A: *Niji han ni TENISU no GEEMU wa hajimarimasu.*
O: *Ee to, niji ni Obaasan no uchi ni ikimasu ga . . .*
A: *Kite kudasai. GEEMU wa taihen taisetsu desu.*
     Ato de Obaasan no uchi ni itte kudasai.
O: *Ja, GEEMU ni ikimasu.*
A: *Arigatoo gozaimasu. Niji juugofun ni kite kudasai.*
O: *Hai. Omoshiroi deshoo ka.*
A: *Mochiron. Watashi wa ii TENISU o shimasu!*
     Ato de watashi mo Obaasan no uchi ni ikimasu.

Check your understanding of the conversation.
A: Mom, today is important. Today I'm going to play tennis at the town park. The game is important. Please come and watch.
M: What time will you play?
A: The game starts at two-thirty.
M: Um . . . at two o'clock I'm going to go to Grandma's but . . .
A: Please come. The game is very important.
     Please go to Grandma's afterwards.
M: All right . . . I'll come to the game.
A: Thank you. Please come at two-fifteen.
M: Yes, I will. Do you think the game will be interesting?
A: Of course. I play good tennis! Afterwards I'll go to Grandma's, too.

STUDY

- The new verb **hajimarimasu** is used for things like concerts, school, parties, etc., starting, not for you starting something; e.g., "School begins at nine o'clock." *Gakkoo wa kuji ni hajimarimasu.*
  "The concert will start at seven."
  KONSAATO wa shichiji ni hajimarimasu.
  "The party began at eight."
  PAATII wa hachiji ni hajimarimashita.
  The topic is always going to be something outside yourself.

- **Taisetsu** is a Qualitative Noun, one of the same group of words as *kirei, HANSAMU, joozu, benri*, that you learned previously. The negative is therefore *taisetsu janai* or *taisetsu dewa arimasen*. (The past: *taisetsu deshita*, the past negative: *taisetsu dewa arimasen deshita*.)

- Using "come" and "go" in Japanese: in the above conversation you may have noticed that mother says **ikimasu** when the English translation says "I'll **come**." The reason for this is that she will have to **go** from where she is in order to get to the park. Her action will be away from where she happens to be at the time. Therefore she will be **going**. It's very logical really. You can't "come" to a place that is away from you!
  In English, however, **come** is used for a movement to the place where the speaker or listener will be, when talking about the past or future. The listener (Anna) will be at the tennis match, and so mother says (in English) "I'll come."

- **Kite, mite kudasai** "please come and watch." You have known this construction for a long time, for making polite requests and giving instructions. The words *kite* and *mite* are in fact a verb form, commonly called the **te** form of their verbs. *Kite* is the *te* form of kimasu, *mite* is the *te* form of *mimasu*. You know the *masu, mashita, masen, masen deshita* and *mashoo* forms of verbs and you have been using the *te* form of verbs with *kudasai* just as learned phrases.

  Here are all the *te* forms of the verbs you know:

come	kimasu	kite
see	mimasu	mite
eat	tabemasu	tabete
speak	hanashimasu	hanashite (when pronouncing the *shite* remember to leave out the "i" – *shte*)
do	shimasu	shite
study	benkyoo shimasu	benkyoo shite
practice	renshuu shimasu	renshuu shite
phone	denwa shimasu	denwa shite
clean	sooji shimasu	sooji shite
be	imasu	ite (things that can move under their own power)
leave	demasu	dete
show	misemasu	misete

(All of the above take off the *masu* and add on *te*.)

meet	aimasu	atte
buy	kaimasu	katte
be/exist	arimasu	atte (for things that can't move under their own power)
go	ikimasu	itte
return	kaerimasu	kaette
begin	hajimarimasu	hajimatte

(These all have double t.)

read	yomimasu	yonde
drink	nomimasu	nonde
play	asobimasu	asonde

(You'll notice that the last three have a **de** ending. Strangely they are still known as the *te* form!)

arrive	tsukimasu	tsuite
listen	kikimasu	kiite

There are rules for learning the *te* forms – a table is given at the end of the book for those who like to see the overall pattern. But at this stage it is probably more practical to learn the *te* form of each verb as it is introduced, as following the rules demands knowledge of the dictionary forms of the verbs which are not introduced until a much later stage. Often too, the rules sound complicated and are themselves difficult to understand and put into practice.

You will also have noticed that *arimasu* and *aimasu* appear to have the same *te* form and you may be wondering how you tell the difference. Eventually when you are reading and writing *kanji* there are different *kanji* for those words. While you are using *hiragana*, the difference is in the context only. You have already gotten used to the fact that you have to use the context in Japanese to work out who is speaking or to whom a sentence applies and will realize that in context the two words will be clearly recognizable. If they are not immediately obvious, try both and see which one fits best for the meaning of the sentence.

You will gradually become aware of the patterns that emerge as you get to know more *te* forms. Learn the *te* forms of all the verbs above by heart and look carefully at the way they are written in *hiragana*: Double the "t" by using a half-size *tsu* in front of the second "t."

- Telling the time with hours and minutes: You know how to tell hours and half-hours answering the question *Ima nanji desu ka*. To give more precise reading of time use the following table of minutes:

いっぷん	*ippun*	one minute
にふん	*nifun*	two minutes
さんぷん	*sanpun*	three minutes
よんぷん	*yonpun*	four minutes
ごふん	*gofun*	five minutes
ろっぷん	*roppun*	six minutes
ななふん	*nanafun*	seven minutes
はっぷん	*happun*	eight minutes
きゅうふん	*kyuufun*	nine minutes
じゅっぷん	*juppun*	ten minutes
じゅういっぷん	*juuippun*	eleven minutes
じゅうにふん	*juunifun*	twelve minutes
じゅうさんぷん	*juusanpun*	thirteen minutes, etc.
にじゅっぷん	*nijuppun*	twenty minutes

Shichiji nifun mae desu

These take a bit of getting used to! Take the trouble to learn them well now and it will prove really useful to you. But until you have them all concretely learned, keep referring to the table. That in itself is a good way to help your memory.

Using these minutes the time is told this way:

Ichiji ippun.　　One minute after one o'clock.
　　　　　　　　　(One o'clock plus one minute)
Sanji juugofun.　Fifteen minutes past three/A quarter past three
　　　　　　　　　(Three o'clock plus fifteen minutes)

Just put the number of minutes after the hour as you did with *han* (half).

To say a time before the hour use "**mae**" in the following way:

Mae means "before" or "in front of."

Niji juppun mae therefore means "ten to two" (ten minutes before two o'clock).

ACTIVITIES

- With a partner test each other on hours and minutes. Take turns making up a time and giving the equivalent in English.

- In groups make a cardboard clock. Each person in the group takes a turn to set the hands. The other people in the group must each give a sentence that includes that time. Each person in turn sets the time and checks the sentences given.

• In pairs: Role play a conversation similar to the one at the beginning of this unit in which two people request things of each other and reach a compromise.

• Make a set of Time cards each or photocopy and cut up the cards on p. 59. Remember to make some of them twenty-four hour time. Use them to test yourself and to test your friends.

• Using these cards plus the ones you've made before, deal out a set of about fifty cards among four people, giving each person seven cards. Leave the rest of the pack face down on the table. Each person should also have a supply of blank cards to use for particles. (The cards will include time words and phrases, activities, objects and verbs – use the activities/places/objects/verbs cards on p. 60.)

   Each person tries to construct a sentence using the words they have in their hands. Particles may be written on the blank cards and inserted where needed to make the sentence make sense. Take turns putting down a sentence. If you can't make one, take a card from the spare card pile and put one of your unwanted cards face upwards beside the spare cards. That was your turn, so if you are now able to make a sentence, you must wait until all the others in your group have had their turn before putting it out. The person who runs out of cards first is the winner.

Which bicycle is mine?

Time words

あした	まいにち	きのう	きょう
いつも	いつ	げつようび	もくようび
すいようび	かようび	にちようび	どようび
きんようび	じゅうじ	くじ	さんじ
にじ	ごじ	よじ	いちじ
ろくじはん	しちじじゅうごふん	はちじにじゅっぷん	じゅういちじ じゅっぷん まえ
くじよんじゅっぷん	よじはん	こんしゅう	らいしゅう
せんしゅう	こんげつ	せんげつ	らいげつ
いちがつ	にがつ	さんがつ	しがつ
ごがつ	ろくがつ	しちがつ	はちがつ
くがつ	じゅうがつ	じゅういちがつ	じゅうにがつ
にじゅうじ	じゅうしちじ	じゅうよじ	ときどき
にじごふん まえ	らいしゅう の かようび	いつも	にがつ むいか

Activities, places, objects, verbs

やきゅう	しょどう	けんどう	からて
すもう	とけい	テニス	かさ
ゴリラ	き	いぬ	はな
ねこ	ノート	えんぴつ	ほん
ライオン	はこ	ペン	うみ
こうえん	としょかん	プール	まち
がっこう	えいが	しんぶん	ざっし
まんが	みせ	みます	みせます
かえります	きます	いきます	あけます
おきます	ねます	かいます	でます
しめます	でんわ　します	れんしゅう　します	よみます

Check your understanding

Use the following exercises to check your memory and your reading of *hiragana*.

A
1 さんじ に ついて ください。
2 レコード を きいて ください。
3 ざっし を よんで ください。
4 ハンバーガー を たべて ください。
5 にほんご を べんきょう して ください。
6 フランスご を れんしゅう して ください。
7 イタリアご で はなして ください。
8 にわ で あそんで ください。
9 ジュース を のんで ください。
10 こうえん に いって ください。
11 わたし の うち に きて ください。
12 ペン を かって ください。
13 おなまえ を かいて ください。
14 くじ に かえって ください。
15 よじ に がっこう を でて ください。
16 しんしつ で ねて ください。
17 だいどころ を そうじ して ください。
18 けんじくん に でんわ して ください。
19 ほん を みて ください。
20 えき で あって ください。

1 *Sanji ni tsuite kudasai.*
2 *REKOODO o kiite kudasai.*
3 *Zasshi o yonde kudasai.*
4 *HANBAAGAA o tabete kudasai.*
5 *Nihongo o benkyoo shite kudasai.*
6 *FURANSUgo o renshuu shite kudasai.*
7 *ITARIAgo de hanashite kudasai.*
8 *Niwa de asonde kudasai.*
9 *JUUSU o nonde kudasai.*
10 *Kooen ni itte kudasai.*
11 *Watashi no uchi ni kite kudasai.*
12 *PEN o katte kudasai.*
13 *Onamae o kaite kudasai.*
14 *Kuji ni kaette kudasai.*
15 *Yoji ni gakkoo o dete kudasai.*
16 *Shinshitsu de nete kudasai.*
17 *Daidokoro o sooji shite kudasai.*
18 *Kenji kun ni denwa shite kudasai.*
19 *Hon o mite kudasai.*
20 *Eki de atte kudasai.*

Katakana words to recognize – find them in the sentences above.
PEN   ペン   *REKOODO*   レコード

| *FURANSU* | フランス | *ITARIA* | イタリア |
| *HANBAAGAA* | ハンバーガー | *JUUSU* | ジュース |

Answers
1   Please arrive at three o'clock.
2   Please listen to the record.
3   Please read the magazine.
4   Please eat the hamburger.
5   Please study Japanese.
6   Please practice French.
7   Please speak in Italian.
8   Please play in the garden.
9   Please drink juice.
10   Please go to the park.
11   Please come to my house.
12   Please buy a pen.
13   Please write your name.
14   Please return at nine o'clock.
15   Please leave school at four o'clock.
16   Please lie down in the bedroom.
17   Please clean the kitchen.
18   Please telephone Kenji.
19   Please look at the book.
20   Please meet at the station.

Using the sentences above write the Japanese equivalent, taking particular note of the particle you need to use. Check against the Japanese version when you finish.

B
Look at the following examples, then do the exercises that follow:
Nijijuugofun ni atte kudasai.   "Please meet me at a quarter past two."
Sanji juppun ni toshokan de atte kudasai.   "Please meet me at the library at ten past three."

(Remember you need **de** after a place if it's the location of your activity; **de** after your means of transportation; **ni** if it's a place you are going to or returning to, or a person you are talking to or meeting, and after times; and **o** if you are using an object.)

1   *Mise de manga o katte kudasai.*
2   *Kyooshitsu de eiga o mite kudasai.*
3   *Toshokan de hon o yonde kudasai.*
4   *PUURU de asonde kudasai.*
5   *Niji gofun no BASU de itte kudasai.*
6   *Machi de shinbun o katte kudasai.*
7   *Densha de kaette kudasai.*
8   *Jitensha de watashi no uchi ni kite kudasai.*
9   *Tabete kudasai.*
10   *BEN san ni hanashite kudasai.*

C

Now work out how you would say the following in Japanese:

(First read the sentences and decide which particle you need and why. Write down the sentences and then check them against the answers given.)

1   Please come to the party on Saturday.
2   Please read the book about Japan.
3   Please return home at six-thirty.
4   Please meet Kawai at seven-twenty at the park.
5   Please do your English homework today.
6   Please practice your guitar at five o'clock.
7   Please go to town on the four minutes past four bus.
8   Please speak to your younger sister.
9   Please telephone at five thirty-five.
10 Please eat the sandwiches.

Reading practice

Listen as your teacher reads the passage aloud, following the *hiragana*, then practice reading it aloud until you are sure that you can read it easily. Work hard to achieve the correct pronunciation.

あ   こんしゅう まち で いい えいが が はじまります。

い   あした えいが に いきましょう か。

あ   はい、いきましょう。なんじ に はじまります か。

い   ごじ じゅっぷん に はじまります。

あ   だいじょうぶ です。さんじ さんじゅうごふん の バス で
      いきましょう。さんじさんじゅっぷん に バスてい で あいます。

い   なんじ に まち に つきます か。

あ   よじ よんじゅっぷん。

い   いい です。ざっし を かいます。じかん が あります。そして
      えいがかん に いきます。

あ   いい です。わたし も ざっし を かいます。

い   なんじ に かえります か。

あ   はちじ にじゅうななふん に バス が あります。

い   いい です。なんじ に うち に つきます か。

あ   くじ さんじゅうにふん に つきます。

A: There's a good movie starting in town this week.
B: Shall we go to the movies tomorrow?
A: Yes, let's. What time does it start?
B: Ten past five.
A: OK. So let's go on the three thirty-five bus. I'll meet you at three thirty at the bus stop.
B: What time will we arrive in town?
A: Four-forty.
B: That's good. I'll buy some magazines. We'll have time. And then we'll go to the movie theater.
A: Good. I'll buy some magazines, too.
B: What time shall we return home?
A: There's a bus at eight twenty-seven.
B: That's good. What time will we arrive home?
A: Nine thirty-two.

BASUtei (bus stop)   **Promoting a new movie**

Writing practice

- Review *TE*, *DE*, *SU* テ デ ス

- Learn *NI* ニ

- Learn *KE* ケ

From *KE* you can make *GE* ゲ

- Learn *MU* ム

- Write *TENISU, GEEMU* テニス　ゲーム

- Find syllables you know in the following lines.
  カサシタチナニハヒマミヤユラリア
  ケセテネヘメワレルヨムフヌツスク
  コソトノホモヲロレンルヨワムメフ
  パトテツチタサシスセソゲクキカネ
  アイウエオコケクキカパプホモヲド
  クスツヌフムヨルリユミヒニチシキ

- Pick out your own country from the following list.
  メキシコ　アフリカ　フランス　イタリア　ドイツ
  イギリス　ロシア　オーストラリア　アメリカ　カナダ

- Are there any names you know in the following selection?
  リサ　アン　ベン　ニキ　スコット
  ジョン　サイモン

- Identify these words.
  テニス　スーパー　プール　デパート　オートバイ　ゲーム

- For interest, here is the *kanji* for "minutes": *fun* or *pun*
  分
  You can put it together with the *kanji* numbers to express, for example:
  五分　　*gofun*　　(five minutes)

分

パチンコ　　*PACHINKO*

PACHINKO, a pinball game, is an incredibly popular pastime. *PACHINKO* parlors can be found in every city and town and often operate for twenty-four hours a day.

In the parlors pinball machines are set up vertically in long rows. The game requires a minimum of skill. Players buy steel balls from the operator, feed them into the machines, and by directing them into the right holes, can win extra balls, which tumble out into small plastic buckets.

As well as the deafening clanging and clatter of the *PACHINKO* balls, pop music blares continuously, and the parlor is filled with cigarette smoke as hardened players puff away – all making it an experience not to be missed!

Some players are so addicted they spend all their leisure time at their favorite parlor. As the game is a form of gambling, entry is restricted to those over eighteen. The parlors are not legally allowed to give cash prizes, so instead the players exchange their buckets of balls for "gifts" – often small boxes of chocolates or other fairly valueless items. These gifts are accepted, and players then go out of the parlor and around the corner to an insignificant little window where the gift is exchanged for cash. The gifts are then sold by the exchange merchant to the parlor. Everyone is happy, and the law has been obeyed!

Unit 2

こうえん に いって、
テニス を みましょう か
kooen ni itte, TENISU o mimashoo ka
Shall we go to the park and
watch the tennis game?

Helen is enjoying an exchange visit in Japan.
Her host father is very obliging and helps her to get to places she wants to visit.

ヘレン　　こうえん　に　いって、テニス　を　みましょう　か。

すみこ　　ええ、そう　しましょう。テニス　が　すき　です。なんじ　に
　　　　　　はじまります　か。

ヘ　　　　にじ　はん　に。

す　　　　どこ　です　か。

ヘ　　　　まち　に　あります。

す　　　　なん　で　いきましょう　か。

ヘ　　　　おとうさん　の　くるま　で。

す　　　　なんじ　に　でます　か。

ヘ　　　　おとうさん　は　いちじ　はん　に　まち　に　いきます。

す　　　　いちじ　にじゅうごふん　に　あなた　の　うち　に
　　　　　　いきます。だいじょうぶ　です　か。

ヘ　　　　はい、だいじょうぶ　です。じゃ　また。

す　　　　じゃ　また。

In pairs read the above conversation. Try not to look at the *roomaji* version unless you have real difficulty.

Helen: *Kooen ni itte, TENISU o mimashoo ka.*
Sumiko: *Ee, soo shimashoo. TENISU ga suki desu. Nanji ni hajimarimasu
          ka.*

H: *Nijihan ni.*
S: *Doko desu ka.*
H: *Machi ni arimasu.*
S: *Nan de ikimashoo ka.*
H: *Otoosan no kuruma de.*
S: *Nanji ni demasu ka.*
H: *Otoosan wa ichiji han ni machi ni ikimasu.*

S: *Ichiji nijuugofun ni anata no uchi ni ikimasu.*
     Daijoobu desu ka.
H: *Hai, daijoobu desu. Ja mata.*
S: *Ja mata.*

Check your understanding of the conversation.
H: Shall we go and watch the tennis game?
S: Yes, let's (do that). I like tennis. What time does it start?
H: 2:30.
S: Where is it?
H: In town.
S: How shall we go?
H: In my father's car.
S: What time will you leave?
H: My father is going to go to town at one thirty.
S: I'll come to your house at one twenty-five. Is that OK?
H: Yes. See you later.
S: Bye.

STUDY

- *Kooen ni itte, TENISU o mimashoo ka.* In this sentence the **te** form is used to join two sentences. **Itte** in this sentence, without *kudasai* or any other ending means "go and." The tense of the whole sentence is taken from the final verb of the sentence: *mimashoo* "let's watch/look/see."

  The **mashoo ka** ending means "Shall we . . ." **mimashoo ka** "Shall we watch?" Therefore the whole sentence reads:
  "Shall we go to the park and watch the tennis game?"

  The first action in the English sentence should come first in the Japanese sentence: "(Shall we) go to the park" *Kooen ni itte,* "watch the tennis game" *TENISU o mimashoo ka.* Put a Japanese comma after the **te** form.

  Study the following examples:
  Watashi wa gakkoo ni itte, benkyoo shimashita.
  I went to school and studied.
  Toshokan ni itte, hon o yomimashita.
  I went to the library and read a book.
  DAN kun ni atte, eiga ni ikimashita.
  I met Dan and (we) went to the movies.
  Asagohan o tabete, heya o sooji shimasu.
  I'll have (eat) breakfast and clean my room.

ACTIVITIES

- Work in pairs. Student One constructs a sentence aloud. Student Two listens and constructs a second sentence that could logically be an action following the first sentence. Student One then joins the two sentences using the **te** form of the verb used in the first sentence. Take turns making the first sentence. Vary your sentences as much as possible.

- Work in two teams. Team One offers a sentence. Team Two changes the verb to a **te** form and adds on another sentence. Team One then gives the meaning of the complete sentence in English.

- Review the following from *Level 1*:
  Nan de ikimasu ka.   "How will you go?" "By what means will you go?"
  Nan   "what" is used with particle **de** to express "by means of"; e.g.,
  Jitensha de ikimasu.   I'll go by bike.
  Densha de ikimasu.   I'll go by train.
  Hikooki de ikimasu.   I'll go by plane.
      Another use of **de** also meaning "by means of" is as follows: I watched the film on TV. (I watched the film by means of TV.) *TEREBI de eiga o mimashita.*
  I heard it on the radio.   *RAJIO de kikimashita.*

Check your understanding

How would you say in Japanese:
1   I'll go to town by bus and watch a movie.
2   Jon went to the park and met Julie.
3   I went to the pool with my friend Sandra and played.
4   The dog saw the hotdog and ate it (saw and ate the hotdog).
5   I'll have (drink) coffee and (eat) a hamburger.
6   I listened to it on the radio and then read the book.

Writing practice

- Practice the words you already know in *katakana*: your name, your friends' names and your country.

- Which of the following do you know?
  ス　ア　イ　オ　ケ　セ　テ　ト　ハ
  フ　ム　リ　ル　ン　パ　バ　プ　ゲ

- Learn **RE**　レ

- Learn **HE** へ

- From **HE** you can make **BE** and **PE**   ベ   ペ

- Learn **HI** ヒ

- From **HI** you can make **BI** and **PI**   ビ   ピ

- Review **FU** フ
  Learn **BU** ブ

- Write the following:

ヘレン	スー	ペン	ベン	テレビ	プール
HEREN	*SUU*	*PEN*	*BEN*	*TEREBI*	*PUURU*

デパート	スーパー	テーブル	オートバイ	テープ
DEPAATO	*SUUPAA*	*TEEBURU*	*OOTOBAI*	*TEEPU*

スープ
SUUPU (soup)

- In the following lines, find words that you have learned.

  1   ソステーブルクシオ
  2   コサマタテープイア
  3   スープハマヤミワフ
  4   デパートフヨユヤヲ
  5   セツチタオートバイ
  6   クサプールタマヒハ
  7   ケキニセールテキア

  8   コウテレビシタハエ
  9   エテニスアカサタナ
  10   ゲームユヤラルリヒ
  11   イシマペンキカサハ
  12   オケスツニハベンコ
  13   ヘレントキタハヤフ

Reading practice

Read the following passage to yourself and see how much you understand the first time you read it through by writing a brief outline of the story. After that, read the story through a second time and check your accuracy.

きのう　がっこう　で　テニス　の　ゲーム　が　ありました。わたし
の　どうきゅうせい　の　カレン　ちゃん　は　その　ゲーム　を
しました。ゲーム　は　さんじはん　に　はじまりました。そして
にじゅうごふん　の　バス　で　がっこう　に　いきました。ゲーム　で
ともだち　に　あいました。いい　ゲーム　でした。カレン　ちゃん　は
テニス　が　じょうず　です。たいへん　おもしろかった　です。がっこう
で　はなしました。ごじ　に　バス　で　かえりました。わたし　は
あした　テニス　を　れんしゅう　します。

ゴルフ　　GOLF

The Japanese have developed the "small culture" and have a reputation for being able to pack an enormous amount into a small space.

Playing golf on a real golf course is very expensive in Japan, but most people can afford some practice time on a golf driving practice range. (Similar practice grounds exist for baseball and other sports, too.) They are usually netted compounds looking like huge aviaries with booths at one end. The participants stand in their allotted spaces hitting balls out into the compound, watching their own ball with intense concentration as others hit at the same time (sometimes from an upper level as well). The compounds are covered with white balls massed around the main green area, looking like confetti. At night these driving ranges are floodlit and often operate for twenty-four hours, offering availability for shiftworkers and the sleepless, too.

Unit 3

こうえん は どこ です か
kooen wa doko desu ka
Where is the park?

NEW WORDS

みち	*michi*	street/road
どちら へ いきます か	*dochira e ikimasu ka*	which way (where) do I go?
どちら	*dochira*	very polite way to say "which" or "where"
から	*kara*	from
まっすぐ	*massugu*	straight ahead
はし	*hashi*	bridge
わたります	*watarimasu*	cross over
わたって	*watatte*	*te* form of *watarimasu*
ひだり	*hidari*	left
ひだりがわ	*hidarigawa*	left-hand side
まがります	*magarimasu*	turn
まがって	*magatte*	*te* form of *magarimasu*
わかります	*wakarimasu*	understand
そして	*soshite*	and then
みぎ	*migi*	right
みぎがわ	*migigawa*	right-hand side

Helen's host father drops the two girls off by the station in town, as he hasn't time to take them all the way.

Before he drives off, Helen asks him for directions to get to the park:

ヘレン おとうさん、こうえんに いきます。どちら へ いきますか。

おとうさん ここ から まっすぐ いって、はし を わたって、そして ひだり に まがって、こうえん は ひだりがわ です。

ヘレン わかりました。ありがとう。

Helen: *Otoosan, kooen ni ikimasu. Dochira e ikimasu ka.*
Otoosan: *Koko kara massugu itte, hashi o watatte, soshite hidari ni magatte, kooen wa hidarigawa desu.*
Helen: *Wakarimashita. Arigatoo.*

Check your understanding of the conversation.
Helen: Dad, I'm going to the park. Which way do I go?
Father: From here go straight ahead, cross over the bridge and turn left. The park is on your left-hand side.
Helen: I understand/I've got it. Thanks.

STUDY

- ***Dochira e ikimasu ka*** is a very useful polite phrase for asking the way. You have already learned *kochira*, another word from the same "family" to say "this way" very politely.

  Remember that **e** and **ni** are for the most part interchangeable. Write **e** particle with **he** *hiragana*.

- **kochira**   this way
  sochira   that way (relatively closer to the person speaking)
  achira   that way over there (away from both people)
  dochira   which way, where
  Koko, soko, asoko, doko are already familiar to you for saying here, there, over there and where. Add the word *kara* "from" to any of them to say "from here," "from there," etc.

- You will notice all the **te** forms that have been used to join the sentences into a flowing passage. Don't put too many into your sentences or it gets a bit boring, but two or three are fine.

  Because Helen's father is obviously familiar, he doesn't use overly polite language. If Helen had asked a stranger, the same conversation would probably have been like this:
  Helen: *Sumimasen ga, kooen wa dochira e ikimasu ka.*
  Stranger: *Koko kara massugu itte, hashi o watatte soshite hidari ni magatte kudasai.*
                    Kooen wa hidarigawa desu.
  Helen: *Wakarimashita. Arigatoo gozaimashita. Sayonara.*

- **Wakarimashita**. The past tense has been used because by that time the information has been digested and the message has been understood. In English we would more often say "I understand," meaning a continuing state. The Japanese use both but prefer to use the past with the assumption that if you have understood, you will continue to understand.

  (In other situations *wakarimasu* usually takes the particle **ga**, because when you say you understand, you are focusing on one particular thing out of the many things you understand to comment on. So they say for example: *Hiragana ga wakarimasu. Eigo ga wakarimasu.* But remember if you want to use the negative, the particle will be **wa**; e.g., *Eigo wa wakarimasen.*)

- Note that when you use *hidari* and *migi* the particle **ni** follows: "**to** the left," "**to** the right," but *massugu* never has **ni** after it. The kanji for left and right are: 左 (*hidari*)   右 (*migi*)

ACTIVITIES

- Choose one student to move like a pawn in a game and take turns ordering him/her around the classroom.

- When you have become sufficiently familiar with the basic directions, send one student out of the room and secretly choose an object to direct him/her towards. The student returns to the room and asks *Dochira e ikimasu ka*. The class responds, directing him/her around the room. When the student arrives close to the chosen object, he/she tries to guess what it is with *Koko desu ka* "Is it here?"; *Kore desu ka* "Is it this?"; *Sore desu ka* "Is it that?"; or the Japanese name of the object.

The class says *chigaimasu* if it's not correct or answers with hot (*atsui*), cold (*samui*), warm (*atatakai*), cool (*suzushii*) appropriately, until the object has been guessed. If you want to say "very hot," etc., use *taihen atsui*.

- Move the desks into "town" blocks. In pairs, direct each other around the room. When you are in danger of bumping into someone else, remember to say *Sumimasen*, and holding your hand (thumb up) in front of you on its edge, with a chopping movement, pass by.

- With a partner role play one of the conversations from the beginning of the unit.

- In a small group role play a similar conversation, but add to it, asking different strangers for information or chatting about your week's activities or your friends as you go, as in normal conversation.

- Make maps and, with a partner, practice finding your way around.

Check your understanding

How would you say the following in Japanese?
1   From here turn left and then go straight ahead.
2   I'll read the map (*chizu*), and I'll understand.
3   Cross over the bridge and then turn left. The park is on the left-hand side.
4   Which way do I go to your house?
5   Excuse me please, where is the library?

Writing practice

- Learn **SA** サ

- From **SA** you can make **ZA** ザ
- Learn **NO** ノ

- Learn **RA** ラ

- Learn **SHI** シ

- From **SHI** you can make **JI** ジ

- Match the *katakana* words with their *ROOMAji* equivalents.

1	ラジオ	11	テレビ
2	リサ	12	ゲーム
3	ノート	13	オレンジ
4	スーパー	14	スープ
5	パン	15	オートバイ
6	デパート	16	サラリー
7	セール	17	バス
8	テープ	18	アイス
9	テーブル	19	スーザン
10	トースト	20	テスト

a	*TEEPU*	k	*TOOSUTO* (toast)
b	*NOOTO*	l	*TESUTO* (test)
c	*SUUPAA*	m	*SEERU*
d	*TEREBI*	n	*ORENJI* (orange)
e	*OOTOBAI*	o	*RISA* (Lisa)
f	*SARARII*	p	*SUUZAN* (Susan)
g	*SUUPU*	q	*DEPAATO*
h	*BASU*	r	*GEEMU*
i	*PAN*	s	*TEEBURU*
j	*AISU* (ice)	t	*RAJIO* (radio)

- Write sentences in *kana*, with each sentence containing a *katakana* word. Write the English equivalent below each sentence so that your intention is clear. Ask a friend to check it and identify errors before asking your teacher to mark it for you.

Unit 4

デパート は この まち に あります か
DEPAATO wa kono machi ni arimasu ka
**Is there a department store
in this town?**

NEW WORDS

あるきます	*arukimasu*	walk
あるいて	*aruite*	*te* form of *arukimasu*
かきます	*kakimasu*	write or draw
かいて	*kaite*	*te* form of *kakimasu*
ぐらい	*gurai*	about
かど	*kado*	corner
ちず	*chizu*	map
ぎんこう	*ginkoo*	bank
ゆうびんきょく	*yuubinkyoku*	post office
とおい	*tooi*	far/distant (adjective)
ガソリン スタンド	*GASORIN SUTANDO*	gas station
ちかい	*chikai*	close/near
みえます	*miemasu*	can/able to see
えいがかん	*eigakan*	movie theater

ブラウン   すみません が、デパート は この まち に あります
か。

ひと   はい、あります。

ブ   とおい です か。

ひ   はい、あるいて いきます か。

ブ   はい。

ひ   ちず を かきます。かみ が あります か。

ブ   はい、どうぞ。

ひ   みて ください。その かど を みぎ に まがって、まっす
ぐ あるいて ください。ガソリン スタンド を ひだり に
まがって ください。そこ から かわ の はし が みえま
す。その はし は わたりません が はし を みぎ に
まがって、じゅっぷん ぐらい まっすぐ あるいて、えいがか
ん の かど を ひだり に まがって、デパート は みぎ
がわ です。デパート の なまえ は みつこし です。

ブ　　　とおい　です　ね。ありがとう　ございました。

ひ　　　どう　いたしまして。さよなら。

BURAUN:　　　*Sumimasen ga, DEPAATO wa kono machi ni arimasu ka.*

Machi no hito:　*Hai arimasu.*

B:　*Tooi desu ka.*

M:　*Hai, aruite ikimasu ka.*

B:　*Hai.*

M:　*Chizu o kakimasu. Kami ga arimasu ka.*

B:　*Hai. Doozo.*

M:　*Mite kudasai. Sono kado o migi ni magatte, massugu aruite kudasai. GASORIN SUTANDO o hidari ni magatte kudasai. Soko kara kawa no hashi ga miemasu. Sono hashi wa watarimasen ga hashi o migi ni magatte, juppun gurai massugu aruite, eigakan no kado o hidari ni magatte, DEPAATO wa migigawa desu. DEPAATO no namae wa Mitsukoshi desu.*

B:　*Tooi desu ne. Arigatoo gozaimashita.*

M:　*Doo itashimashite. Sayonara.*

Check your understanding of the conversation.

Brown:　Excuse me please . . . Is there a department store in this town?

Town person:　Yes, there is.

B:　Is it far?

T:　Yes, are you going to go on foot/Are you walking?

B:　Yes.

T:　I'll draw a map. Have you got some paper?

B:　Yes. Here you are.

T:　Please watch. At that corner turn right and walk straight ahead. At the gas station/garage turn left. From there you can see the river bridge. You don't cross the bridge, but at the bridge turn right and walk straight ahead for about ten minutes, at the movie theater turn left and the department store will be on your right-hand side. The name of the department store is Mitsukoshi.

B:　It is a long way! Thank you very much.

T:　Don't mention it. Goodbye.

STUDY

- To say "At the corner turn . . ." you use the **o** particle. The **o** particle is used, with verbs of motion, to indicate where the activity takes place. It will be a point that you turn at, an object like a traffic light at which you will change direction, a point you will pass through. Imagine the **o** particle as a circle on the pavement that reminds you to turn at that point.

  Practice using that particle after all the places that you know and request someone to change direction.

- **Miemasu** is a new verb to learn. It always takes the **ga** particle because, as you have learned before, **ga** particle focuses on a particular thing. *Miemasu* means "able to see/can see" and may be labeled an ability verb like *wakarimasu* in the last unit. Understanding is an ability, too. Use it like any other verb, but remember always to use **ga** in front of it.

- The difference between **mimasu** and **miemasu**: *Mimasu* is a fact – you see/watch/look at something. *Miemasu* is the ability to do those things: I am able to see/I can watch the dog.

    Study the following examples:

Hana o mimasu.	(I) look at the flowers.
Hana ga miemasu.	(I) am able to see/look at the flowers.
TEREBI o mimashita.	watched television
TEREBI ga miemashita.	was able to watch television
TENISU wa mimasen deshita.	did not watch the tennis
TENISU wa miemasen deshita.	was not able to watch the tennis

- **Aruite ikimasu** means "Walk and go" or "Go on foot."

- **Gurai** means "about" when you are speaking of a length of time or a distance. It cannot be used to say "about" a specific time; e.g., "about one o'clock." The word for that situation is **goro**: *Ichiji goro*.

EXERCISE

How would you say the following in Japanese?
1 At the corner turn right.
2 Will you walk? (go on foot)
3 I'll go by bus.
4 Turn left at the gas station.
5 Go straight ahead and then turn right at the corner.

ACTIVITIES

- Look at the town map on p. 81. Learn the names of the various places. Work out how you would say what there is in this town; e.g., *Toshokan ga arimasu*. Take turns in groups or around the class, as if you are trying to tell a stranger of all the facilities your town offers. The following list will assist you.

デパート	*DEPAATO*	department store
こうえん	*kooen*	park
びょういん	*byooin*	hospital
しょうがっこう	*shoogakkoo*	primary/elementary school
ちゅうがっこう	*chuugakkoo*	intermediate school
こうとうがっこう	*kootoogakkoo*	high school
としょかん	*toshokan*	library
えき	*eki*	(railway) station
えいがかん	*eigakan*	movie theater
おてあらい	*Otearai*	toilet(s)
ぎんこう	*ginkoo*	bank
ゆうびんきょく	*yuubinkyoku*	post office
ガソリン　スタンド	*GASORIN SUTANDO*	gas station
しんごう	*shingoo*	signal/traffic lights
バスてい	*BASUtei*	bus stop
こうさてん	*koosaten*	intersection

- Using the map on p. 81 work with a partner. Ask for directions to get to places, and give directions.

- Photocopy the map on p. 81, one sheet for each student. The teacher or a student calls out directions and the class draws the route taken. The original of the map can be drawn on the blackboard, so that you can compare your efforts.

- Listen as the teacher reads the following instructions and match the end point of each direction (A, B, C, D, E) with the number of the sentence read.

1　えき　から　まっすぐ　いって、スー　さん　の　うち　は　ひだりがわ　です。

2　えき　から　まっすぐ　いって、デパート　の　かど　を　ひだり　に　まがって、ガソリン　スタンド　を　みぎ　に　まがって、ケン　さん　の　うち　は　みぎがわ　です。

3　えき　から　まっすぐ　いって、デパート　を　まがりません。まっすぐ　いって、こうえん　が　みえます。こうえん　の　はし　を　わたりません。みぎ　に　まがって、パム　さん　の　うち　は　みぎがわ　です。

4　えき　から　みぎ　に　まがって、ぎんこう　を　ひだり　に　まがって、はし　を　わたって、かど　を　みぎ　に　まがって、ベン　さん　の　うち　は　ひだりがわ　です。

5　えき　から　みぎ　に　まがって、しょうがっこう　を　ひだり　に　まがって、まっすぐ　いって、はし　を　わたって　ください。パット　さん　の　うち　は　ひだりがわ　です。

1 *Eki kara massugu itte, SUU san no uchi wa hidarigawa desu.*
2 *Eki kara massugu itte, DEPAATO no kado o hidari ni magatte, GASORIN SUTANDO o migi ni magatte, KEN san no uchi wa migigawa desu.*
3 *Eki kara massugu itte, DEPAATO o magarimasen. Massugu itte, kooen ga miemasu. Kooen no hashi o watarimasen. Migi ni magatte, PAMU san no uchi wa migigawa desu.*
4 *Eki kara migi ni magatte, ginkoo o hidari ni magatte, hashi o watatte, kado o migi ni magatte, BEN san no uchi wa hidarigawa desu.*
5 *Eki kara migi ni magatte, shoogakkoo o hidari ni magatte, massugu itte, hashi o watatte kudasai. PATTO san no uchi wa hidarigawa desu.*
(Check with the English translation on p. 84)

- Using the same sentences, read the directions to your partner, who will sketch a route to the places for each sentence.

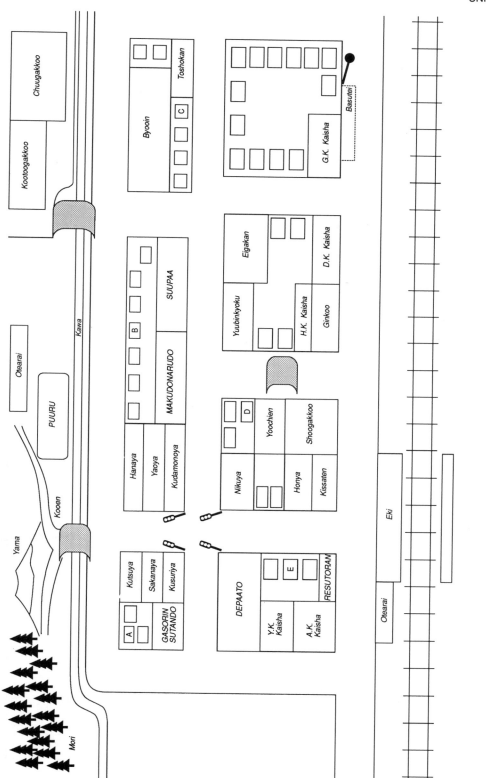

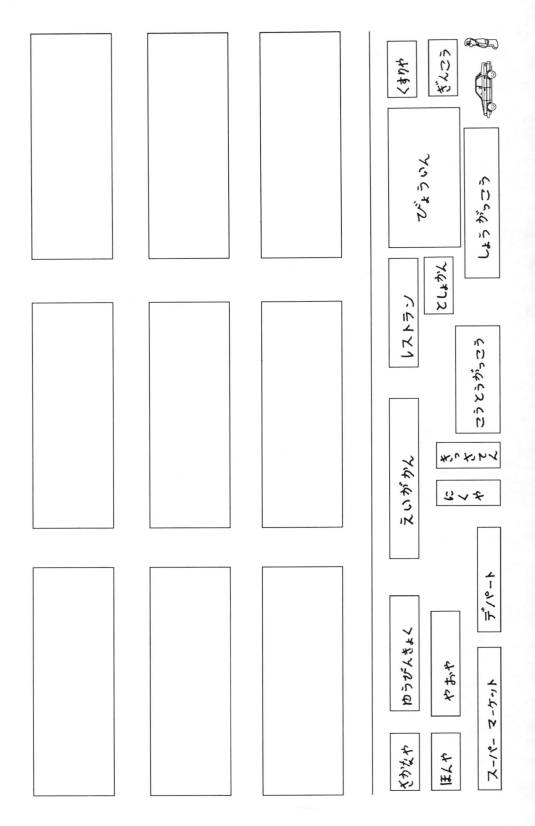

くすりや

ぎんこう

びょういん

こうばん

レストラン

バスてい

えいがかん

こうばんこうえん

きっさてん

ホテル

デパート

ゆうびんきょく

やおや

スーパーマーケット

ほんや

さかなや

Reading practice

Read the *hiragana* passage and find out where two students are meeting, on what day, at what time, and why.

A: らいしゅう の すいようび に テニス の ゲーム に
いきます。はちがつ じゅうよっか です。あなた も きて ください。
ゲーム は にじ はん に はじまります。わたし の がっこう
の アナ ちゃん は ゲーム を します。アナ ちゃん は テニ
ス が じょうず です。まいにち アナ ちゃん は テニス を
れんしゅう します。ときどき わたし は がっこう で アナ ち
ゃん を みます。わたし は テニス を しません が すき で
す。きのう がっこう に いって、アナ ちゃん の れんしゅう
を みました。きょう の ゲーム は たいへん いい でしょう。
ゲーム は まち の こうえん で します。わたし は いちじは
ん の バス で いきます。デパート で にじにじゅっぷん に
あなた に あいます。いきます か。だいじょうぶ です か。

B: ええ、だいじょうぶ です。わたし も いきます。

A: *Raishuu no suiyoobi ni TENISU no GEEMU ni ikimasu.*
Hachigatsu juuyokka desu. Anata mo kite kudasai. GEEMU wa niji han ni
hajimarimasu. Watashi no gakkoo no ANA chan wa GEEMU o shimasu.
ANA chan wa TENISU ga joozu desu. Mainichi ANA chan wa TENISU o
renshuu shimasu. Tokidoki watashi wa gakkoo de ANA chan o mimasu.
Watashi wa TENISU o shimasen ga suki desu. Kinoo gakkoo ni itte, ANA
chan no renshuu o mimashita. Kyoo no GEEMU wa taihen ii deshoo.
GEEMU wa machi no kooen de shimasu. Watashi wa ichiji han no BASU
de ikimasu. DEPAATO de nijinijuppun ni anata ni aimasu. Ikimasu ka.
Daijoobu desu ka.

B: *Ee, daijoobu desu. Watashi mo ikimasu.*

Writing practice

• Learn **KA** カ

From **KA** make **GA** ガ

- Learn **SO**   ソ

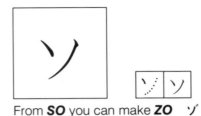

From **SO** you can make **ZO**   ゾ

- Learn **TA**   タ

From **TA** you can make **DA**   ダ

- Learn **MA**   マ

- Read the following words. Some are new. Read them over until you can "hear" the words and recognize them.

  マーケット   マット   マンディ   ガス   バス   テスト
  パーティー   スーパーマーケット   テレビ   プール

- You now know enough *katakana* to write all the following *katakana* words:

  TENISU   GEEMU   TEREBI   PUURU   TEEBURU   BASU
  RAJIO   NOOTO   GASORIN   GASU   TESUTO
  DEPAATO   PAATII   SUUPAAMAAKETTO

Translation of direction sentences on p. 80

1 From the station go straight ahead, Sue's house is on the left-hand side.
2 From the station go straight ahead, turn left at the department store, turn right at the gas station, Ken's house is on the right-hand side.
3 From the station go straight ahead, don't turn at the department store. Go straight ahead and you'll be able to see the park. Don't cross the park bridge. Turn right, Pam's house is on the right-hand side.
4 From the station turn right, turn left at the bank, cross over the bridge, turn right at the corner. Ben's house is on the left-hand side.
5 From the station turn right, turn left at the primary school, go straight ahead, cross the bridge. Pat's house is on the left.

Unit 5

どこ で あいましょう か
doko de aimashoo ka
Where shall we meet?

NEW WORDS

まえ	*mae*	in front of/before/ago
えいがかん	*eigakan*	movie theater
もっと	*motto*	more
だいすき	*daisuki*	like a lot
した	*shita*	under
わたしたち	*watashitachi*	we

Rie and Juuichiroo make arrangements to go out.

りえ	らいしゅう まち に いきましょう か。
じゅういちろう	はい、らいしゅう えいがかん で あたらしい えいが が あります。
り	おかね が あります か。
じゅ	えいが は いくら でしょう か。
り	せんえん ぐらい でしょう。
じゅ	あります。あなた は。
り	ええ、わたし も あります。
じゅ	では、えいが に いきましょう か。
り	ええ、わたし は えいが が だいすき です。なんようび に いきましょう か。
じゅ	きんようび は いい でしょう。きんようび の しゅくだい は たいせつ では ありません。しゅうまつ に します。
り	きんようび は いい です。なん で いきましょう か。
じゅ	でんしゃ で いきましょう か。バス で いきましょう か。
り	でんしゃ は もっと はやい です。
じゅ	そう です。どこ で あいましょう か。
り	えき の まえ で あいましょう。

じゅ	そう です ね。えいが は ごじ に はじまります。なんじ に あいましょう か。
り	よじ じゅうごふん に うち を でます。よじ はん に えき の まえ で あいましょう。
じゅ	いい です。じゃ また。
り	じゃ また。

Rie: *Raishuu machi ni ikimashoo ka.*
Juuichiroo: *Hai, raishuu eigakan de atarashii eiga ga arimasu.*
R: *Okane ga arimasu ka.*
J: *Eiga wa ikura deshoo ka.*
R: *Senen gurai deshoo.*
J: *Arimasu. Anata wa?*
R: *Ee, watashi mo arimasu.*
J: *Dewa, eiga ni ikimashoo ka.*
R: *Ee, watashi wa eiga ga daisuki desu. Nanyoobi ni ikimashoo ka.*
J: *Kinyoobi wa ii deshoo. Kinyoobi no shukudai wa taisetsu dewa arimasen. Shuumatsu ni shimasu.*
R: *Kinyoobi wa ii desu. Nan de ikimashoo ka.*
J: *Densha de ikimashoo ka. Basu de ikimashoo ka.*
R: *Densha wa motto hayai desu.*
J: *Soo desu. Doko de aimashoo ka.*
R: *Eki no mae de aimashoo.*
J: *Soo desu ne. Eiga wa goji ni hajimarimasu. Nanji ni aimashoo ka.*
R: *Yoji juugofun ni uchi o demasu. Yoji han ni eki no mae de aimashoo.*
J: *Ii desu. Ja mata.*
R: *Ja mata.*

Check your understanding by answering the following questions:

1   When and where does Rie suggest they go at the beginning of the conversation?
2   What attraction is there for them in town?
3   Have they got enough money to go?
4   What day do they decide to go? Why?
5   What means of transportation will they use? Why?
6   Where do they decide to meet?
7   At what time?
8   What time will Rie leave home?

STUDY

- As you know, adjectives in Japanese are placed in front of the noun in the same way as in English: *atarashii eiga* "new movie" or you can say *Eiga wa atarashii desu.* "The movie is new."

- *Motto hayai desu.* "It is faster." *Hayai* is an adjective (fast), *motto* means more. In English we don't say "more fast," we add "er" – "faster." *motto ookii* bigger, *motto chiisai* smaller, *motto omoshiroi* more interesting.

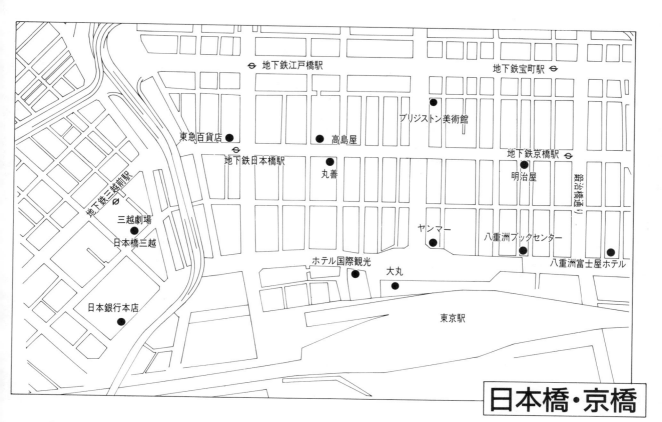

地下鉄江戸橋駅
地下鉄宝町駅
ブリジストン美術館
東急百貨店
高島屋
地下鉄日本橋駅
地下鉄京橋駅
丸善
明治屋
地下鉄三越前駅
三越劇場
ヤンマー
八重洲ブックセンター
日本橋三越
ホテル国際観光
大丸
八重洲富士屋ホテル
日本銀行本店
東京駅

日本橋・京橋

Notice the block arrangement of this central city area. Use this map to give directions to each other. Photocopy it and mark in shops, etc., where you wish.

- With your partner, practice giving sentence choices; e.g.,
  BASU de ikimasu ka. Jitensha de ikimasu ka.
  Will you go by bus **or** by bike?
  In your answer choose one and use *desu kara* to say "because." Remember, when you give a reason in Japanese, the reason goes first:
  Motto hayai desu kara BASU de ikimasu.
  I'll go by bus, because it's faster.
  Eiga ni ikimasu ka, PUURU ni ikimasu ka.
  Will you go to the movies or to the swimming pool?
  I'll go to the movies, because it's more interesting/entertaining.

- Use all the adjectives you know, with and without *motto*; and use adjectives with *desu*; and adjectives in front of a noun. For example:
  Densha wa hayai desu.
  Hayai densha desu.
  Densha wa motto hayai desu.

- **USING POSITION PHRASES**. There are two basic patterns.
  Basic pattern 1:
  *Eki **no mae de** aimashoo ka.*
  "Shall we meet in front of the station?"
  You are talking about the position that belongs to a particular place or object: "the station in front of." In comparison with English, the phrase is backwards.

Look at the following examples:

Enpitsu wa tsukue no mae ni arimasu.

The pencil is in front of the desk.

In using these position "packages," it's important to sort out first what your topic is, or you can easily get things backwards. In this example we are talking about the pencil. We want to say where it is. Its position is "in front of the desk." That is why the position phrase has been called a "package," because all the words relating to the position must be kept together. So we have two separate items of information: the topic (the pencil); and its position (in front of the desk), and the verb on the end of the sentence as usual. Look at the following examples.

1   *Hon wa/TEREBI no mae ni/arimasu.*
2   *Chizu wa/RISA no mae ni/arimasu.*
3   *NOOTO wa/TEEBURU no shita ni/arimasu.*

1   The book is in front of the TV.
2   The map is in front of Lisa.
3   The notebook is under the table.

Try the following examples:
1   The pen is under the desk.
2   The paper is in front of the box.
3   The blackboard is in front of the desks.
4   Jon's pencil is under the table.
5   The book is in front of the bookshelf.
6   The river is in front of the school.

In all of these examples the phrase was **no . . . ni**. If any activity follows, however, the particle **ni** must be changed to **de**, just as you have learned in other situations. So if you want to say that you will meet someone or do something in front of a place or object, you must remember to use **no . . . de** as your phrase:

Eki no mae de aimashoo ka.

Gakkoo no mae de hanashimashita.

Kooen no mae de asobimashita.

Here are some more position words:

うえ	*ue*	on top of/over/above
うしろ	*ushiro*	behind
なか	*naka*	inside
そば	*soba*	beside
そと	*soto*	outside

These are used in the same way, with **no . . . ni** or **no . . . de**; e.g.,

Hon wa tsukue no ue ni arimasu.

The book is on the desk.

BEN san ni mise no naka de aimashita.

I met Ben inside the shop.

Try the following examples:

Ki wa uchi no ushiro ni arimasu.

Hako wa kyooshitsu no naka ni arimasu.

Kooen wa gakkoo no soba ni arimasu.

Jitensha wa uchi no soto ni arimasu.

- **USING POSITION PHRASES: Basic pattern 2.**

  In English we have different basic patterns to describe where things are:

  "The book is on the table."

  "There is a book on the table."

  These two sentences have a subtle difference in meaning:

  "The book is on the table." – a definite book that someone may be needing and that we know about already.

  "There is a book on the table." – suggests new information and can be any book.

  These two situations have been dealt with in the past section in Japanese as:

  Hon wa TEEBURU no ue ni arimasu.

  The verb *arimasu* may be translated "is/are" or "there is/are" or "exists"; e.g., "The book is/exists on the table."

  The second pattern starts from naming the position first: "On top of the desk there is a book." To produce sentences like this, begin with the whole package of the position: "on top of the car," "under the bus," "beside the river."

  (Kuruma no ue ni) kami ga arimasu.

  (BASU no shita ni) hon ga arimasu.

  (Kawa no soba ni) kuruma ga arimasu.

  Two things have been done differently: The position has been stated first, and the particle used in front of *arimasu* is **ga**.

  Ga has been used to focus on a particular thing and is always used for topics in front of **arimasu** and **imasu**. If you want to speak about things that can move under their own volition, you will of course be using the verb *imasu*.

  If you want to say:

  Inu wa kuruma no shita ni imasu. "The dog is under the car." It is very important to keep clear in your mind what the "position package" is and what the topic is. You don't want to put the car under the dog by mistake. *(Kuruma wa inu no shita ni arimasu.)*

ACTIVITIES

- Set up situations for each other by putting articles on top of, under, behind, beside your desks. Get your partner to tell you where they are in response to your questions; e.g.:

  Enpitsu wa doko desu ka. Enpitsu wa tsukue no soba ni arimasu.

- In pairs or as a class, using the illustration of a classroom on the next page, describe the position of people and objects.

- In teams or as individuals, listen as each team or person in turn gives the position of someone or something, using the classroom illustration. The person or first of the listening teams to identify what, where, or who gains a point.

● **Pair work**

Label students A and B to work from the A and B sheets below. You are not allowed to look at each other's information sheets! Your task is to find the information that is missing from your sheet by questioning your partner.

Question patterns: *(Kaban) wa doko ni arimasu ka.*
(Tsukue no soba ni) nani ga arimasu ka.
Heya no naka ni (kaban) ga arimasu ka.

Answer patterns: *Hai, (kaban) wa heya no naka ni arimasu.*
Iie, (kaban) wa heya no naka ni arimasen.
Tsukue no soba ni (kaban) ga arimasu.
(Kaban) wa tsukue no soba ni arimasu.

Sheet A

Here is a list of objects that may be in the room:
kaban isu tsukue BEDDO hon hana REKOODO manga
1 *Heya no naka ni wa . . . . ya BEDDO ya . . . . ya tsukue ya . . . . ga arimasu.*
Now find out where they are in the room:
2 *. . . . . wa tsukue no ushiro ni arimasu.*
3 *BEDDO wa . . . .*
4 *. . . . . wa BEDDO no ue ni arimasu.*
5 *Tsukue wa . . . .*
6 *. . . . . wa tsukue no shita ni arimasu.*

Sheet B

Things that may be in the room:
kaban isu tsukue hon hana REKOODO manga
1 *Heya no naka ni wa isu ya . . . . ya hon ya . . . . ya kaban ga arimasu.*
Now find out where they are in the room:
2 *Isu wa . . . .*
3 *. . . . . wa mado no mae ni arimasu.*
4 *Hon wa . . . .*
5 *. . . . . DOA no soba ni arimasu.*
6 *Kaban wa . . . .*

STUDY

- *Mae* may be used to say "in front of": *Eki no mae ni arimasu*, or in time phrases to express "before": *Niji gofun mae*. (Five minutes to/before two o'clock), and also to express "ago": *Gofun mae ni mimashita*. (I saw it five minutes ago.)

  Practice together making sentences that use *mae* in those three different ways.

- There is a difference in understanding between *Kooen wa doko desu ka* "Where is the park?" (you know that there is one but don't know where exactly to find it) and *Kooen wa doko ni arimasu ka* which may be translated "Where is there a park?"

  Often the use of *arimasu* suggests the words "there is/are" as well as saying something exists/is in that place. Try both translations to find the one that feels best in that situation in English.

EXERCISE

Work out what the following sentences mean in English.

1　きょうしつ　の　なか　に　せんせい　が　います。
2　ノート　は　ほん　の　した　に　あります。
3　わたし　の　えんぴつ　は　どこ　です　か。
4　ぎんこう　は　どこ　に　あります　か。
5　かみ　の　うえ　に　ペン　が　あります。
6　ねこ　の　うえ　に　いぬ　が　います。
7　ジョン　さん　は　しんしつ　の　なか　に　います。
8　かわ　の　そば　に　き　と　はな　が　あります。
9　うち　の　そと　で　おとこ　の　こ　は　あそびました。
10　くるま　の　うしろ　に　おんな　の　こ　が　いました。

1　*Kyooshitsu no naka ni sensei ga imasu.*
2　*NOOTO wa hon no shita ni arimasu.*
3　*Watashi no enpitsu wa doko desu ka.*
4　*Ginkoo wa doko ni arimasu ka.*
5　*Kami no ue ni PEN ga arimasu.*
6　*Neko no ue ni inu ga imasu.*
7　*JON san wa shinshitsu no naka ni imasu.*
8　*Kawa no soba ni ki to hana ga arimasu.*
9　*Uchi no soto de otoko no ko wa asobimashita.*
10　*Kuruma no ushiro ni onna no ko ga imashita.*

ACTIVITIES

- **The Pile**. In groups, pile articles up, one on top of the other. As you get each thing on top of the pile, you all say what has gone before; e.g., you have a pile that has a book, a notebook, a pencil case, a pencil, and are about to add a pen, so everyone "reads" the pile: *Hon no ue ni NOOTO ga arimasu, NOOTO no ue ni fudebako ga arimasu, fudebako no ue ni enpitsu ga arimasu*. As you add the pen you say: *Enpitsu no ue ni PEN ga arimasu* and so on until the pile collapses.

- (In groups or as a class)
  Assemble a collection of ten objects on a table. Put them in positions that allow you to use all the position words. Choose a student to try out his/her memory and give a minute to memorize the items in the collection and their relative positions.

  The student is blindfolded or faces away from the collection. The class asks: *Enpitsu wa doko desu ka*. The student answers: *PEN no soba ni arimasu,* etc. Give credit for correct answers and say *chigaimasu* if the answer is wrong.

- The teacher or a student sets up a selection of objects. Take turns describing the position of different objects.

- Look at the map on p. 81 and describe where places are in relation to one another, as a written or oral exercise.

- Use the same map to ask, as if you were a stranger to the town, where places are. In the reply say where that place is in relation to other places, as well as giving directions on how to get there from a specified point.

Unit 6

ゆうびんきょく は ちかく
に あります か
yuubinkyoku wa chikaku ni arimasu ka
Is there a post office near here?

NEW WORDS

ちかく　に	*chikaku ni*	near here
まちます	*machimasu*	wait
まって	*matte*	te form of *machimasu*
Interest		
みつこし	*Mitsukoshi*	name of chain of department stores

Sumiko is looking for a post office.

すみこ　　　すみません が、ゆうびんきょく は ちかく に あります か。

まちのひと　はい、あります。

す　　　　　どちら へ いきます か。

ま　　　　　デパート が みえます か。

す　　　　　みつこし です か。

ま　　　　　はい、そう です。その デパート の うしろ に ゆうびんきょく が あります。

す　　　　　ありがとう ございます。ゆうびんきょく は なんじ から です か。

ま　　　　　じゅうじ から です。いま じゅうじごふん まえ です。ごふん ぐらい まって ください。

す　　　　　ありがとう ございました。

ま　　　　　どう いたしまして。さよなら。

Sumiko:　　　　　*Sumimasen ga, yuubinkyoku wa chikaku ni arimasu ka.*
Machi no hito:　*Hai, arimasu.*
S:　*Dochira e ikimasu ka.*
M:　*DEPAATO ga miemasu ka.*
S:　*Mitsukoshi desu ka.*
M:　*Hai, soo desu. Sono DEPAATO no ushiro ni yuubinkyoku ga arimasu.*
S:　*Arigatoo gozaimasu. Yuubinkyoku wa nanji kara desu ka.*

M: *Juuji kara desu. Ima juujigofun mae desu. Gofun gurai matte kudasai.*
S: *Arigatoo gozaimashita.*
M: *Doo itashimashite. Sayonara.*

Check your understanding of the conversation.
S: Excuse me please, is there a post office close by?
M: Yes, there is.
S: Where is it? (In which direction do I go?)
M: Can you see that department store?
S: Is that Mitsukoshi?
M: Yes, that's it. Behind that department store there's a post office.
S: Thank you. What time does the post office open?
M: Ten o'clock. It's five to ten now. Please wait about five minutes.
S: Thank you.
M: You're welcome. Goodbye.

STUDY

• **Speaking of lengths of time.**
Gofun matte kudasai.   "Please wait five minutes."
You have learned already that when you speak of numbers of people you always put the number directly in front of the verb; e.g.,
Imooto ga futari imasu./Kazoku wa yonin imasu.

It is the same principle with any numbers or amounts. The number or amount always goes directly in front of the verb with no particles in between; e.g., It's five to six.   *Rokuji gofun mae desu.*

Using position words and *machimasu* in all the verb forms that you know, how would you say:
1   I'll wait for you in front of the station at three-thirty.
2   Shall we wait outside?
3   Please wait until five-fifteen.
4   Simon won't wait outside the library.
5   Bob waited five minutes in front of the department store.
6   Kenji did not wait outside school yesterday.

ACTIVITIES

• Look around whichever room you happen to be in and in your mind work out how you would say, for example: "The chair is beside the table," "My school bag is under the desk." Go through ten items.

• Practice with a partner explaining where things are in the classroom in relation to each other. When you have practiced it, write ten sentences in your book. Get your partner to check your work. Discuss any differences of opinion before checking it over with your teacher.

● Work in groups.

Now you can describe in much more detail about what is in each room of your home and where things are in the room. Review the vocabulary for objects and rooms of a house as you tell each other about one room in your house each. No one may use the same room to describe.

Listen·carefully to each other and ask each other questions about the room if there is anything left unexplained.

● Write about your bedroom, saying what is in the room and where specific articles are.

Asking directions at a police box (*kooban*) (top left)
Kutsuya (lower left)
Kasaya (top right)
A *kissaten* advertises its cheap coffee (lower right)

**Choosing tiny turtles to take home
as pets**

Kimonoya. **Kimono are sold as
lengths of material in rolls**

Writing practice

- Review **HE**, **BE**, **PE**, **N**   へ　べ　ぺ　ン

- Write *PEN, BEN, PETTO*

- Find the words you know that must be written in *katakana* from the following list:
  here, pencil, pen, bus, train, bicycle, flower, department store, gas station, television, park, radio, tennis, basketball, football, soccer, hockey, do, play, see, tree, dog, cat.

- Write all the words you have picked out in *katakana*.

Unit 7

おかね が いります から ぎんこう に いきます

okane ga irimasu kara ginkoo ni ikimasu

I need some money so I'm going to the bank

NEW WORDS

いります	*irimasu*	need
ぎんこう	*ginkoo*	bank
はじめ に	*hajime ni*	first
あと で	*ato de*	after that/afterwards
（と）いっしょ に	*(to) issho ni*	together (with)
Interest		
かんがえ	*kangae*	idea/thought

A bank. Learn to recognize the last two *kanji*

Darryl and Simon meet on the street as both are hurrying towards the center of town.

ダリル　サイモン くん、おはよう。おひさしぶり です ね。おげんき です か。

サイモン　ああ、ダリル。そう です ね。おかげ さま で げんき です。あなた は。

ダ　げんき です。ありがとう。
いま どこ に いきます か。

サ　おかね が いります から ぎんこう に いきます。あなた は。

ダ　はじめ に ゆうびんきょく に いって そして くつや に いきます。あたらしい くつ が いります。らいしゅう がっこう は はじまります ね。

サ　そう です ね。きょう わたし も くつ を かいます。

ダ　じゃ、はじめ に ぎんこう に いきます。あと で いっしょ に くつや に いきましょう か。

サ　はい、ぎんこう の まえ で まって ください。

ダ　それ は いい かんがえ です。いま なんじ です か。

サ　　　じゅうじ　じゅうごふん　です。

ダ　　　じゃ、じゅうじ　はん　に　ぎんこう　の　まえ　で
　　　　あいましょう。

サ　　　そう　しましょう。じゃ　また。

DARIRU:　　SAIMON kun, ohayoo. Ohisashiburi desu ne. Ogenki desu ka.
SAIMON:　　Aa, DARIRU. Soo desu ne. Okage sama de genki desu.
　　　　　　　Anata wa.
D:　Genki desu. Arigatoo. Ima doko ni ikimasu ka.
S:　Okane ga irimasu kara ginkoo ni ikimasu. Anata wa.
D:　Hajime ni yuubinkyoku ni itte soshite kutsuya ni ikimasu. Atarashii kutsu
　　ga irimasu. Raishuu gakkoo wa hajimarimasu ne.
S:　Soo desu ne. Kyoo watashi mo kutsu o kaimasu.
D:　Ja, hajime ni ginkoo ni ikimasu. Ato de issho ni kutsuya ni ikimashoo ka.
S:　Hai, ginkoo no mae de matte kudasai.
D:　Sore wa ii kangae desu. Ima nanji desu ka.
S:　Juuji juugofun desu.
D:　Ja, juuji han ni ginkoo no mae de aimashoo.
S:　Soo shimashoo. Ja mata.

Check your understanding of the conversation.
D:　Simon! Hi (Good morning). I haven't seen you for ages. How are you?
S:　Ah, Darryl! You're right (It's been a long time). I'm fine thanks. How
　　about you?
D:　I'm well, thanks. Where are you going now?
S:　I need some money so I'm going to the bank. What about you?
D:　First I'm going to the post office and then I'm going to the shoe store.
　　I need some new shoes. School starts next week.
S:　That's right (You don't need to tell me!). Today I'm going to buy shoes,
　　too.
D:　Well then, first I'll go to the bank. After that shall we go to the shoe store
　　together?
S:　Yes, please wait in front of the bank.
D:　That's a good idea. What's the time now?
S:　Ten fifteen (A quarter past ten).
D:　OK then, let's meet in front of the bank at half-past ten.
S:　OK, let's do that. See you later.

STUDY

- **Irimasu** "need" is another verb that always takes the particle **ga**. You
  now know *wakarimasu, miemasu, arimasu, imasu,* and *irimasu* that always
  take **ga**. Put it with them in your mind as a group that have to be
  remembered together.

Writing practice

- Learn **KO**　コ

- Learn **E**　エ

- Review **SHI**　シ

- Learn **NU**　ヌ

- Learn **TSU**　ツ

Look at the difference between *SHI* and *TSU*. Imagine a stroke upwards for *SHI*, a stroke downwards for *TSU*.

- Don't confuse *TA* and *NU*:
  TA　タ
  NU　ヌ

  Write: *KOOHII*　コーヒー
  　　　SHIKAGO　シカゴ

Unit 8

どんな まち に すんで います か
donna machi ni sunde imasu ka
What kind of town do you live in?

NEW WORDS

よく	*yoku*	often/well
のうじょう	*noojoo*	farm(s)
うし	*ushi*	cow
ひつじ	*hitsuji*	sheep
みずうみ	*mizuumi*	lake
たくさん	*takusan*	many/a lot of
すいえい を します	*suiei o shimasu*	swim
つり	*tsuri*	fishing
しゅうまつ	*shuumatsu*	weekend
Review		
なつ	*natsu*	summer
ふゆ	*fuyu*	winter
ゆき	*yuki*	snow

Read the following description of a town.

わたし の まち は きれい です。ちいさい です が みせ は たいへん いい です。まち は おおきい こうえん と プール と としょかん が あって、きれいな かわ が あります。かわ の なか に さかな が たくさん います。なつ は よく つり に いきます。まち の うしろ に たかい やま が あります。ふゆ は やま の うえ に ゆき が あります。まち の そと に のうじょう が あります。うし と ひつじ が たくさん います。うみ は とおい です が やま の みずうみ が ちかく に あります。なつ は ときどき ともだち と まち の プール で すいえい を します。ときどき やま の みずうみ で すいえい を します。まち から みずうみ まで あるいて にじゅっぷん ぐらい です。わたし の まち が すき です。

Watashi no machi wa kirei desu. Chiisai desu ga mise wa taihen ii desu. Machi wa ookii kooen to PUURU to toshokan ga atte, kireina kawa ga arimasu. Kawa no naka ni sakana ga takusan imasu. Natsu wa yoku tsuri ni ikimasu. Machi no ushiro ni takai yama ga arimasu. Fuyu wa yama no ue ni yuki ga arimasu. Machi no soto ni noojoo ga arimasu. Ushi to hitsuji ga takusan imasu. Umi wa tooi desu ga yama no mizuumi ga chikaku ni arimasu. Natsu wa tokidoki tomodachi to machi no PUURU de suiei o shimasu. Tokidoki yama no mizuumi de suiei o shimasu. Machi kara mizuumi made aruite, nijuppun gurai desu. Watashi no machi ga suki desu.

Check your understanding of the passage.

My town is beautiful. It's small but the shops are very good. The town has a big park, swimming pool and library, and there's a beautiful river. There are lots of fish in the river. In the summer I often go fishing. Behind the town there are high mountains. In the winter there is snow on the mountains. Outside the town there are farms. There are lots of cows and sheep. The sea is a long way away but there are mountain lakes nearby. In the summer I sometimes swim in the pool with my friends. Sometimes we swim in the mountain lakes. From the town to the lakes on foot is about twenty minutes. I like my town.

STUDY

- Previously you learned how to use qualitative nouns like *kirei* with *desu* in phrases like: *Kirei desu*. It's beautiful./*Joozu desu*. She's clever./*Benri desu*. It's convenient./and the negative: *HANSAMU janai desu*. He's not handsome./*Suki dewa arimasen*. I don't like it.

  Now learn how to use these words in front of a noun. When you use them in front of a noun they must have **na** after them. They are telling you something about the quality of the noun, answering the question "What kind of . . .?"; e.g.,

  It is a beautiful town.   *Kireina machi desu.*
  She is a clever student.   *Joozuna seito desu.*
  It's a convenient house.   *Benrina uchi desu.*

  You may remember that adjectives most often tell you a fact about a noun: it's red, big, tall, etc. Qualitative Nouns, however, give an opinion. You may like to remember Qualitative Nouns as **na** words and to think of the **na** as a "noun addition." You must add it every time you use one of these words in front of a noun.

  Look at the following:

  Hito wa kirei desu.   The person is beautiful.
  Kireina hito desu.   She's a beautiful person.
  Uchi wa benri desu.   The house is convenient.
  Benrina uchi desu.   It's a convenient house.

  Notice that when you use **na**, the describing word in the English is directly in front of the noun. You never use **na** in front of a verb.

  Now look at the following examples:

  Kireina hito wa uchi no mae ni imasu.
  Watashi wa benrina uchi ni sunde imasu.

- **Te imasu.** This is a new verb form to learn, developing from your knowledge of the **te** form. The **imasu** ending is one that you know as a verb in its own right. In this situation, however, it opens up the opportunity to say something "is happening at this minute." In English we say "What are you doing?" to ask someone what they are actually doing **at this moment**. In Japanese you add the *imasu* to the **te** form of the verb and it gives you the "ing" part of the English expression. Remember *imasu* means "exist/be" and is of course usually a continuing state. It is the verb that is used with people, animals, fish and insects, and all things that can move under their own volition.

Think of *imasu* after a **te** form as "ing" and it helps to keep it straight in your mind. Be careful not to get confused by English expressions like "I am going to the store" which actually mean, a lot of the time, not that I am on my way now, but that I am going in the future.

• Look at the following and work out how you would express the same in English:

tatte imasu	*hanashite imasu*
suwatte imasu	*tabete imasu*
kiite imasu	*shite imasu*

Imagine someone calls out to you: *Nani o shite imasu ka.* "What are you doing?"

You may answer:

Hon o yonde imasu.   I'm reading a book.

HANBAAGAA o tabete imasu.   I'm eating a hamburger.

Shukudai o shite imasu.   I'm doing homework.

TEEBURU no ue ni tatte imasu.   I'm standing on the table.

Learn the question by heart: *Nani o shite imasu ka.* Remember to pronounce the *shite* as if it has no "i," "*shte.*"

• To make the negative; e.g., "I'm not doing" use ***imasen*** after the **te** form:

shite imasen   (leaving the *te* form alone)

shite imashita   (works on the same principle and therefore means "was doing")

shite imasen deshita   ("was not doing")

• Practice using all the verbs you know with these four new verb forms. Brainstorm the list of verbs you know, writing them on the board as you go or in your book. Leave space to fill in the **te imasu** forms alongside.

• Try the following.
  1   I was reading.
  2   He was going to the bank.
  3   She was not studying yesterday.
  4   I am not practicing now.
  5   Are you eating?

Note: Don't use *itte imasu* about yourself or the person you are talking to, only about a third person.

• Have a polite disagreement! Student One chooses to give a sentence made with any verb and any of its continuing action "ing" forms; e.g., *KAREN san wa HANBAAGAA o tabete imasu.*

Student Two makes a sentence following this, that disagrees; e.g., *KAREN san wa tabete imasen.*

Student Three says: *KAREN san wa HANBAAGAA o tabete imashita.*

Student Four says: *KAREN san wa HANBAAGAA wa tabete imasen deshita.*

Student Five chooses a new verb and makes a sentence with the **te imasu** form and so on.

- When we use the verb "live" in English, we can say "I live in Tokyo" to talk about a permanent situation. We can also say "I'm living in Chicago at the moment" to suggest a more temporary situation. However, in Japanese, the "I am living . . ." (*sunde imasu*) form is generally used for both temporary and permanent situations.

ACTIVITIES

Make up a role play with a partner or a small group.

You are busy doing something and a visitor comes to the house. You:
- greet appropriately for the time of day;
- make a comment about the weather;
- invite him/her into the room in which you are working;
- and the visitor asks what you are doing;
- you reply;
- the visitor suggests that you go out together;
- you say you won't go, thank you;
- the visitor, realizing you are busy, says sorry he/she must go and says goodbye;
- or you are pleased to be interrupted and agree to go.

Variations

1   The visitor offers to get something you need.
2   Or you tell the visitor of something you need and go off together to buy it.
3   (If you decide to continue the idea further, move all the desks to the side of the room to give yourselves maximum space, perhaps setting up your meeting points behind groups of desks: "houses.")

- Chat on the way about all the things you have done in the past few days and what you plan to do tomorrow/next week, etc.

- Take turns making sentences with the following pattern:
  Machi wa (kirei) desu.
  kirei   kirai   benri   joozu   genki   HANSAMU   ookii
  chiisai   suki   taisetsu   daijoobu   hen (strange/peculiar)

- Next use the same list to make sentences using **na**; e.g.,
  Genkina hito wa suiei o shimashita.

- Write a simple description of your town or village (*mura*) and say what you do there.

  If each person writes about a different feature, you will be able to put them together as a simple book about your town. This will not only be good for you to read but will be good for future students in your school to use as reading material.

- Draw a picture or map of your ideal town. Label the places of interest. Work in pairs to tell each other about your imaginary town.

- Collect all the pictures and maps, and give them out randomly. When you receive a map or picture, work out five things you could say about it. Take turns showing the illustrations to the group.

- Photocopy p. 82 (enlarge if necessary). If possible, glue the illustrations on cardboard. Cut out the shops and services, people and objects so that they will stand up, or lay them on top of the street plan if they are not on cardboard. Read the following and place the items in the positions suggested by the passage.
  Kutsuya wa toshokan no soba ni arimasu.
  Kuruma wa toshokan no mae ni arimasu.
  Ginkoo wa toshokan no migigawa desu.
  Shoogakkoo wa toshokan no ushiro ni arimasu.
  Kusuriya wa byooin no soba ni arimasu.
  BURAUN sensei wa ginkoo no mae de matte imasu.
  (Check with each other that you are correct.)

- Use the cutouts to request your partner to put things in particular positions; e.g., *Ginkoo wa toshokan no soba ni oite kudasai.* (Please put the bank next to the library, etc), until you have placed all the items where you choose.

- Using your cutouts again, with a partner take turns commenting on each place; e.g., *Toshokan wa ii desu. Kireina hanaya desu.*

- Make up a role play with one or two other people:
  Greet each other. Ask about each other's health if you haven't seen each other for a while or one of you has been ill. Ask about families. Suggest that you go somewhere together, and discuss how you would get there. One of you is not familiar with the district and asks if there is a (bank/library, etc) in this vicinity. Talk about what there is in the town and about what you have been doing since you last saw each other.

Reading practice

みずうみ は おおきい です

わたし の まち の そば に おおきい みずうみ が あります。みずうみ で すいえい と ヨット と つり を します。みずうみ は きれい です。みずうみ に さかな が たくさん すんで います。みず は きれい です。はる は みず が やま から みずうみ に たくさん はいります。みずうみ の そば に もり が あります。たかい き が たくさん あります。ときどき みずうみ の そば で ピクニック を します。

ヨット	YOTTO	yacht/yachting
きれい	kirei	beautiful/clean
はる	haru	spring
ピクニック	PIKUNIKKU	picnic
もり	mori	forest

まち の がっこう

まち の がっこう は こうえん の そば に あります。こうとうが
っこう は がくせい が せんにん います。がくせい は おんな の
こ と おとこ の こ です。いい がっこう です。その こうとうが
っこう の がくせい は だいがく に たくさん はいります。ちゅう
がっこう は あたらしい です。ちゅうがっこう も おとこ の せい
と と おんな の せいと が います。しょうがっこう は ふるい
です。わたし の おとうさん は その しょうがっこう で べんきょ
う しました。ようちえん も あります。

| はいります | hairimasu | enter |
| だいがく | daigaku | university |

プール は いい です ね。

わたし の がっこう は プール が あります が ちいさい です。
でも まち は おおきい プール が あります。にちようび は とも
だち と その おおきい プール で すいえい を します。その ま
ち の プール は あたらしい です。たかかった です が いま み
な は プール が すき です。いま たいせつな すいえい の スポ
ーツ が わたしたち の プール で みえます。たいへん おもしろい
です。

わたし の まち の としょかん

わたし の まち の としょかん は ふるい です。ほん が たくさ
ん あります。ふゆ は としょかん の なか が あたたかい です。
なつ は すずしい です。ときどき としょかん で ざっし を よみ
ます。ざっし は たかい です から かいません が としょかん は
たくさん あります。べんり です。としょかん の ひと は あたま
が いい です。ほん の なまえ を いつも おぼえて います。とき
どき としょかん で しゅくだい を します。

| おぼえて います | oboete imasu | remember (te form) |
| おぼえます | oboemasu | remember |

やま は たかい です

わたし の まち の うしろ に たかい やま が あります。いつも
きれい です。ふゆ は いつも やま の うえ に ゆき が ありま
す。スキー を します。なつ は やま で さんぽ を します。やま
の かわ で すいえい を します。やま の した に おおきい も
り が あります。もり に ふくろう が すんで います。ふくろう
は よる おきます。あさ ねます。もり の なか は いつも すずし
い です。いつも しずか です。でも とり が たくさん います。とき
どき やま と もり に は たき が みえます。

スキー	SUKII	ski
さんぽ	sanpo	a walk
しずか	shizuka	quiet, peaceful
ふくろう	fukuroo	owl
とり	tori	bird
たき	taki	waterfall

CROSSWORD (TOPIC ELEVEN REVIEW)

Write in *ROOMAji*.

ACROSS

4 mountain
6 here
9 swimming
10 below/under/ beneath
11 The season that follows winter
13 *te* form of verb wait
15 farm
19 a minute
21 close/near
22 about (length of time or distance)
23 after
25 please cross over
27 left-hand side
28 ten minutes
31 OK
34 at first
35 like a lot
41 I'll walk
42 lake
44 a very popular Japanese pinball game
45 top, above, up
46 six minutes
47 I'm going (at this moment)

DOWN

1 . . . . . . is the coldest season of the year
2 where?
3 In . . . . the leaves change color
5 I want to go fastER
7 in front of
8 Most people take vacations in this season
10 let's do that
12 To find the way look at a . . .
13 can see
14 far/distant
16 person who pushes people into trains
17 left
18 road
20 two minutes
24 The *te* form of this verb is *magatte*
26 Place that stores money
29 cow
30 straight ahead
32 together with
33 Most enjoyable time of the week for most people
34 sheep
36 *te* form of *arukimasu*
37 8:08 is . . . . . . past eight o'clock
38 three minutes to boil my egg
39 right
40 horse
43 inside

Vocabulary checklist (Topic Eleven)

Introduction
Interest

おしや	*oshiya*	pusher (onto trains)
パチンコ	*PACHINKO*	pinball game

Unit 1

いっぷん	*ippun*	one minute
にふん	*nifun*	two minutes
さんぶん	*sanpun*	three minutes
よんぶん	*yonpun*	four minutes
ごふん	*gofun*	five minutes
ろっぷん	*roppun*	six minutes
ななふん	*nanafun*	seven minutes
はっぷん	*happun*	eight minutes
きゅうふん	*kyuufun*	nine minutes
じゅっぷん	*juppun*	ten minutes
じゅういっぷん	*juuippun*	eleven minutes
じゅうにふん	*juunifun*	twelve minutes
にじゅっぷん	*nijuppun*	twenty minutes
バスてい	*BASUtei*	bus stop
はじまります　はじまる	*hajimarimasu (hajimaru)*	start/begin
ゲーム	*GEEMU*	game
おばあさん	*Obaasan*	grandmother
たいせつ	*taisetsu (na)*	important (Qualitative Noun)
もちろん	*mochiron*	of course
あと　で	*ato de*	afterwards
まえ	*mae*	before
ふん　ぶん	*fun/pun*	minutes
じゅうごふん	*juugofun*	fifteen minutes
で	*de*	particle: for location of activity; by means of

Unit 2

そう　しましょう	*soo shimashoo*	let's do that
だいじょうぶ	*daijoobu (na)*	OK/all right (Qualitative Noun)

Unit 3

どちら　へ　いきます　か	*dochira e ikimasu ka*	which way?
こちら	*kochira*	this way
そちら	*sochira*	that way
あちら	*achira*	that way over there
まっすぐ	*massugu*	straight ahead
はし	*hashi*	bridge
みち	*michi*	road/street
わたります　わたる	*watarimasu (wataru)*	cross over
わたって	*watatte*	*te* form of *watarimasu*
ひだり　に	*hidari ni*	to the left
みぎ　に	*migi ni*	to the right

ひだりがわ	*hidarigawa*	left-hand side
みぎがわ	*migigawa*	right-hand side
まがります　まがる	*magarimasu (magaru)*	turn
まがって	*magatte*	*te* form of *magarimasu*
わかります　わかる	*wakarimasu (wakaru)*	understand
そして	*soshite*	and then

Unit 4

あるきます　あるく	*arukimasu (aruku)*	walk
あるいて	*aruite*	*te* form of *arukimasu*
かきます　かく	*kakimasu (kaku)*	write
かいて	*kaite*	*te* form of *kakimasu*
ぐらい	*gurai*	about (distances/ lengths of time)
かど	*kado*	corner
ちず	*chizu*	map
ちかい	*chikai*	close/near
みえます　みえる	*miemasu (mieru)*	can/able to see
えいがかん	*eigakan*	movie theater (building)
ぎんこう	*ginkoo*	bank
ゆうびんきょく	*yuubinkyoku*	post office
とおい	*tooi*	distant/far
ガソリン　スタンド	*GASORIN SUTANDO*	gas station
Interest		
こうさてん	*koosaten*	intersection
しんごう	*shingoo*	signal/traffic lights

Unit 5

まえ	*mae*	in front of/before/ago
した	*shita*	under/below
うしろ	*ushiro*	behind
うえ	*ue*	on top/above
そば	*soba*	beside
なか	*naka*	inside
そと	*soto*	outside
もっと	*motto*	more
だいすき	*daisuki*	like a lot
わたしたち	*watashitachi*	we

Unit 6

ちかく　に	*chikaku ni*	neighborhood/nearby
まちます　まつ	*machimasu (matsu)*	wait
まって	*matte*	*te* form of *machimasu*
Interest		
みつこし	*Mitsukoshi*	a chain of department stores

Unit 7

いります/いる	*irimasu (iru)*	need
いって	*itte*	*te* form of *need*
はじめ　に	*hajime ni*	at first/first/in the beginning
あと　で	*ato de*	afterwards
（と）いっしょ　に	*(to) issho ni*	together (with)
Interest		
かんがえ	*kangae*	thought/idea

Unit 8

よく	*yoku*	well/often
のうじょう	*noojoo*	farm
やま	*yama*	mountain
ひつじ	*hitsuji*	sheep
うし	*ushi*	cows
うま	*uma*	horse
みずうみ	*mizuumi*	lake
たくさん	*takusan*	many/a lot
すいえい　を　します　する	*suiei o shimasu (suru)*	swim
つり　を　します　する	*tsuri o shimasu (suru)*	go fishing
して	*shite*	*te* form of *shimasu*
しゅうまつ	*shuumatsu*	weekend
おぼえます　おぼえる	*oboemasu (oboeru)*	remember
おぼえて	*oboete*	remember (*te* form)

Interest

スキー	*SUKII*	ski/skiing
さんぽ	*sanpo*	a walk
しずか	*shizuka (na)*	quiet, peaceful
とり	*tori*	bird
たき	*taki*	waterfall

TOPIC TWELVE
eating and drinking

Introduction

ACHIEVEMENTS

By the end of this topic, you will be able to:
- offer food and drink politely;
- accept or reject food politely;
- say what you have for a meal;
- know some of the differences between food in Japan and in your own country;
- know how to cook and eat some Japanese food;
- ask for food and drink in a restaurant or coffee bar.

いただきます   *itadakimasu*

Japanese say *itadakimasu* before a meal to give thanks to the person who has prepared it, or to thank the host when being treated to a meal. *Gochisoosama deshita* is an expression of thanks used at the end of the meal.

Eating in Japan is a marvelous adventure. Visitors find that the choice of food is tremendously varied and it is easy to sample good traditional food (*washoku*) or foreign food (*yooshoku*) inexpensively.

The "safest" way to eat out in Japan is to look in the restaurant windows where incredibly true-to-life plastic models of the food offered, along with prices, are displayed. These models are called *shokuhin SANPURU*. (To be sure of what you will pay, add on three percent for Government tax, as on any purchases in Japan.) There is no obligatory tipping in Japan.

If you are not confident about using your Japanese to order food, it is always possible to take a waiter or waitress outside and show them what you would like from the window.

When your meal arrives, it will look unbelievably like the plastic model, often down to the exact number of peas or pieces of tomato.

There are many very exclusive restaurants in Japan that don't advertise their prices and do have high cover charges, but if you are on a budget, it is easy to avoid the embarrassment of perhaps being in a restaurant you can't afford by using the method above.

Eating in tourist hotels is usually expensive, and many visitors are unwilling to venture out and try the local restaurants. Often they don't realize that in Japan there is an enormous number and variety of eating places – over

40,000 in Tokyo alone! Visitors can usually find places serving familiar food, including numerous American and European style fast-food outlets.

Japanese people eat and entertain in restaurants much more than most other nationalities. (It is, in fact, a real privilege to be invited to a Japanese person's home for a meal, as particularly for business contacts, it is more usual to take visitors to restaurants.)

A family meal (top left)
Plastic models in the display window (top right)
Inside an *udon* noodle restaurant (lower right)
A mobile street stall (lower left)

あさごはん   *asagohan*   breakfast

In the mornings there are good value breakfasts called *MOONINGU SETTO* (morning set meal) in many restaurants. These usually include toast (*TOOSUTO*) and boiled eggs or ham, salad, coffee and juice. Toast, jam and scrambled egg is often offered as a continental breakfast. These often cost hardly more than a cup of coffee bought alone. A traditional Japanese breakfast will consist of rice, miso soup, fish and salad with fruit juice or vegetable juice and Japanese tea.

For many visitors even the Westernized versions are unusual to contemplate at breakfast time! Japanese toast is an experience not to be missed. Slices can be anything from 1 to 2 inches thick!

During the day

Department store basements are usually food halls and have an amazing variety of prepared food on sale. Many of the counters have free taste samples readily available. If you need a light snack at some time while shopping, this is a way of sampling everyday Japanese food and replenishing your energy at the same time! Ice creams and the usual Western-style snacks are readily available in most places. There are lots of coffee bars (*kissaten*) and cake shops, too.

ひるごはん   *hirugohan*   lunch

Lunchtime offers an opportunity to try simple, cheap, traditional food like *soba* noodles, simple *sushi* or *obentoo*.

Soba noodles are served in a soup, and many visitors are astonished at the noises they hear around them, as the other customers show their appreciation by slurping and sucking loudly as they eat.

If you have been brought up not to slurp, it's actually very difficult to do it! (A class noodle slurping competition is fun and easy to do in the classroom if you have access to an electric kettle to boil the water and everyone brings a bowl and a packet of instant noodles. If you are able to get chopsticks as well, it gives you good practice, using them in a non-threatening situation.)

Sushi of various sorts is delicious. The main ingredient is a slightly sweet, vinegared cooked rice. *Nigirizushi* is made by squeezing the seasoned, vinegared, cooked rice into a rectangular shape and then pressing some raw or cooked fish onto the top. They are usually decorated with bamboo grass.

Makizushi is made by spreading the *sushi* rice onto a sheet of baked seaweed called *nori* that has been laid out on a bamboo mat. (The mat is rather like those sold for place mats that consists of slender rods of bamboo linked together into a flat mat with thread, that roll up smoothly and easily.) Seafood and vegetables are placed on top, and the mat is then rolled up tightly. The roll is lifted off the mat and cut into slices with a sharp knife and is ready to eat.

There are hundreds of different kinds of *sushi* with the same basic components as these, each area having its own specialty.

Obentoo/Bentoo are lunch packs. They always look most attractive and tempting because Japanese people take such care with the presentation of food. In a lunch box there are usually some sorts of *sushi* and *onigiri*, and fruit or celery, carrot, tomato and leftover *tempura*, etc.

Bentoo may be bought at railway stations too, and are called *ekiben*.

Traditionally the *obentoo* was packed up and then wrapped in a *furoshiki* to be carried to school or work. The *furoshiki* is a square of fabric, often very beautiful, about the size of a headscarf.

Onigiri are rice cakes. They are very filling and surprisingly tasty and are also easy to make. They are often made with cold cooked rice left over from the meal of the night before. The rice is rolled into elongated or round balls or triangles, between hands that have been dipped in cold water and lightly salted. Sometimes they have fish or Japanese salted plums pressed into the middle. Sometimes they are rolled in sesame seeds or wrapped in baked seaweed. These are the staple lunch food for Japanese students.

Yakitori

ばんごはん   *bangohan*   **evening meal**

In the rush of working days, eating quickly is important. Evening meals are, however, much more relaxed affairs and provide a time for the family to come together and talk.

In the home a lot of time is spent preparing the evening meal, and it is usually beautifully presented. A variety of foods will be offered in an array of dishes of every shape, size and color. Rice is nearly always served. As well, there will be numerous small bowls of sauces and dressings into which food may be dipped.

The Japanese place a lot of importance on the visual aspect of food, as well as allowing the subtle flavors of each dish to be savored separately.

A family meal at home

Eating *obentoo* in the park (above)

A *RAAMEN* noodle restaurant. The curtain over the doorway shows that the shop is open (right)

Etiquette

It is important to learn a little about Japanese table manners in order to avoid giving offense.

First, practice sitting Japanese style: a woman sits with legs tucked under her; men sit cross-legged. Those not used to this find it quite uncomfortable. Japanese people won't mind if you put your legs to one side or even if you stretch them out under the table. However, it is considered impolite to point your toes directly at anyone.

Ohashi or *hashi* (chopsticks) are important to master before you start experimenting with Japanese food. It can be embarrassing to have your food fly out over the table!

Try out the recipes in this topic and get your chopstick practice while enjoying the food. Also look at the instructions for using chopsticks on p. 126.

Using chopsticks, transfer the food from the small bowls to your mouth. It is not proper to mix other food with rice or to put sauces on rice (unless it is *KAREERAISU* – curry and rice). If food is served in a large communal bowl, as is the case with *sukiyaki*, use the back end of your chopsticks to take food to your own plate, and carefully distinguish between the end you are putting to your mouth and the "clean end."

Larger pieces of food can be cut up with chopsticks – though this requires practice! While taking a break during the meal and after eating, chopsticks are placed on chopstick rests, not left in the bowl. If there are no rests, place them neatly across the top of the bowl on the side away from you. Never stand them up in the rice, as this is the way food is placed on shrines for the dead! Don't gesture with your chopsticks or point them at others.

Sip soups and liquid dishes straight from the bowl. If food arrives in a dish with a lid, replace the lid after taking what you want.

If Japanese people give you a meal or take you to a restaurant, they will appreciate it if you try the food that is offered, even if it doesn't look appealing to you. Certainly do your best to look interested and don't make "yuk" faces. If you can't honestly say something is delicious, you can say it's "interesting" or "unusual"!

However, be wary of enthusing over things you don't like, for two reasons: you may be offered it over and over again, and people may spend more than they can really afford to give you more of the same.

Unit 1

コーヒー は いかが です か
KOOHII wa ikaga desu ka
Would you like some coffee?

NEW WORDS

ごめん　ください	Gomen kudasai	Is anyone home?
いいえ、けっこう　です	iie, kekkoo desu	no, thank you
まだ	mada	still/not yet
まだ　へた　です	mada heta desu	still no good at
		not yet good at
へた	heta	not good at/not clever/
		unskillful
はいります	hairimasu	enter
とけい	tokei	watch/clock
きっさてん	kissaten	coffee shop
アイスクリーム	AISUKURIIMU	ice cream
みず	mizu	water
おちゃ	ocha	tea
コーヒー	KOOHII	coffee
ジュース	JUUSU	juice
Interest		
ミルク	MIRUKU	milk
ミルクセーキ	MIRUKUSEEKI	milkshake
コカコーラ	KOKAKOORA	Coke
じゅく	juku	cram school
この　ごろ	kono goro	these days
ひま	hima	free
のど　が	nodo ga	Are you thirsty?
かわきました　か	kawakimashita ka	
この　まえ	kono mae	before this

Yooko's friend Kenji has just come to her house to see her. He has just returned home after a year in Australia. He calls out the standard greeting for letting people in the house know that he is there. (Japanese people don't knock on doors very often.)

けんじ　ごめん　ください。

ようこ　おはいり　ください…ああ、けんじ　くん　おひさしぶり　です　ね。

け　そう　です　ね。おげんき　です　か。

よ　おかげ　さま　で　げんき　です。けんじ　くん　は。

け　げんき　です。ありがとう。

よ　こちら　へ　どうぞ…さむい　です　ね。

け　はい、きょう　とても　さむい　です。

よ　どうぞ…ここ　に　すわって　ください。コーヒー　は　いかが
　　です　か。のど　が　かわきました　か。

け　いいえ、けっこう　です。すみません　が　じかん　が
　　ありません。まち　に　いって、かいしゃ　に　いきます。

よ　そう…この　まえ　なに　を　しました　か。

け　オーストラリア　に　すんで　いました。

よ　そう　です　か。べんきょう　して　いました　か。

け　はい、えいご　を　れんしゅう　して　いました。

よ　いい　です　ね。この　ごろ　えいご　が　じょうず　です　ね。

け　まだ　へた　です　が　まいにち　れんしゅう　して　います。

よ　じゃ…しがつ　に　だいがく　に　はいります　か。

け　いいえ、はいりません。かいしゃ　に　はいります。そろそろ
　　しつれい　します　が　あした　また　あいましょう　か。

よ　はい、にちようび　です　から　ひま　です。どこ　で
　　あいましょう　か。

け　えき　の　まえ　に　おおきい　とけい　が　あります。その
　　とけい　の　した　で　ごじ　に　あいましょう。きっさてん　に
　　いきましょう。

よ　ありがとう。ごじ　に　えき　の　とけい　の　した　で…じゃ
　　また。

け　あした　また。

K:　*Gomen kudasai.*
Y:　*Ohairi kudasai . . . aa, Kenji kun Ohisashiburi desu ne.*
K:　*Soo desu ne. Ogenki desu ka.*
Y:　*Okage sama de genki desu. Kenji kun wa.*
K:　*Genki desu. Arigatoo.*
Y:　*Kochira e doozo . . . samui desu ne.*
K:　*Hai, kyoo totemo samui desu.*
Y:　*Doozo . . . koko ni suwatte kudasai. KOOHII wa ikaga desu ka. Nodo ga
　　kawakimashita ka.*
K:　*Iie, kekkoo desu. Sumimasen ga jikan ga arimasen.
　　Machi ni itte, kaisha ni ikimasu.*
Y:　*Soo . . . kono mae nani o shimashita ka.*
K:　*OOSUTORARIA ni sunde imashita.*
Y:　*Soo desu ka. Benkyoo shite imashita ka.*
K:　*Hai, eigo o renshuu shite imashita.*
Y:　*Ii desu ne. Kono goro eigo ga joozu desu ne.*

K: *Mada heta desu ga mainichi renshuu shite imasu.*
Y: *Ja . . . shigatsu ni daigaku ni hairimasu ka.*
K: *Iie, hairimasen. Kaisha ni hairimasu. Sorosoro shitsurei shimasu ga ashita mata aimashoo ka.*
Y: *Hai, nichiyoobi desu kara hima desu. Doko de aimashoo ka.*
K: *Eki no mae ni ookii tokei ga arimasu. Sono tokei no shita de goji ni aimashoo. Kissaten ni ikimashoo.*
K: *Arigatoo. Goji ni eki no tokei no shita de . . .*
Y: *Ashita mata.*

STUDY

- **Gomen kudasai** is usually answered with **O hairi kudasai** "Please enter" or **O agari kudasai** "Please step up" (Remember that there is a step up from the *genkan* into the house.)

   This means that the person who has come to call enters the *genkan*, and waits there until the person inside comes to the entrance hall. People don't march in further until invited.

- **Kenji kun wa**. This is sometimes difficult for non-Japanese to understand. Kenji is there in front of her, but she doesn't say "How are you?" she says "How is Kenji?" as if she is speaking about a mutual friend of theirs. Until this point of time *Anata wa* has been the expression offered to you for this situation. It is, however, more common in Japan to use people's names or titles instead of "you."

   Study the following:

   Sensei wa. Depending on the context, this can mean "How about you?" if you are speaking to the teacher, or "How about the teacher?" if the teacher is not present.

   Doctors, teachers, university professors and many professional people are addressed as *sensei*. As you learn more of the language, you will gradually absorb the titles by which to address people politely.

- **Hairimasu** is a new verb: "enter." It is used in many situations in Japan, where in English we use a different verb. In English we "take" a bath or "have" a bath. The Japanese "enter" a bath, because they in fact immerse their whole bodies. They enter the bath literally.

   The same verb is used for "going into" the hospital. If someone says to you *Byooin ni ikimasu*, he means that he will go to the hospital, maybe to visit a friend or for a quick check, but if he says *Byooin ni hairimasu* he is being admitted as a patient.

   The same verb is used for a new situation like going to high school for the first time or entering (going to) a university.

- **KOOHII wa ikaga desu ka**. *KOOHII* is a *katakana* word, because coffee has only become popular since the American occupation period after the war. Learn **Ikaga desu ka** as a phrase for asking people what they would like. Just put the topic, followed by **wa**, in front of it.

   Using all the food and drink vocabulary that you know, take turns asking each other "Would you like . . . . . .?" Each person asks the question of her neighbor and the neighbor answers before asking her other neighbor, until everyone has had a turn.

- **Hen** and **heta** are both Qualitative Nouns. Add them to your Qualitative Noun list.

  Heta, like *joozu*, usually has **ga** in front of it, because you will be picking out a specific thing that you are poor/unskillful at.

  ITARIAgo ga heta desu. I'm no good at Italian.

  How many Qualitative Nouns do you now know? Brainstorm them and write them on the board. Once you have the complete list, practice making sentences using:

  1 Topic/*ga*/Qualitative Noun/*desu*.

      e.g.: *Watashi wa TENISU ga joozu desu.*

          Watashi no nihongo ga heta desu.

  2 Qualitative Noun/*na*/noun/*desu (dewa arimasen)*.

      e.g.: *Henna inu desu ne.*   It's a peculiar/funny dog, isn't it?

          Henna inu janai desu/dewa arimasen.   It's not a funny dog.

          Kirei na yama deshita.   It was a beautiful mountain.

                            They were beautiful mountains.

ACTIVITIES

- Take turns asking your neighbor if he/she would like

  tea   coffee   juice   milk   water

  The answer may be *lie, kekkoo desu* or *arigatoo*.

- An alternative for offering a guest a drink is to use the negative of *nomimasu: nomimasen* and say:

  Ocha o nomimasen ka   Won't you have some tea?

  Practice using this way of inviting someone to have a drink using the same list as before.

- Practice reading through the conversation aloud with a friend. Then make your own substitutions for: names; what Kenji has been doing or what he studied; the time and place of meeting. Next, role play the situation.

Check your understanding

けさ ろくじ に おきました。あさごはん を たべて しんぶん を
よみました。しちじ はん に うち を でました。えき に いって、
でんしゃ で がっこう に いきました。いちにちじゅう たいへん
べんきょう しました。よじ に スポーツ の れんしゅう を
しました。そして ともだち と でんしゃ で かえりました。でんしゃ
の なか で しゅくだい を しました。ともだち と えいご の
しゅくだい を しました。えいご の ほん を よみました。ろくじ

はん　に　うち　に　つきました。ばんごはん　の　あと　で　じゅく　に
いきました。くじ　に　うち　で　おふろ　に　はいりました。そして
しゅくだい　を　しました。いま　じゅうにじ　ごふん　です。ねます。

Kesa rokuji ni okimashita. Asagohan o tabete shinbun o yomimashita. Shichiji han ni uchi o demashita. Eki ni itte, densha de gakkoo ni ikimashita. Ichinichijuu taihen benkyoo shimashita. Yoji ni SUPOOTSU no renshuu o shimashita. Soshite tomodachi to densha de kaerimashita. Densha no naka de shukudai o shimashita. Tomodachi to eigo no shukudai o shimashita. Eigo no hon o yomimashita. Rokuji han ni uchi ni tsukimashita. Bangohan no ato de juku ni ikimashita. Kuji ni uchi de ofuro ni hairimashita. Soshite shukudai o shimashita. Ima juuniji gofun desu. Nemasu.

(Bangohan no ato de – after dinner/evening meal)

ACTIVITY

Have a Japanese tea party. Make a cup of Japanese tea and drink it in class, if you are able to buy Japanese tea locally, or use weak ordinary tea and drink it Japanese style. Everyone will need a small bowl.

There are many varieties of Japanese tea. When you see it growing alongside roads and railways, it looks very attractive, because the long lines of knee-high bushes are so neatly clipped. Only the tips of the shrub are used for tea, so the bushes are constantly manicured.

If you try one tea and don't like it, don't be put off, because you may like the next one you try. Japanese green tea is not made with boiling water, but with water just before boiling. The hostess pours the tea around all the cups a little at a time so that everyone gets the same strength of brew, and tops up the teapot with fresh hot water (*Oyu*) as it runs out. It is drunk without milk and sugar or any other additives and is a very healthy refreshing drink. English style tea is also drunk in Japan and is called *koocha* (black tea).

You may like to try sitting around on the floor Japanese style drinking tea from small bowls like Japanese tea bowls (*chawan*). Japanese tea bowls are often very treasured and valuable, so hold one hand under the bowl and the other hand around the bowl to be sure that you won't drop it, and sip a little at a time.

(Please note: This is not a "Tea Ceremony." It is an everyday "drinking tea with friends" situation. A tea ceremony has very formal ritual to be observed by hosts and visitors.)

if you wish, your tea party can take the form of a whole class role play: Visitors arrive in twos and threes.
One student plays hostess and greets the visitors, invites them inside, they take off their shoes, are taken through to the *ima* and asked to sit down, and are offered tea. While waiting for the kettle to boil, chat about the weather; while drinking it, chat with neighbors about what they've been doing or their families' news.

Unit 2

コーヒー を みっつ ください
KOOHII o mittsu kudasai
Three coffees please

NEW WORDS

ひとつ	hitotsu	one
ふたつ	futatsu	two
みっつ	mittsu	three
よっつ	yottsu	four
いつつ	itsutsu	five
むっつ	muttsu	six
ななつ	nanatsu	seven
やっつ	yattsu	eight
ここのつ	kokonotsu	nine
とお	too	ten
じゅういち	juuichi	eleven, etc.
しょうしょう	Shooshoo omachi	very polite for "Please
おまち ください	kudasai	wait a minute"
おまたせ しました	Omatase shimashita	Sorry to have kept you
		waiting

Interest

いちご	ichigo	strawberry
りんご	ringo	apple
バニラ	BANIRA	vanilla
チョコレート	CHOKOREETO	chocolate
バナナ	BANANA	banana
オレンジ	ORENJI	orange
ケーキ	KEEKI	cake
ハンバーガー	HANBAAGAA	hamburger
ホットドッグ	HOTTO DOGGU	hotdog

Review

おなか が すきました	Onaka ga sukimashita	I'm hungry
のど が	nodo ga	I'm thirsty
かわきました	kawakimashita	
ひとり で	hitori de	by myself/alone
ふたり で	futari de	two people (only)

Interest

マクドナルド	MAKUDONARUDO	McDonalds

Some school friends go to McDonalds after school.
みせ の ひと いらっしゃいませ。

Many Western food chains now operate in Japan

みちこ	ミルクセーキ を ふたつ、コーヒー を みっつ くだ さい。
みせ の ひと	ミルクセーキ は チョコレート です か、いちご で す か。
みちこ	チョコレート は ひとつ、いちご は ひとつ くださ い。
みせ の ひと	しょうしょう おまち ください。

Michiko collects the money from her friends

みちこ	ミルクセーキ も コーヒー も ひとつ にひゃくごじ ゅうえん です。にひゃくごじゅうえん を ください。
せいと	どうぞ。
みせ の ひと	おまたせ しました。せん にひゃくごじゅうえん で す。
みちこ	だいじょうぶ です。ありがとう。ここ に すわりまし ょう か うえ に すわりましょう か。
せいと	うえ に いきましょう。

Mise no hito: *Irasshaimase.*
Michiko: *MIRUKU SEEKI o futatsu, KOOHII o mittsu kudasai.*
Mise no hito: *MIRUKU SEEKI wa CHOKOREETO desu ka, ichigo desu ka.*
Michiko: *CHOKOREETO wa hitotsu, ichigo wa hitotsu kudasai.*
Mise no hito: *Shooshoo o machi kudasai.*
(While they are waiting the students collect up their money.)
Michiko: *MIRUKU SEEKI mo KOOHII mo hitotsu nihyakugojuuen desu.*
                Nihyakugojuuen o kudasai.

(The students each hand over two hundred and fifty yen.)

Seito:	*Doozo.*
Mise no hito:	*Omatase shimashita. Sen nihyaku gojuuen desu.*
Michiko:	*Daijoobu desu. Arigatoo.*
	Koko ni suwarimashoo ka, ue ni suwarimashoo ka.
Seito:	*Ue ni ikimashoo.*

STUDY

- **Japanese numbers.** You have learned one set of numbers and have seen some words that look very similar to the ones in this unit when learning dates. These, however, are not the ones used for dates. These are used for counting objects up to ten when you have not learned a particular counter to use. You already know the counters for time, *ji,* for people, *nin,* for languages, *go.*

  But there are many more which are fun to learn and use. Because there are so many, only a few basic ones are included in this course, and you will be understood if you use the Japanese numbers for counting cakes, cups of tea, etc, even though they may have a specific counter of their own. You will not be easily understood if you ask for coffee with *ichi, ni, or san!*

  The pattern to use when ordering food and drink is:

  (KOOHII) o (futatsu) kudasai.

  Note that the number/quantity word is placed directly in front of the verb. Think back to other situations in which the pattern is the same:

  When counting people   *sannin imasu*   There are three people.
  takusan arimasu   There are a lot.

  If you want to state the flavor of, for example, a milkshake, *BANIRA no MIRUKU SEEKI* is a vanilla flavor milkshake. Because vanilla flavor is a noun, the **no** particle must be used between that and the next noun – milkshake; e.g.,

  Ichigo no MIRUKU SEEKI – a strawberry flavor milkshake.
  BANANA no MIRUKU SEEKI – a banana flavor milkshake.

  If, however, you are fortunate enough to have a strawberry milkshake made with real strawberries the **no** is not needed. Orange juice does not need the **no** either, because it is one complete noun – the name of that beverage is "orange juice": *ORENJI JUUSU,* pineapple juice *PAIN-APPURU JUUSU,* apple juice: *ringo JUUSU.* (The reason *ringo* is written in *hiragana* is that apples were known in Japan long ago, whereas some other fruits have been introduced to Japan during the past four hundred years.)

- Learn the polite phrases that store clerks use to apologize for keeping you waiting or to ask you to "please wait."

  When **you** ask someone to wait, the polite phrase is *chotto matte kudasai.* The clerk's phrase is super polite because the customer is, in Japanese terms, "above" the clerk who is offering the service. This is another example of different language for different status situations. It does not mean that Japanese people look down on people who are doing service jobs as people, only that when performing that service they are acting in a situation that calls for respect for the customer or client. There are situations in English, too, where we modify our language depending upon the person to whom we are speaking or the job we are doing. Discuss this together.

Once you have learned the basics of communication in Japanese, you will begin to learn this "super polite" level for addressing people of higher status than yourself in given situations.

EXERCISE
1   *Ichigo no MIRUKU SEEKI o hitotsu nomimashita.*
2   *CHOKOREETO no MIRUKU SEEKI wa suki janai desu. Anata wa.*
3   *ORENJI JUUSU o mittsu kudasai.*
4   *HANBAAGAA o futatsu kudasai.*
5   *Chiisai KOKA KOORA o hitotsu kudasai.*
6   *Ookii ORENJI JUUSU o futatsu kudasai.*
7   *ORENJI JUUSU ga arimasu ka . . . . . mittsu kudasai.*
8   *KOOHII o hitotsu, Ocha o futatsu kudasai.*
9   *Kyoo KEEKI o hitotsu tabemashita.*
10 *Onigiri ga daisuki desu. Kyoo itsutsu tabemashita.*

ACTIVITIES
• Learn the Japanese numbers by heart. Chanting them to a clapping rhythm is fun, as is dancing them to a rhythm. Anything that helps you to fix them in your memory is worth trying. Be particularly careful with similar ones.

   Statistically it has been proven that if you learn an incorrect pattern or fact it may take as many as two hundred repetitions to undo the damage. So save yourself effort by learning accurately each step of the way!

• Practice asking for a specific number of hamburgers, etc. Around the group each person adds on one and repeats the sentence: *HANBAAGAA o (hitotsu) kudasai.* After twelve, start again at the beginning with a different item. See how fast you can go with everyone being absolutely ready to add their sentences.

• Around the group make a mammoth order for an unfortunate clerk to remember! Each person adds on items to the list, remembering to adjust the sentence pattern:
   Student One: *MIRUKU SEEKI o hitotsu kudasai.*
   Student Two: *MIRUKU SEEKI o hitotsu, JUUSU o futatsu kudasai.*
   Student Three: *MIRUKU SEEKI o hitotsu, JUUSU o futatsu, mizu o mittsu kudasai.*
   How many items can you add before someone gets mixed up?

• In small groups role play entering a coffee bar and each order something to eat or drink. Pay for what you order, and sit down to chat.

Using *hashi*

Japanese start learning to use chopsticks as small children (using half-size chopsticks) and become very adept at the task. As well as for eating, chopsticks are used for all sorts of cooking tasks, including stirring, cutting and whisking.

In most households each person has their own pair(s) of chopsticks. Restaurants, however, provide disposable wooden ones called *waribashi.*

Though there is supposedly a "correct" way of holding *hashi,* you will see a wide variety of styles used.

The upper stick is held between the thumb and the index and middle fingers. This stick is the one that is moved up and down.

The lower stick is held reasonably firmly and is not moved.

Check your understanding

- Sort out the following list into sequence from one to ten:
  muttsu, mittsu, yattsu, hitotsu, too, kokonotsu, futatsu, itsutsu, nanatsu, yottsu.

- Sort the following *hiragana* list into reverse order from largest number to smallest.
  むっつ　　ひとつ　　とお　　　ここのつ　　ふたつ　　やっつ
  みっつ　　よっつ　　ななつ　　いつつ

• Read the following passage and answer the questions that follow.

きのう　ともだち　と　スポーツ　を　しました。スポーツ　の　あと　で
たいへん　おなか　が　すきました。マクドナルド　に　いきました。
ハンバーガー　は　ひとり　で　みっつ　たべました。わたし　の
ともだち　の　ピーター　くん　は　ビッグ　マック　を　ふたつ
たべました。のど　も　かわきました。コカコーラ　は　ふたり　で
よっつ　のみました。

*Kinoo tomodachi to SUPOOTSU o shimashita. SUPOOTSU no ato de tai-
hen onaka ga sukimashita. MAKUDONARUDO ni ikimashita. HANBAAGAA
wa hitori de mittsu tabemashita! Watashi no tomodachi no PIITAA kun wa
BIGGU MAKKU o futatsu tabemashita. Nodo mo kawakimashita. KOKA
KOORA wa futari de yottsu nomimashita.*
(*BIGGU MAKKU* – no prizes for guessing that it means "Big Mac"!)
1   How many hamburgers did the writer eat?
2   How many Cokes did they drink between them?
3   What had they been doing to get so hungry?
4   How many people went to the restaurant?

• Write a short passage in which you say how many of various foods and
drinks you ate after an activity.

• Have a vocabulary/spelling quiz in teams to check all your vocabulary so
far. Each team makes a list to test the other teams. (Decide on the number of words: 20..50..100?) You will, of course, need to know your own list
very well to be sure of marking other teams accurately.

• Organize a vocab/spellathon using the combined vocabulary lists that
you have just compiled in teams, or use the vocabulary lists at the back
of each book.
     If you are allowed to seek sponsorship, it is a way of raising money for
buying the ingredients to make a Japanese meal or to visit a Japanese
restaurant for a meal or . . . to start fundraising for a trip to Japan!

Recipes

(Simplified recipes for school use)

Beef Sukiyaki
(Quantities of meat need to be adjusted to the size of the group. Allow 1 tablespoon of meat per person.)

Vegetables: Onions, carrots, spinach, pumpkin, broccoli, mushrooms. Bring prepared vegetables to school, one cup per person. (Vegetables of any kind should be cut into small pieces so that they will cook in the same time as one another.)

Meat: Wiener Schnitzel, top side or rump steak cut into thin strips. Marinate in a little soy sauce.

Rice: Boil white rice until soft. Don't wash the rice, leave it sticky.

You will need an electric skillet, oil, a little white wine or rice wine, 2 tablespoons of sugar and soy sauce.

Heat the skillet, add 3 tablespoons of oil, 3 tablespoons of soy sauce, sugar and 3 tablespoons of wine. Stir well. When bubbling and well mixed add vegetables. After 2 or 3 minutes add meat and simmer gently until the vegetables are tender. Serve the rice in separate bowls. Do not put sauce or sukiyaki in with the rice. Take the sukiyaki from the skillet with chopsticks.

Sushi
You will need baked dried seaweed (*yaki nori*) (which can be bought in Oriental foodshops), a small can of salmon or tuna, carrots, parsley, lettuce, and some mayonnaise.

Boil two cups of white rice until soft. When cool add 2-3 tablespoons of vinegar and 2 tablespoons of sugar. Stir well and allow to cool.

On a bamboo mat lay out one sheet of baked seaweed. Spread rice onto seaweed, leaving a one-inch strip uncovered on the front edge. Across the middle lay out a strip of fish; on top of that lay out strips of carrot, parsley and lettuce and smear with mayonnaise. Roll firmly into a tidy roll. Wet the seaweed strip that has no rice on it and it will stick to itself. Leave for a few minutes, then cut into slices with a sharp knife. Each slice will have a colorful fish and carrot center. (One sheet of nori makes 5-6 slices.)

Onigiri
Boil rice as for sukiyaki. Dip hands into cold water and sprinkle with salt. Roll rice between hands to form a cylindrical shape. The onigiri can also be rolled in sesame seeds or have fish in the center.

Unit 3

なに を たべて います か
nani o tabete imasu ka
What are you eating?

NEW WORDS

いれます	*iremasu*	put in
いれて	*irete*	put in (*te* form)
おいしい	*oishii*	delicious
おいしかった です	*oishikatta desu*	it was delicious
まずい	*mazui*	unpalatable/not nice
Interest		
なに も	*nani mo*	nothing
けしごむ	*keshigomu*	eraser
ごみばこ	*gomibako*	waste basket
ガム	*GAMU*	chewing gum

せんせい カイルさん、なに を たべて います か。

カイル なに も だべて いません。

せんせい カイルさん、なに を たべて います か。

ガイ グリーン せんせい、すみません…カイルさん は ガム を たべて います。

せんせい そう です か。

カイル そう では ありません。わたし の けしごむ を たべて います。

せんせい なに!

カイル けしごむ です。けしごむ が すき です。おいしい です。

せんせい まずい でしょう。それ は ごみばこ の なか に いれて ください。

S: *KAIRU san, nani o tabete imasu ka.*
K: *Nani mo tabete imasen.*
S: *KAIRU san, nani o tabete imasu ka.*
G: *GURIIN sensei, sumimasen.*
　　KAIRU san wa GAMU o tabete imasu.
S: *Soo desu ka.*
K: *Soo dewa arimasen. Watashi no keshigomu o tabete imasu.*
S: *Nani!*
K: *Keshigomu desu. Keshigomu ga suki desu. Oishii desu.*
S: *Mazui deshoo. Sore wa gomibako no naka ni irete kudasai.*

Check your understanding of the conversation.

Teacher: Kyle, what are you eating?
Kyle: Nothing!
Teacher: Kyle, what are you eating?
Guy: Excuse me, Mr. Green . . . . Kyle's eating chewing gum.
Teacher: Is that so?
Kyle: No, I'm not. I'm eating my eraser.
Teacher: What!
Kyle: It's an eraser. I like erasers. They're delicious.
Teacher: They're probably awful. Put it in the waste basket, please.

STUDY

- ***Nani mo*** is a colloquial expression for "Nothing."
  Nani! "What!" – on its own is not very polite, but it is used in exclamation or by young people talking among themselves.

Check your understanding

Review the names of Japanese foods that you learned in Units 1 and 2.
How many foods and drinks do you now know?
Who can make the longest list in two minutes?
Don't forget that spelling accuracy is really important.
Which are written in *hiragana* and which in *katakana*?
How many of the *katakana* ones can you write? Who can write the most, accurately.

How would you say the following in Japanese?
1   The sushi was delicious.
2   Yesterday I ate a delicious orange.
3   The breakfast was not nice.
4   I ate hot tempura.
5   The tea was hot.
6   The onigiri was tasty.
7   The soba was not unpalatable.
8   The sashimi was expensive.
9   The packed lunch was not expensive.
10 Was the set breakfast cheap?
11 That restaurant's sushi is not cheap.
12 The fish is not big/large.

Students help to serve meals in a *chuugakkoo* school canteen

ACTIVITIES

- Role play the conversation.

- Write the story of Kyle eating her eraser in class as if you were telling your friend about it after school.

    Add in as many details as you can. Where did the action take place? What lesson was it? Was she hungry? Does she always eat erasers?

- Write a conversation between two students, one of whom was taken out to a Japanese restaurant last Saturday. After saying where he went, his friend asks who he went with, what he ate, was it fish or meat and if he liked it.

    Maybe you'd like to role play it on tape with a friend for others to listen to.

- Listen to the following story of an unwary tourist.
  Who can tell the outline of the story to the class in English afterwards?
  How many other details do you remember as a class?

スコット せんせい は にがつ に にほん に ひこうき で
いきました。よる の しちじ に なりた くうこう に つきました。
ふゆ でした から さむかった です。ひこうき の なか で ねて
いました。ばんごはん は たべません でした。それから しちじ に
おなか が たいへん すきました。くうこう の レストラン で
ばんごはん を たべました。てんぷら を たべました。テーブル の
うえ に わさび が ありました。みどり いろ でした。はし で
スコット せんせい は その わさび を てんぷら の うえ に
たくさん おきました。…てんぷら を ひとつ たべました。…いや
でした ね！くち が あつかった です。かお が あかかった です。
のど が いたかった です。みず を たくさん のみました が まだ
くち が あつかった です。さんじゅっぷん あと でも くち が

まだ いたかった です。レストラン を でました が おなか が
すいて いました。このごろ わさび は いつも たべません。

なりた くうこう	*narita kuukoo*	Narita airport (Tokyo)
ひこうき	*hikooki*	airplane
すいて	*suite*	*te* form of *sukimasu*
おきます	*okimasu*	put, place (don't confuse with the verb "get up")
おいて	*oite*	*te* form of *okimasu*
わさび	*wasabi*	very hot, green horseradish

SUKOTTO sensei wa nigatsu ni nihon ni hikooki de ikimashita. Yoru no shichiji ni Narita kuukoo ni tsukimashita.
Fuyu deshita kara samukatta desu.
Hikooki no naka de nete imashita. Bangohan wa tabemasen deshita. Sorekara shichiji ni onaka ga taihen sukimashita.
Kuukoo no RESUTORAN de bangohan o tabemashita.
Tempura o tabemashita. TEEBURU no ue ni wasabi ga arimashita. Midori iro deshita. Hashi de SUKOTTO sensei wa sono wasabi o tempura no ue ni takusan okimashita . . .
Tempura o hitotsu tabemashita . . .
Iya deshita ne! Kuchi ga atsukatta desu. Kao ga akakatta desu. Nodo ga itakatta desu. Mizu o takusan nomimashita ga mada kuchi ga atsukatta desu. Sanjuppun ato de mo kuchi ga mada itakatta desu.
RESUTORAN o demashita ga onaka ga suite imashita.
Kono goro wasabi wa itsumo tabemasen!

Listen to the story again to see if you were all correct. Read it again on your own to understand the things you didn't pick up when it was read to you.

- Write ten sentences of your own using a different adjective for each sentence. Check them with a partner. Any you are not sure about, discuss with your teacher.

- Write your own story or conversation about someone who goes to a coffee bar or restaurant.
    What did they choose? How much was it? Was it good? Expensive? Cheap? What happened?
Remember, as always in your own role plays and stories, to stick to the vocabulary that you have learned in the course, so that everyone will understand.

Writing practice

- Learn **CHI** チ

- Learn **YU** ユ

- From **CHI** you can make **CHU**, using a half-size **YU**: チュ

- Learn **YO** ヨ

- Using a half-sized **YO**, you can write **CHO** チョ

- Write *CHOKOREETO* チョコレート

Unit 4

へんな なまえ です
henna namae desu
It's a peculiar name

NEW WORDS

ポカリ スエット	*POKARI SUETTO*	"Pocari Sweat," an isotonic health drink
からだ	*karada*	health, body
のみもの	*nomimono*	drink
つめたい	*tsumetai*	cold to taste or touch

Two students are choosing a drink from a vending machine.

アン　　あつい です ね。なに を のみましょう か。

さちこ　ポカリ スエット が すき です か。

ア　　　ポカリ スエット！へんな なまえ です ね。なん です か。

さ　　　からだ の のみもの です。からだ に いい です。
　　　　おいしい です。

ア　　　わかりません。えいご で ポカリ スエット は なん です
　　　　か。

さ　　　ポカリ は かいしゃ の なまえ です。「スエット」 は
　　　　えいご で 「sweat」 です。それ を のんで ください。
　　　　いい です。

ア　　　いいえ、けっこう です。りんご ジュース を のみます。
　　　　ポカリ スエット は いやな なまえ です ね。

さ　　　わたし は ポカリ スエット が すき です。あつい
　　　　おてんき です から いい のみもの です。

ア　　　そう です か。じゃ、それ を のみます。いくら です か。

さ　　　ひゃくえん です。やすい です ね。いい です か。
　　　　つめたい です か。

ア　　　つめたい です。すき じゃない です が おもしろい です。

さ　　　にほんじん は その のみもの が すき です。

ア　　　そう…でも、わたし は にほんじん じゃない です。

Ann:　　*Atsui desu ne. Nani o nomimashoo ka.*
Sachiko:　*POKARI SUETTO ga suki desu ka.*
A:　　*POKARI SUETTO! Henna namae desu ne. Nan desu ka.*

S: *Karada no nomimono desu. Karada ni ii desu. Oishii desu.*
A: *Wakarimasen. Eigo de POKARI SUETTO wa nan desu ka.*
S: *POKARI wa kaisha no namae desu. SUETTO wa eigo de "sweat" desu.*
    Sore o nonde kudasai. Ii desu.
A: *Iie, kekkoo desu. Ringo JUUSU o nomimasu. POKARI SUETTO wa iyana*
    namae desu ne.
S: *Watashi wa POKARI SUETTO ga suki desu. Atsui otenki desu kara ii*
    nomimono desu.
A: *Soo desu ka. Ja, sore o nomimasu. Ikura desu ka.*
S: *Hyakuen desu. Yasui desu ne.*
(Ann puts in her money, gets out a can of drink and tries it.)
S: *Ii desu ka. Tsumetai desu ka.*
A: *Tsumetai desu. Suki janai desu ga omoshiroi desu.*
S: *Nihonjin wa sono nomimono ga suki desu.*
A: *Soo . . . demo, watashi wa nihonjin janai desu.*

Check your understanding of the conversation.
Ann: It's hot, isn't it? What shall we drink?
Sachiko: Do you like Pocari Sweat?
Ann: Pocari Sweat? What a peculiar name. What is it?
Sachiko: It's a health drink. It's good for your health. It's delicious.
Ann: I don't understand. What is "Pocari Sweat" in English?
Sachiko: Pocari is the company/trade name. "*SUETTO*" is "sweat" in
          English. Have some. It's good.
Ann: No, thanks. I'll have apple juice!
          Pocari Sweat! What a terrible name!
Sachiko: I like Pocari Sweat. Because it's hot weather, it's a good drink.
Ann: Is that so? . . . well, I'll drink that then.
          How much is it?
Sachiko: One hundred yen. It's cheap, isn't it? . . .
          Is it good? Is it cold?
Ann: It's cold. I don't like it, but it's interesting.
Sachiko: Japanese people like that drink.
Ann: Is that so? . . . but . . . I'm not Japanese.

STUDY

• Pocari Sweat is supposed to be a very good health drink, specially
  recommended for hot weather or to drink after exercise to rebalance the
  ions in the body.

• **_Eigo de_** "In English/by means of English"; e.g.,
  Eigo de nan desu ka.   What is it in English?
  Nihongo de nan desu ka.   What is it in Japanese?
  FURANSUgo de nan desu ka.   What is it in French? etc.
  Answer: *FURANSUgo de . . . desu.*
  Extension: A more advanced way of saying the same thing is:
  Eigo de nan to iimasu ka.   "What do you call it in English?/How do you
                                    say it in English?"

The answer then is: *Eigo de . . . to iimasu.*
If you would like to do so, learn this phrase now. If you prefer to leave it until that verb is taught, that's fine.

- ***Tsumetai***. This adjective may only be used for things that are cold to touch or taste; e.g., ice cream, water that you touch or swim in.

- ***Karada ni ii desu***. "It's good for the health."
In this phrase the ***ni*** still means "to." It's good **to** your health. In English we use the word "for." Learn it as a phrase and keep in the back of your mind that "to" can sometimes mean the same as "for."
Karada ni warui desu.   It's bad for/to your health.

ACTIVITIES

- Make up a menu in Japanese. Be careful to write the names in *hiragana* or *katakana* appropriately.

- Use your menu for a restaurant or snack bar role play with a group of five people. Try foods and drinks that you haven't tried before and comment on them. Persuade others.

- Look at the following sentences to check your understanding. When you have read through, cover the *roomaji* and try to give the Japanese.

1	The water is cold.	*Mizu wa tsumetai desu.*
2	It is cold today.	*Kyoo wa samui desu.*
3	The ice cream was very cold.	*AISUKURIIMU wa taihen tsumetakatta desu.*
4	The drink was interesting.	*Nomimono wa omoshirokatta desu.*
5	Smoking (*TABAKO*) is bad for your health.	*TABAKO wa karada ni warui desu.*
6	Exercise (*undoo*) is good for your health.	*Undoo wa karada ni ii desu.*
7	That drink was delicious.	*Sono nomimono wa oishikatta desu.*
8	I drank a strange drink.	*Henna nomimono o nomimashita.*
9	The drink was peculiar.	*Nomimono wa hen deshita.*
10	Did you like that?	*Sore ga suki deshita ka.*

- In small groups of 3 or 4, use the following menu and role play visiting a coffee shop. One person will be the waiter/waitress. Some suggestions on what your conversation could cover are:
Saying you are hungry/thirsty and suggesting going to a coffee shop.
Being greeted by the waiter/waitress as you enter.
Asking or suggesting what you like and dislike.
Commenting on the prices.

Deciding on your order and giving your order to the waiter/waitress.
Commenting on your food and drink as you consume it.
Suggesting and deciding what you will do after you have finished eating and
drinking.
Paying the waiter/waitress.
Receiving your change from the waiter/waitress.

メニュー
MENU

のみもの DRINKS			たべもの EATS		
コーヒー	Coffee	¥250	ホット ドッグ	Hot dog	¥300
おちゃ	Green tea	¥200	ハンバーガー	Hamburger	¥300
こうちゃ	English tea	¥200	カレー ライス	Curry Rice	¥300
ミルク セーキ	Milkshake	¥200	トースト	Toast	¥100
• バニラ	• Vanilla		サンドイッチ	Sandwich	¥200
• チョコレート	• Chocolate		• ハム	• Ham	
• バナナ	• Banana		• トマト	• Tomato	
• オレンジ	• Orange		パンケーキ	Pancake	¥250
• いちご	• Strawberry		ケーキ	Cake	¥300
• りんご	• Apple		• バナナ	• Banana	
ジュース	Juice	¥180	• チョコレート	• Chocolate	
• オレンジ	• Orange		アイスクリーム	Ice cream	¥250
• りんご	• Apple		• バニラ	• Vanilla	
			• いちご	• Strawberry	

Unit 5

にほん の たべもの
nihon no tabemono
Japanese food

NEW WORDS

ゆうめい	*yuumei*	famous (qualitative noun)
おんがく	*ongaku*	music
おと	*oto*	sound/noise
うるさい	*urusai*	noisy
ごはん	*gohan*	cooked rice
そば	*soba*	buckwheat noodles
すし　すきやき	*sushi, sukiyaki,*	Japanese foods
さしみ	*sashimi*	
Interest		
なま	*nama*	raw
のり	*nori*	baked seaweed
ヌードル	*NUUDORU*	noodles

Jackie has just returned from a visit to Japan. She has been asked to tell her class what the food in Japan was like.

にほん の たべもの は おいしかった です。ゆうめいな たべもの が たくさん あります。たべもの の なまえ は すし や すきやき や そば や さしみ です。すし は ごはん と やさい と さかな と のり です。すきやき は にく と やさい です。そば は スープ と ヌードル です。ときどき そばや で そば を たべました。レストラン の なか は うるさかった です。おんがく では ありません でした。ひと は そば を たべて いました。おおきな おと が しました。レストラン の まど の なか に しょくひん モデル が みえました。にほんじん は あたらしい さかな を たくさん たべます。さしみ は あたらしい さかな です。たいへん あたらしい です。なま です。さしみ を たべました が すき では ありません でした。

Nihon no tabemono wa oishikatta desu. Yuumeina tabemono ga takusan arimasu. Tabemono no namae wa sushi ya sukiyaki ya soba ya sashimi desu. Sushi wa gohan to yasai to sakana to nori desu.
Sukiyaki wa niku to yasai desu.
Soba wa SUUPU to NUUDORU desu. Tokidoki sobaya de soba o tabemashita.
RESUTORAN no naka wa urusakatta desu.
Ongaku dewa arimasen deshita.
Hito wa soba o tabete imashita. Ookina oto ga shimashita!
RESUTORAN no mado no naka ni shokuhin MODERU ga miemashita.
Nihonjin wa atarashii sakana o takusan tabemasu. Sashimi wa atarashii sakana desu.

Taihen atarashii desu! Nama desu!
Sashimi o tabemashita ga suki dewa arimasen deshita.

Check your understanding of Jackie's story.
"Japanese food was delicious. There are lots of famous foods.
The names of the foods are sushi, sukiyaki, soba, sashimi, etc.
Sushi is cooked rice, vegetables, fish and baked seaweed.
Sukiyaki is meat and vegetables. Soba is soup and noodles.
Sometimes I went to a soba shop and had soba noodles.
Inside the restaurant it was noisy.
It wasn't music. People were eating soba. They made a loud noise.
In the restaurant windows you could see plastic models of the food.
Japanese people eat a great deal of fresh fish. Sashimi is fresh fish. Very fresh fish! It's raw! I ate sashimi but I didn't like it."

STUDY

* **Yuumei (na)** is another Qualitative Noun to add to your list.

* **Ookii/ookina**. *Ookii* and *chiisai* are two words that can be either adjectives or Qualitative Nouns. Because they sound a bit awkward in front of some nouns (the sound does not flow) add the **na**. E.g.: *ookina uchi desu/chiisana uchi* rather than *ookii uchi, chiisai uchi*. In front of some words there is not that awkwardness: *ookii neko, chiisai neko*. (Those that begin with a vowel usually take the "**na**.")

  Ookii and words that have double "o" at the beginning, like Oosaka city, are written with two *hiragana* o's.

* **Gohan** means cooked rice. You have met it in *asagohan* (morning cooked rice/breakfast), *hirugohan* (noon cooked rice) and *bangohan* (evening cooked rice). The Japanese traditionally had cooked rice at every meal, but that pattern is changing as eating habits incorporate more and more foreign ideas. (Uncooked rice is called *kome*.)

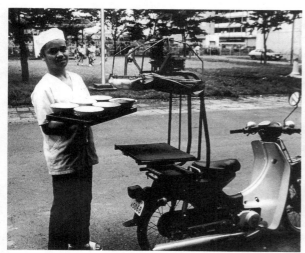
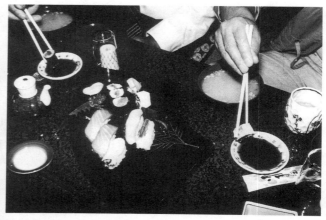

Noodle meal delivery (left)
Eating *sushi* (right)

Dinner in a Western style home

EXERCISES
True or false?

- 1 *Onigiri wa gohan desu.*
  2 *Sushiya de kutsu o kaimasu.*
  3 *Yasai wa yaoya de kaimasu.*
  4 *Sashimi wa niku desu.*
  5 *Hanayasan wa hana ga takusan arimasu.*

- Rewrite the sentences in *hiragana* and *katakana*, inserting the words or particles given in their correct place within the sentence.
  1 *(wa) SUMISU san nihon ni ikimashita.*
  2 *(hon) Honya de o kaimashita.*
  3 *(sakana)Kinoo o tabemashita.*
  4 *(o) Getsuyoobi wa TENISU shimashita.*
  5 *(takusan) Inu o mimashita.*
  6 *(takusan) Sushi wa tabemashita.*
  7 *(totemo) Onna no ko wa kirei desu.*
  8 *(hitotsu) HANBAAGAA o kudasai.*
  9 *(futari)Otoko no hito wa ikimashita.*
  10 *(ni) Goji aimashita.*

Round up time

- Have a quiz on (or brainstorm on the board) all the background information that you have learned in this book. In groups prepare twenty questions and answers and cut them into strips. Put everyone's questions into a box. A question master may then take out one at a time for the quiz to find the cultural background champions of your class.

- In teams, compose sentences to test each other. Check that your sentences are correct, of course, before you begin. Each member of the team should know his/her team questions thoroughly and be able to answer them in order to check the other team's answers.

- In pairs test your vocabulary.

- Test yourself on all the *katakana* that you should know by now.

- Look at the achievements list and see if you can do everything on the list without looking up anything. If there are ones you can't do, help your own future satisfaction by reviewing and learning it now. Then do that exercise again to prove that you can do it. *Ganbatte kudasai!*

Reading practice

1 Read the following sentences.
a　それ　を　ください。
b　どれ　です　か。
c　その　かばん　です。
d　これ　です　か。
e　はい、そう　です。

1 Who do you think the two people are in this conversation?
2 Suggest a sentence, word or phrase that would usually come before sentence *a*.
3 Suggest a sentence or phrase to follow sentence *e*.

2 これ　と　これ　を　ください。
いくら　です　か。
1 How many things are required?
2 Suggest an answer to the question and complete the conversation in 3 sentences.

3

Name	Item bought	Price
たろう	りんご	にひゃくえん
なおみ	かさ	ごひゃくえん
やすこ	とけい	さんぜんえん
けんじ	じてんしゃ	にまんえん
まさお	ジュース	ひゃくごじゅうえん
ゆり	しんぶん	ひゃくよんじゅうえん

1 Who bought what? (Answer in English.)
2 Make two sentences for each person, saying what they bought and how much it cost.
3 How would you say:
Taroo bought one (apple).

Naomi bought two (   ).
Yasuko bought three (   ).
Kenji bought four (   ).
Masao bought five (   ).
Yuri bought six (   ).

4 *a* Make sentences to give the price of the following toys and objects.

ゴリラ	ごひゃくえん
カンガルー	せんさんびゃくえん
はな	ろっぴゃくえん
ペン	ひゃくななじゅうえん
ほん	はっぴゃくえん
え	さんぜんえん
いす	いちまんえん
はこ	よんひゃくえん
かばん	にせんえん
えんぴつ	きゅうじゅうえん

b Make two-sentence dialogues with each pair, asking, for example,
(   ) *wa ikura desu ka.*
(   ) *desu.*

c Make short stories about someone buying two items at a time; e.g., a
pen and a box. Say how much they spent.

d Make sentences; e.g., "I bought two boxes" and give the total price.

5 Read the information and answer the questions.
この おんな の ひと は モリッソン せんせい です。ともだち
に でんわ して います。
つくえ の うえ に かみ と でんわ の ほん が あります。
この ひと は うれしい です。きょう の ろくじ に その
ともだち に あいます。レストラン で ばんごはん を たべます。
あと で えいが に いきます。

モリッソン	*MORISSON*	Morrison
レストラン	*RESUTORAN*	restaurant

a Who is the person in the photo?
b To whom is she talking?
c What is on the desk?

d   What time will they meet?

e   What do they plan to do?

CROSSWORD (TOPIC TWELVE REVIEW)

Write in *ROOMAji.*

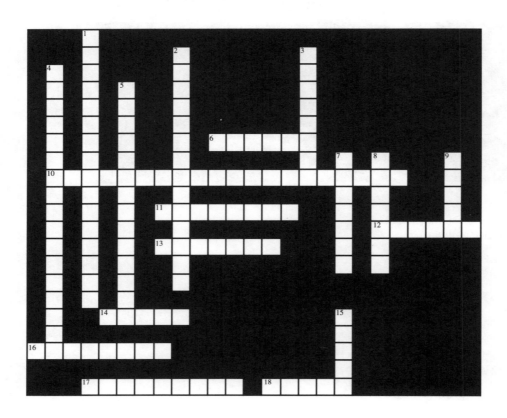

ACROSS

6 A soba noodle shop is called a . . . .
10 Please eat with chopsticks
11 will eat
12 delicious
13 deep fried food
14 vinegared rice, fish and vegetables often wrapped in seaweed
16 Japanese dish of meat and vegetables
17 restaurant
18 knife

DOWN

1 I like cooking
2 It was delicious
3 will drink
4 It is not fresh
5 I cook
7 raw fish
8 Japanese food
9 unpalatable
15 fork

Writing practice

- You now know enough *katakana* to write the following words:

CHOKOREETO	*SEERU*
SUUPAA	*PETTO*
OOTOBAI	*DEPAATO*
TOOSUTO	*PUURU*
PAN	*TENISU*
GEEMU	*TEREBI*
TEEBURU	*TEEPU*
RAJIO	*BASU*
TESUTO	*PAATII*
GASORIN	*PEN*

- Sketch some of the above words and label them in *katakana*.

Vocabulary checklist (Topic Twelve)

Introduction

いただきます	*itadakimasu*	said before eating
わしょく	*washoku*	Japanese food
ようしょく	*yooshoku*	foreign food
しょくひん　サンプル	*shokuhin SANPURU*	window samples
あさごはん	*asagohan*	breakfast
ひるごはん	*hirugohan*	lunch
ばんごはん	*bangohan*	dinner/evening meal
モーニング　セット	*MOONINGU SETTO*	morning set meal
トースト	*TOOSUTO*	toast
きっさてん	*kissaten*	coffee bar
おべんとう	*Obentoo*	lunch boxes
おはし	*Ohashi*	chopsticks
おしぼり	*Oshibori*	moist towels
ごちそうさま	*gochisoo sama*	Thank you (for the meal)
でした	*deshita*	

Interest

えきべん	*ekiben*	lunch boxes bought at a station
にぎりずし　まきずし	*nigirizushi/makizushi*	types of sushi
のり	*nori*	baked seaweed
おにぎり	*Onigiri*	rice cakes
ふろしき	*furoshiki*	wrapping cloth
わさび	*wasabi*	horseradish
そばや	*sobaya*	soya noodle restaurant
うどんや	*udonya*	udon noodle restaurant
やきとりや	*yakitoriya*	barbecue chicken shop
うなぎや	*unagiya*	eel restaurant
すきやき	*sukiyaki*	Japanese dish
すし	*sushi*	Japanese dish
さしみ	*sashimi*	Japanese dish
てんぷら	*tenpura*	Japanese dish

Unit 1

コーヒー　は　いかが　です　か	*KOOHII wa ikaga desu ka*	Will you have a cup of coffee? (Would you like a cup of coffee?)
ごめん　ください	*Gomen kudasai*	Anyone home?
おはいり　ください	*O hairi kudasai*	Please come in
おあがり　ください	*O agari kudasai*	Please step inside
いいえ、けっこう　です	*iie, kekkoo desu*	No, thank you
まだ	*mada*	not yet
へた	*heta*	not good, unskillful at
はいります　はいる	*hairimasu (hairu)*	enter
はいって	*haitte*	*te* form of *hairimasu*

とけい	*tokei*	watch/clock
アイスクリーム	*AISUKURIIMU*	ice cream
みず	*mizu*	water
おちゃ	*Ocha*	tea (Japanese)
コーヒー	*KOOHII*	coffee
ジュース	*JUUSU*	juice
きっさてん	*kissaten*	coffee shop
Interest		
ひま	*hima*	free (time)
のど　が	*nodo ga*	Are you thirsty?
かわきました　か	*kawakimashita ka*	
この　まえ	*kono mae*	before this
ミルク	*MIRUKU*	milk
ミルクセーキ	*MIRUKU SEEKI*	milkshake
コカコーラ	*KOKAKOORA*	coca cola
じゅく	*juku*	cram school
この　ごろ	*kono goro*	these days
ちょっと	*chotto*	a little bit

Unit 2

ひとつ	*hitotsu*	one
ふたつ	*futatsu*	two
みっつ	*mittsu*	three
よっつ	*yottsu*	four
いつつ	*itsutsu*	five
むっつ	*muttsu*	six
ななつ	*nanatsu*	seven
やっつ	*yattsu*	eight
ここのつ	*kokonotsu*	nine
とお	*too*	ten
しょうしょう　おまち　ください	*shooshoo Omachi kudasai*	Please wait a moment (very polite)
おまたせ　しました	*Omatase shimashita*	Sorry to have kept you waiting
Interest		
いちご	*ichigo*	strawberry
りんご	*ringo*	apple
バニラ	*BANIRA*	vanilla
チョコレート	*CHOKOREETO*	chocolate
バナナ	*BANANA*	banana
オレンジ	*ORENJI*	orange
ケーキ	*KEEKI*	cake
ホット　ドッグ	*HOTTO DOGGU*	hotdog
マクドナルド	*MAKUDONARUDO*	McDonald's
ハンバーガー	*HANBAAGAA*	hamburger

Unit 3

いれます　いれる	*iremasu (ireru)*	put in
いれて	*irete*	*te* form of *iremasu*
おいしい	*oishii*	delicious/tasty
まずい	*mazui*	unpalatable/not nice
そう　では　ありません	*soo dewa arimasen*	I don't agree (opposite of *soo desu*)

Interest

ガム	GAMU	chewing gum
なに　も	nani mo	nothing
けしごむ	keshigomu	eraser
ごみばこ	gomibako	waste basket
ひこうき	hikooki	airplane
なりた　くうこう	Narita kuukoo	Narita airport
おきます　おく	okimasu (oku)	put, place
おいて	oite	te form of okimasu

Unit 4

ボカリ　スエット	POKARI SUETTO	Pocari Sweat (drink)
いや	iya (na)	horrible, disgusting
からだ	karada	health, body
のみもの	nomimono	beverage/drink
つめたい	tsumetai	cold to touch

Unit 5

はし	hashi	chopsticks
むずかしい	muzukashii	difficult (adjective)
ゆうめい	yuumei (na)	famous (Qualitative Noun)
おんがく	ongaku	music
おと	oto	sound
うるさい	urusai	noisy (adjective)
ごはん	gohan	meal/cooked rice
こめ	kome	uncooked rice
そば	soba	buckwheat noodles

Interest

| なま | nama | raw |
| ヌードル | NUUDORU | noodles |

TOPIC THIRTEEN
leisure, sports and hobbies

Introduction

ACHIEVEMENTS

By the end of his topic you will be able to:
- Tell about your hobbies and leisure time interests.
- Ask about others' hobbies and leisure time interests.
- Say what you can and cannot do.
- Say what you've already done and what you haven't done yet.
- Ask permission to do things.
- Refuse permission (option).
- Say what you wear.
- Describe what others are wearing.
- Describe the colors of objects.
- Say what you own and ask what others own.
- Make a phone call and answer a call simply.
- Learn to write more *katakana* syllables and combined sounds.

Leisure

There are as many activities available in Japan for leisure time as in any country anywhere, with the addition of many that are traditional to Japan or have been adapted to allow for the lack of space and time in Japan. As they strive to improve their school grades and work positions, *hima*, or free time, is less readily available to Japanese people than to many other nationalities. Free time in Japanese terms is usually time outside school or work that is heavily programmed with "improvement" activities. In a recent survey people gave the following priorities for their choice of leisure activity:
1   Getting rid of stress and maintaining good health.
2   Enjoying life.
3   Improving and maintaining friendships.
4   Improving knowledge.

Work, school, and holidays

Japanese students have many hobbies and interests but, compared with other nationalities, they have only limited time to devote to them. School hours are from 8:30 to 3:30 or 4 o'clock, with compulsory club activities for most students four nights a week until five or six o'clock, followed by practices on Saturdays and Sundays, and of course homework, which keeps high school students busy until the early hours of the morning.

Students go to school for half a day on Saturdays.

Usually, there are school breaks three times a year: in summer from mid-July until the end of August; in winter for two weeks, beginning Dec. 25; and after the end of the school year, in March, there is a two-week vacation before the beginning of the new school year.

Working hours in Japan have been reduced in the past few years, and many companies now give Saturdays off and about two weeks paid vacation a year: four or five days in summer and the rest at New Year, as well as public holidays.

The most popular way to spend free time, according to a recent survey, is watching TV, but sports is increasing in popularity. The most popular sports are baseball, physical exercises, swimming and jogging. The most popular hobbies are going to the movies, gardening, fishing, knitting and dress-making.

In previous topics you have read about festivals, bonsai, ikebana, kendo, judo, karate, pachinko, calligraphy, music, golf, fishing, sports, movies, records, books, activities with friends and other ways of enjoying life after school hours. Add to these activities like collecting stamps, keeping insects in cages, butterfly and moth hunting, Japanese dancing and western dancing, evening classes, clubs in pottery and art, and parties, and you will realize that the possibility exists to have a very varied selection of interests, both inside and outside the home.

The real drawback is the exam system and the competition for jobs that puts pressure on people to study all of their waking hours, leaving them little time to pursue other interests. This is particularly true of students who are studying an instrument and who must spend hours each week in serious practice, or those who play sports and must practice regularly or lose their places on teams.

Martial arts

The martial arts (*budoo*) include *juudoo, kendoo, karate, aikidoo* and *kyuudoo* (archery). They develop tremendous concentration and singlemindedness and are therefore seen as excellent backups to good study habits. The mental and emotional side of these activities is as important as the physical. The strategy employed in all of them is to take advantage of opponents' power by making it work against them.

The martial arts in Japan developed for people to protect themselves from personal attack, but religious influences, particularly from Buddhism and Confucianism, caused them to develop into disciplines of the mind as well as of the body.

They teach the principles of fair play, loyalty and honor and are encouraged in schools, where they are offered as part of the physical education program and as club activities.

Judo (*Juudoo*) is an original Japanese sport and uses throws and holds.

Karate, thought to have originated in China or Korea, uses bare hands and feet. The name literally means "empty hand."

Kendo (*Kendoo*) is a form of fencing using a wooden sword.

Aikidoo uses throws and concentrates on the art of bending and twisting the joints, using power efficiently.

Kyuudoo (archery) uses a traditional long bow and emphasizes form.

Yabusame is archery performed on horseback. Although only a few people are able to participate these days, it makes an impressive display. "Warriors," dressed in colorful and elaborate clothing, fire their arrows at targets while galloping at full speed.

Shodoo

Shodoo (calligraphy), *ikebana* and *bonsai* develop an eye for balance and harmony according to Japanese traditional aesthetic taste.

Shodoo is a traditional art form in Japan and is very popular. It uses a brush (*fude*) and traditionally used ink made from soot that had been compressed into a solid block. Before attempting to write, the calligrapher used to spend an hour or more mixing the ink with water to the perfect density and blackness. Perfectionists nowadays do the same, though most people use ready mixed ink. After that, it is necessary to sit quietly to still the mind before starting.

It may take a long time for each stroke, as each one must be considered so carefully that you know exactly where your brush will move and exactly how you will angle your wrist to produce the stroke you want, before any ink is transferred from the brush to the paper. This is taken as seriously as deciding upon moves in chess.

Shodoo takes a lot of patience. Children at school, in the days when they wrote with a *fude*, used to spend as long as an hour mixing their ink every day under the teacher's careful scrutiny. During that time, they did not speak and were expected to concentrate totally on what they were doing even when they were only six or seven years old.

Ikebana

In *ikebana* flower arranging, also known as *kadoo*, the same patience and stillness of mind is necessary to follow the rules of the art. *Ikebana* originated from ritual flower offerings by Buddhist priests and became an established art form around the sixteenth century, with various schools developing over the years, each emphasizing different styles of arrangement.

In one traditional style three main heights are incorporated, symbolizing heaven, earth, and mankind. The aim is to arrange them in such a way that the three achieve natural harmony and represent the universe.

Modern *ikebana*, however, places more emphasis on artistic aspects and doesn't always follow the three-symbol concept. Even inorganic materials like plastic, glass, metal, and so on, are used these days.

Bonsai

In *bonsai*, landscapes are miniaturized so that they can be enjoyed in a small space. The roots and branches of trees are carefully pruned and the branches trained to grow in aesthetically pleasing but natural shapes. A solitary tree or a group of plants is grown in a shallow container. Sometimes rocks or other miniaturized plants are placed around them to make a whole garden in miniature. Some *bonsai* trees have been tended for more than a hundred years. It is interesting to think of the loyal and tender care that they must have received from a succession of people over the years to keep them healthy and beautiful.

You may like to make miniature gardens of your own for the classroom or to keep at home. Choose plants that will be in proportion to one another in size and then be willing to maintain them carefully through the year. To keep them going takes regular care. You may like to see how long you can maintain a class miniature garden or even a genuine *bonsai* tree. If you undertake such an activity you will soon gain respect for the people who have looked after the old bonsai trees, and for those who take it up as a long-term hobby, as you realize the amount of attention you need to give the plants to keep them healthy.

Music and dance

Japanese dancing is enjoyed by many people, male and female, and is still regularly practiced in Japan, particularly around the Obon festival in August. Japanese traditional musical instruments and music are widely enjoyed and practiced, too. The most well-known instruments are *koto* (harp), *shamisen* (lute) and *shakuhachi* (flute).

KARAOKE

KARAOKE is singing along with a pre-recorded tune and is a very popular pastime, particularly for men, either at home or in the many special *KARAOKE* bars that have sprung up all over Japan. In the bars, adults may sing along to a tape or video and be much more exhibitionist than would normally be possible. Almost all popular songs, both Japanese and foreign, are available on *KARAOKE* tapes. The most popular music for *KARAOKE*, however, is *enka*, an original Japanese kind of "blues" music – mostly relating sad and melancholy tales and love stories.

Card games

The three most popular traditional card games are *irohaKARUTA*, *hanafuda*, and *hyakunin isshu*.

IrohaKARUTA (or *irohaGARUTA*) makes use of the *hiragana* syllabary and is a game often enjoyed by families during New Year. *Iroha* means the *hiragana* syllabary and *KARUTA*, as you may guess, is a general term for various card games.

Two sets of cards are used. One set has pictures and a *hiragana* syllable on each card. The other has forty-eight reading cards with a proverb or saying written on the back. These have been chosen so that the first letter of each proverb, if arranged in order, will make up the *hiragana* syllabary.

To play, a reader reads from a card and the other players must identify the picture card that relates to the reading.

The one who identifies it first wins that card, and the player who picks up the most cards is the winner.

Hanafuda (flower cards) uses forty-eight cards, four for each month of the year. Each month is represented by one of twelve flowers or plants. Each card has a different number of points in accordance with the picture.

The game is played by several people matching the various kinds of pictures in order to make some combination with higher points. *Hanafuda* is usually played for money.

Hyakunin isshu is a card game which uses 100 *tanka* poems by 100 poets, dating from the seventh to thirteenth centuries.

The players compete in matching two cards: one is a reading card with a complete poem printed on it, while the other is a matching card with only the second half of the same poem. All the cards are spread out on the floor to be picked up by the players as the reader recites one poem after another. The winner is the one who matches the most poems.

Origami

Origami is the traditional art of paper folding, now well-known around the world as a creative and stimulating hobby. *Origami* products were used long ago for decorating ceremonial tools at Shinto shrines, and they are still used in wedding ceremonies. *Origami* is taught at kindergartens and in the lower grades of elementary school to cultivate an aesthetic sense and a feeling for form. The result is that practically every Japanese person can produce an *origami* creation within a few minutes.

The ideal of *origami* is to simply fold a square sheet of paper and create forms without drawing, cutting, or gluing; however, cutting or painting is sometimes permissible. The most popular shapes include cranes and helmets, but almost any shape is possible.

You may like to try the *origami* example on p. 167.

Mushi

A less formal activity is the keeping of insects (*mushi*). Japanese children often keep crickets (*koorogi*) in bamboo cages as pets. Large beetles are also popular. There is one very large black beetle that has scissor-like jaws. When confronted by a sheet of paper this creature munches its way quickly from one side to the other, leaving two neatly cut halves – a pet to be wary of!

Company outing – waiting for the bus (left)
Ikebana (right)

Learning a language

Karaoke bar (top left)
Going to the movies (top right)
Wendy's – a place to meet friends (lower left)
Exhibition poster (lower right)

A lot of the activities described in this introduction demand obedience to set rules, patience, and continual practice. If any of the activities interest you, you may like to adopt one as a hobby, to be enjoyed alongside your Japanese study. There are numerous books available and clubs to join.

Reading books and magazines about Japan and practicing one of these activities will give you extra enjoyment in your study. Language cannot be separated from the way of life and the activities of the people of a nation, and the more you learn about these things, the greater your enjoyment of the language will become, because your understanding of the reasons behind words and actions will grow.

If you have the opportunity to watch Japanese films or cartoons, or to listen to Japanese music, take it. Even if you understand little or nothing of what is said, you will pick up useful information or ideas about the culture. Also, listening to the sounds and rhythms of the language will assist you in producing a more natural sound when speaking.

You may not be able to see a tangible result quickly, but all the background information that you store away will, in time, enrich your ability to communicate.

Unit 1

えいが に いって も いい です か
eiga ni itte mo ii desu ka
May I go to the movies?

NEW WORDS

いって も いい です か	*itte mo ii desu ka*	May I go?
おわります おわる	*owarimasu (owaru)*	finish
おわって	*owatte*	*te* form of *owarimasu*
キャンプ に いきます	*KYANPU ni ikimasu*	go camping
クラス	*KURASU*	class
いなか	*inaka*	countryside
の あと で	*no ato de*	afterwards, after
すぐ	*sugu*	soon
つかいます つかう	*tsukaimasu (tsukau)*	use
つかって	*tsukatte*	*te* form of *tsukaimasu*
つまらない	*tsumaranai*	boring
もちろん	*mochiron*	of course

Review

りか	*rika*	science
しゅくだい	*shukudai*	homework
らいしゅう	*raishuu*	next week
いつ	*itsu*	when

Read the following conversation with a friend and only use the English version or the *ROOMAji* if you are unsure about something.

Haruko is unsure whether her mother will allow her to go out for the evening.

はるこ　　きょう わたし の ともだち は えいが に いきます。
　　　　　　わたし も いって も いい です か。

おかあさん　しゅくだい が あります か。

は　　　　はい、でも すぐ おわります。
　　　　　　しゅくだい の あと で えいが に いって も いい です か。

お　　　　はい、いって も いい です が くじ に かえって きて ください。

H: *Kyoo watashi no tomodachi wa eiga ni ikimasu. Watashi mo itte mo ii desu ka.*

O: *Shukudai ga arimasu ka.*

H: *Hai, demo sugu owarimasu.*
      Shukudai no ato de eiga ni itte mo ii desu ka.

O: *Hai, itte mo ii desu ga kuji ni kaette kite kudasai.*

After you and your friend have read the conversation take turns asking each other the following questions and answering in English.

1   Where did Haruko want to go?
2   What did she have to do first?
3   How long did she expect that activity to take?
4   What was the stipulation made by her mother?

Use the English version below to test yourself. Would you be able to say all the same things as Haruko and her mother, in Japanese?

Try a similar conversation without checking back or planning it first. You know the general gist of the conversation, and it's perfectly all right to add in your own ideas.

For those who'd like to check their understanding, here is an English version:

H: Today my friends are going to the movies. May I go?

O: Do you have homework?

H: Yes. I'll finish it soon. After homework may I go to the movies?

O: Yes, you may go, but please come home at nine o'clock.

STUDY

- *te mo ii desu* is another use of the *te* form – to ask permission. The *te* form of any verb may be placed in front of the package *mo ii desu ka* to ask "May I . . . ," "Is it OK for me to . . ."

  e.g.:

Suwatte mo ii desu ka	May I sit down?
Tatte mo ii desu ka	May I stand up?
Kono hon o katte mo ii desu ka	May I buy this book?
Anata no manga o yonde mo ii desu ka	May I read your comic book?

  A new verb that you will find useful here is *tsukaimasu* – "use." (The *te* form is *tsukatte*); e.g.,

  Anata no monosashi o tsukatte mo ii desu ka.

  May I use your ruler?

  Remember that Japanese people prefer to use names rather than *anata*, even though it means looking someone in the face and calling them by name; e.g.,

  KEN kun no monosashi o tsukatte mo ii desu ka.

  How would you say the following:

  Ben: "Excuse me Dan, may I please use your pencil?"

  Dan: "Of course, but please wait a minute."

  Go through a few examples like this together and also answer with the pattern minus **ka** to give permission. At this point you will not be able to refuse permission! (Except by saying *lie, dame desu* – No, it's no good/you can't.)

To give permission, say: *Doozo* or *Hai, suwatte mo ii desu*. "Yes, you may sit down," etc.

- **Ato de/no ato de** (after, afterwards, later)
  You may begin a sentence with *Ato de* (after that); e.g.,
  Ato de RESUTORAN ni ikimashita.
  After that we went to a restaurant.

  Ato de may also be used with the meaning of "see you later," instead of *ja mata*. Remember that these two expressions for saying goodbye are only appropriate when talking to your friends; they'd sound a bit rude if said to adults or people you don't know well.

  If you use **ato** after a noun, you must use the particle **no**;
  e.g.:
  *Hirugohan **no ato de** SUPOOTSU GURAUNDO ni ikimashita.*
  After lunch we went to the Sports Ground.
  *Shigoto **no** ato de kaerimashita*
  After work we went home.
  *Gakkoo **no** ato de PUURU ni ikimashita.*
  After school we went to the pool.
  Practice some sentences like this together.

ACTIVITIES

- Ask permission from the teacher for something you would like to do. An alternative may be suggested if your teacher doesn't think it appropriate to grant your request! See if everyone in the class can think of a different thing to ask. Listen carefully so that you don't repeat a request. (Later, use this request form as often as you can with your friends, and never leave the room without asking permission.)

- An opportunity not to be missed! Write notes in class without getting into trouble.

  Write a note to your friend to ask if he or she will give you permission to do something. When you receive the request, write a note back giving or refusing permission.

- Pairwork.
  Photocopy the two worksheets on pp.158 and 159 and give each partner a different sheet and some scrap paper. Don't allow your partner to see your sheet.

  It's Saturday and your little sister/brother is bored. She (he) keeps asking for permission to do things, nearly driving you crazy. In the activity she (he) asks questions and you give her (him) the replies. Where it says (name) substitute the real name of the person taking the part of the older relative, adding *kun* or *chan*.

  At the end of the activity, sort out into lists the things that she (he) was allowed to do and those not allowed and the reasons given, where appropriate.

Compare your answers with those of other pairs. You may like to change roles and practice again.

Pairwork Sheet A (little sister/brother)
(Write your older sister's (brother's) replies in the space provided.)

1   なに を して も いい です か。
    Nani o shite mo ii desu ka. _____

2   テレビ は つまらない です。
    え を かいて も いい です か。
    TEREBI wa tsumaranai desu.
    E o kaite mo ii desu ka. _____

3   ペン を つかって も いい です か。
    PEN o tsukatte mo ii desu ka. _____

4   にわ に いって も いい です か。
    Niwa ni itte mo ii desu ka. _____

5   （なまえ） の ほん を よんで も いい です か。
    (Namae) no hon o yonde mo ii desu ka. _____

6   （なまえ） の へや に おおきい むし が います。
    （なまえ） は むし が すき です か。
    (Namae) no heya ni ookii mushi ga imasu.
    (Namae) wa mushi ga suki desu ka. _____

7   むし は いません！
    だいどころ に いって も いい です か。
    Mushi wa imasen!
    Daidokoro ni itte mo ii desu ka. _____

8   ケーキ を たべて も いい です か。
    KEEKI o tabete mo ii desu ka. _____

9   （なまえ） と はなして も いい です か。
    (Namae) to hanashite mo ii desu ka. _____

10 つまらない です。
    （なまえ） の へや で あそんで も いい です か。
    Tsumaranai desu.
    (Namae) no heya de asonde mo ii desu ka. _____

11 はい、しゅくだい が あります。
    Hai, shukudai ga arimasu. _____

Pairwork Sheet B (older sister/brother)

1　テレビ　を　みて　も　いい　です。
　TEREBI o mite mo ii desu. _____

2　いいえ、えんぴつ　は　ありません。
　Iie, enpitsu wa arimasen. _____

3　いいえ、だめ　です。
　Iie, dame desu. _____

4　いいえ、あめ　です　から　へや　で　ほん　を
　よんで　も　いい　です。
　Iie, ame desu kara heya de hon o yonde mo ii desu. _____

5　いいえ。
　Iie. _____

6　なに！　むし　は　どこ　に　います　か。
　Nani! Mushi wa doko ni imasu ka. _____

7　はい、だいどころ　に　いって　ください。
　Hai, daidokoro ni itte kudasai. _____

8　はい、ケーキ　を　たべて　も　いい　です。
　Hai, KEEKI o tabete mo ii desu. _____

9　いいえ、レコード　を　きいて　ください。
　Iie, REKOODO o kiite kudasai. _____

10　いいえ、しゅくだい　が　あります　か。
　Iie, shukudai ga arimasu ka. _____

11　では　しゅくだい　を　して　ください。
　Dewa shukudai o shite kudasai. _____

- You may like to see if you could do the next pairwork activity (as homework) over the phone (use the sheets on pp. 160 and 161).
  Make sure that you only look at the sheet that has been allotted to you!
  In school ask in Japanese for the phone number of your partner. Arrange a time in Japanese for phoning each other. When you phone, introduce yourself in Japanese as soon as your partner answers, and suggest doing the homework (*shukudai o shimashoo ka*). Make it fun for yourselves by playing by the rules and not speaking any English! (When you get to school the next day, check against your partner's sheet to see if you got the correct answers.)
  Imagine one of you is the parent and one the student who is away from home staying at a friend's place.

You call up, ask questions, receive and give answers. Fill in the answers you are given.

Try to listen so well that you don't need to ask for a repeat (*moo ichido itte kudasai*). Give each other time to write quick answers in Japanese.

Pairwork Sheet A

1   *(Okaasan/Otoosan) desu ka.*
     (Answer) _____

4   *Hai, daijoobu desu.*
     Ashita tomodachi to eiga ni itte mo ii desu ka.
     (Answer) _____

6   *"Grease" desu.*

8   *Hai, ii ongaku desu.*
     Itte mo ii desu ka.
     (Answer) _____

10   *Senroppyakuen desu.*
     Itte mo ii desu ka.
     (Answer) _____

12   *Hai, machi ni arimasu.*
     Itte mo ii desu ka.
     (Answer) _____

14   *Yukiko chan to Junji kun desu.*
     Itte mo ii desu ka.
     (Answer) _____

16   *Ii seito desu. Yukiko chan no otootosan desu.*
     Itte mo ii desu ka.
     (Answer) _____

18   *Arigatoo.*
     Eiga no ato de kissaten ni itte mo ii desu ka.
     (Answer) _____

20   *Hai, arimasu.*

22   *Juuji ni . . . BASU de kaerimasu. Ja mata ne.*

- With a partner practice giving one half of the sentence each in Japanese. Take turns giving the first part of the sentence.

   1   After swimming (*suiei*) ....   I went home by bus
   2   After the party ....   I talked to George
   3   After the examination ....   I met Ken
   4   After the film ....   I read the book
   5   After camp ....   I left the countryside

---

Pairwork Sheet B (*Okaasan / Otoosan*)

2 *Hai (Okaasan/Otoosan) desu.*
3 *Hitori de daijoobu desu ka.*
   (Answer) _____
5 *Eiga no namae wa nan desu ka.*
   (Answer) _____
7 *Soo desu ka. "Grease" ga suki desu ka.*
   (Answer) _____
9 *Kippu wa ikura desu ka.*
   (Answer) _____
11 *Sono eiga wa machi ni arimasu ka.*
   (Answer) _____
13 *Tomodachi wa dare ga ikimasu ka.*
   (Answer) _____
15 *Junji san wa donna hito desu ka.*
   (Answer) _____
17 *Hai, itte mo ii desu.*
19 *Hai. Okane ga arimasu ka.*
   (Answer) _____
21 *Nanji ni kaerimasu ka.*
   (Answer) _____
23 *Ashita mata ne.*

- With a partner make sentences similar to the ones in the activity at the bottom of p.160, without working them out on paper first. Student One gives half a sentence, Student Two finishes that sentence with anything that would make sense. Student Two then gives the first half of a new sentence, and so on. Which pair keeps going longest? Keep a tally of the number of sentences. (Brainstorm a list of verbs learned previously, with their **te** forms first, if you are still a bit shaky on them.)

- In pairs, make up a role play in which one person asks permission of another for some activity. Remember that Japanese people are very obliging towards one another!
   Again, don't plan it first. Just start and see where the conversation goes as you listen and genuinely answer.

- You meet a friend on the way to school, who tells you that he/she plans to go to the pool after school this evening for a swim. You ask if you may go with him or her and arrange a place and time to meet.

- Write the conversation you have practiced into your notebook in *hiragana* and *katakana*. Ask your friend to check it over for accuracy while you check his or hers. Discuss any differences and, if necessary, ask for your teacher's opinion.

STUDY TIPS

Try to use your Japanese as much as you can in speaking with others who study Japanese. Every time you use a word, phrase or sentence, you are consolidating what you know and helping yourself towards genuine, natural communication and helping yourself to forget your inhibitions.

You could be very useful now to new or younger students. Think about setting up a ***senpai-koohai*** system in your school for all those who study Japanese. You will find that helping someone else to understand is a marvelous way of helping yourself to understand more fully. The opportunity it will give you for using your Japanese is also important.

Have you got a Japanese club in your school yet where you can:
- meet with others to watch Japanese films or travel films?
- learn some Japanese hobbies?
- invite Japanese nationals to come and talk to you about Japan, (in English or Japanese) or make conversation with you in Japanese?

Think about ways in which you can learn more about Japanese people, their way of life, the country and the language. Are there tourists or Japanese nationals living in your area with whom you can talk?

If you do invite Japanese nationals to visit you and to talk with you in Japanese, there are two ways of preparing: You can ask a visitor to come in to speak to you in natural, normal speed Japanese. (If you make your request in Japanese you will gain some practice.) This is excellent for helping you to hear the usual flow of the language, but you will probably not understand very much.

A second way is to explain very carefully to your visitor what you would like him/her to talk about, and give the visitor a list of the vocabulary and grammar structures that you know, a week or two before he/she comes. Suggest a time limit if they are speaking to you in Japanese; e.g., one to five minutes. Ask them, too, to speak more slowly than normal so that you can understand.

You need to make concessions, too, and realize that even with this preparation, your visitor may use expressions that you don't know or explain things differently from the way your teacher has explained. Listen politely and ask your questions of your own teacher afterwards to avoid confusing yourself or making others confused.

There are many different ways to express things in any language, and you have only been taught one way so far. Accept your limitations, and also accept that there are other ways to express things that you will learn later. If all the ways were explained to you now, you would never be able to carry your textbooks!

- With a friend work out a different conversation of about ten lines that includes greetings and asking permission to use something; e.g., "May I read your book?" "May I swim in your pool?" "May I write my telephone number in your book?" etc.

  Write it out neatly on paper using a different colored pen for each speaker. Cut the conversation into strips and pass it to another pair, who will give you theirs in exchange.

  At a given signal everyone starts sorting out the strips into logical sequence. The first pair to finish gets their work checked by the original writers and, if there is no dispute, are the winners. If they are not correct and the teacher agrees that their conversation is out of sequence, the next pair to finish has a chance to win. (Remember that sentences can often make sense given in a different order, so be flexible enough to see the other people's way of thinking.)

Reading practice

- Practice reading the following sentences.
  1 すいえい の あと で バス で かえりました。
  2 パーティー の あと で ジョージ さん に
     はなしました。   (JOOJI)
  3 しけん の あと で ケン くん に あいました。(KEN)
  4 えいが の あと で ほん を よみました。
  5 キャンプ の あと で いなか を でました。   (KYANPU)

- Match the words in the two columns.

1	サンフランシスコ	a	*OOTOBAI* (bike)
2	ゲーム	b	*AMERIKA* (America)
3	デパート	c	*DEPAATO* (department store)
4	フランス	d	*SEERU* (sale)
5	テニス	e	*SANFURANSHISUKO* (San Francisco)
6	アメリカ	f	*GEEMU* (game)
7	セール	g	*SUUPAA* (supermarket)
8	クラス	h	*TENISU* (tennis)
9	オートバイ	i	*FURANSU* (France)
10	スーパー	j	*KURASU* (class)

Writing practice

Below are some of the *katakana* syllables that you have learned so far. Practice writing them, and make sure that you know them well.

セ	バ	オ	ア	ニ	ケ
SE	PA	O	A	NI	KE

ル	ト	イ	フ	ゲ	ヘ
RU	TO	I	FU(HU)	GE	HE

ス	バ	テ	リ	ム	ベ
SU	BA	TE	RI	MU	·BE

ハ	デ	プ	ン	レ	ペ
HA	DE	PU	N	RE	PE

ヒ	ビ	ピ	ブ	サ	ジ
HI	BI	PI	BU	SA	JI

ザ	ノ	ラ	シ	カ	ソ
ZA	NO	RA	SHI	KA	SO

ガ	ゾ	タ	マ	コ	エ
GA	ZO	TA	MA	KO	E

ダ	ツ	ヌ	チ	チュ	チョ
DA	TSU	NU	CHI	CHU	CHO

ユ	ヨ
YU	YO

- Practice writing the following words.

1	TEREBI	8	HANBAAGAA
2	HANSAMU	9	SANDOITCHI
3	GEEMU	10	TAKUSHII
4	PETTO	11	SARARIIMAN
5	APAATO	12	AISUKURIIMU
6	FURANSU	13	SUKEETO
7	BEDDO	14	SUUPU

- ### *Hiragana practice crossword*
  Put the *hiragana* clues into *ROOMAji* to solve the following crossword.

ACROSS
5 べんきょう
6 れんしゅうしてください
7 おりがみ
8 かきません
10 はなします
11 ふで
14 ききました
15 たべます
17 しょうがっこう
18 こと
19 よみます
20 りか

DOWN
1 じゅうどう
2 つまらない
3 いけばな
4 こうとうがっこう
9 しゅくだい
12 からて
13 がっこう
16 ぼんさい

- **Katakana practice crossword**
  Put the *katakana* clues into *ROOMAji* to solve the crossword.

ACROSS

3 ニューヨーク
6 ゲーム
9 バーゲンセール
10 デパート

DOWN

1 キャンプ
2 オーストラリア
4 テニス
5 クラス
7 アメリカ
8 セール

Check your understanding

A

Check your understanding of the *Introduction* by writing in *ROOMAji* the Japanese word for the following.

1 A martial art that ends in "e."
2 Japanese flute.
3 Singing along with a tape.
4 Calligraphy.
5 Paper folding.
6 Flower arranging.
7 Brush.
8 *Hiragana* card game.
9 Martial art that uses a wooden sword.
10 Insects.

B

Check your understanding of *Unit 1* by writing in *ROOMAji* the translation of
the following.

1   Use.
2   Next week.
3   Before.
4   Finish.
5   What kind of . . .?
6   After.
7   Camp.
8   *Te* form of *tachimasu*.
9   Science.
10 Boring.

11 Homework.
12 Buy.
13 *Te* form of *suwarimasu*.
14 Countryside
15 *Te* form of *yomimasu*.
16 Why?
17 May I go?
18 *Te* form of *tsukaimasu*.
19 Class.
20 When.

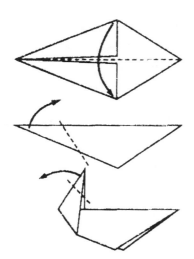

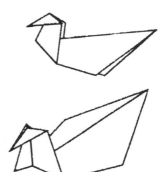

**Follow the steps to
make an origami
crane**

Unit 2

キャンプ に いって も いい です か
KYANPU ni itte mo ii desu ka
May I go camping?

In pairs, read the following conversation between Kaoru and his father, and work out what they are saying to each other. When everyone has finished reading, your teacher or one of your group will question you on the passage in Japanese, and you will answer in Japanese. Your teacher will listen and comment where necessary to help you.

かおる	らいしゅう の げつようび に わたし の クラス は キャンプ に いきます。 キャンプ に いって も いい です か。
おとうさん	どんな キャンプ です か。
か	スポーツ の キャンプ です。
お	キャンプ は どこ です か。
か	ちかく の いなか です。
お	せんせい は だれ が いきます か。
か	いのうえ せんせい と ささき せんせい と ほった せんせい が いきます。
お	キャンプ は いくら です か。
か	ごせんえん です。
お	では いって も いい です。いつ おかね が いります か。
か	きんようび に。だいじょうぶ です か。
お	はい、だいじょうぶ です。
か	ありがとう ございます。

Kaoru:	*Raishuu no getsuyoobi ni watashi no KURASU wa KYANPU ni ikimasu.*
	KYANPU ni itte mo ii desu ka.
Otoosan:	*Donna KYANPU desu ka.*
Kaoru:	*SUPOOTSU no KYANPU desu.*
Otoosan:	*KYANPU wa doko desu ka.*

Kaoru:	*Chikaku no inaka desu.*
Otoosan:	*Sensei wa dare ga ikimasu ka.*
Kaoru:	*Inoue sensei to Sasaki sensei to Hotta sensei ga ikimasu.*
Otoosan:	*Kyanpu wa ikura desu ka.*
Kaoru:	*Gosenen desu.*
Otoosan:	*Dewa itte mo ii desu.*
	Itsu Okane ga irimasu ka.
Kaoru:	*Kinyoobi ni. Daijoobu desu ka.*
Otoosan:	*Hai. Daijoobu desu.*
Kaoru:	*Arigatoo gozaimasu.*

Note: *ga* is used after the teacher's names because the speaker is picking out particular teachers who will go.

Teacher's questions

1 いつ　かおる　さん　の　クラス　は　キャンプ　に　いきます　か。
2 どんな　キャンプ　です　か。
3 せんせい　は　なんにん　いきます　か。
4 せんせい　の　なまえ　は　なん　です　か。
5 キャンプ　は　いくら　です　か。
6 いつ　かおる　さん　は　おかね　が　いります　か。
7 かおる　さん　は　キャンプ　に　いって　も　いい　です　か。
8 キャンプ　は　どこ　です　か。

1 *Itsu Kaoru san no KURASU wa KYANPU ni ikimasu ka.*
2 *Donna KYANPU desu ka.*
3 *Sensei wa nannin ikimasu ka.*
4 *Sensei no namae wa nan desu ka.*
5 *KYANPU wa ikura desu ka.*
6 *Itsu Kaoru san wa Okane ga irimasu ka.*
7 *Kaoru san wa KYANPU ni itte mo ii desu ka.*
8 *KYANPU wa doko desu ka.*

Writing practice

- Learn the *katakana* syllable **YA**　ヤ

- Learn **KI** キ

Write **KYA**　キャ
Write **KYANPU**　キャンプ

- Learn **TII**　ティー
  Write **PAATII**　パーティー

- Learn **DII**　ディー

- Learn **HO**　ホ

From **HO** you can make **BO** and **PO**:　ボ　　ポ

Unit 3

まいにち スポーツ を して も いい
です か
mainichi SUPOOTSU o shite mo ii
desu ka
May I play sports every day?

NEW WORDS

ばん	ban	evening/night
やすみ	yasumi	holiday/rest/vacation
らいねん	rainen	next year
しけん	shiken	examination
ことし	kotoshi	this year
かいしゃ	kaisha	company/business
たいせつな	taisetsu (na)	important
ひつような	hitsuyoo (na)	necessary
Interest		
ほんだ	Honda	company name

Because the following conversation is longer than usual, it has been separated into two parts.

Listen to the story as your teacher reads it to you. At your teacher's direction either close your books and listen or follow the words in your book. At the end of each short section, there are questions to ask each other in pairs to help you to understand the story as it unfolds and to give you practice in listening and answering questions.

Part One
Kazuko and her mother are talking as they do the dishes after dinner.

かずこ　　　あした なつ やすみ が はじまります。まいにち あさ
　　　　　　から ばん まで スポーツ を して も いい です か。

おかあさん　でも かずこ さんは じかん が ありません。

か　　　　　なぜ です か。

Kazuko: *Ashita natsu yasumi ga hajimarimasu. Mainichi asa kara ban
            made SUPOOTSU o shite mo ii desu ka.*
Okaasan: *Demo Kazuko san wa jikan ga arimasen.*
Kazuko: *Naze desu ka.*
しつもん
1 なつ やすみ は いつ はじまります か。
2 かずこ さん は スポーツ を して も いい です か。

Shitsumon (Questions)
With a partner take turns asking and answering.
1   *Natsu yasumi wa itsu hajimarimasu ka.*
2   *Kazuko san wa SUPOOTSU o shite mo ii desu ka.*

おかあさん   らいねん　たいせつな　しけん　が　あります。らいしゅう
の　げつようび　に　じゅく　に　いきます。

かずこ   おかあさん、いや　です。ことし　は　よく　べんきょう
して　います。いい　がくせい　です。じゅく　は　いりません。

Okaasan: *Rainen taisetsuna shiken ga arimasu. Raishuu no getsuyoobi ni juku ni ikimasu.*

Kazuko: *Okaasan iya desu. Kotoshi wa yoku benkyoo shite imasu. Ii gakusei desu. Juku wa irimasen.*

しつもん
1   かずこ　さん　は　いつ　しけん　が　あります　か。
2   かずこ　さん　は　いつ　じゅく　に　いきます　か。

Shitsumon
1   *Kazuko san wa itsu shiken ga arimasu ka.*
2   *Kazuko san wa itsu juku ni ikimasu ka.*

おかあさん   この　やすみ、かずこちゃん　は　じゅく　が　ひつよう
です。
その　しけん　の　あと　で　かずこ　ちゃん　は　いい
かいしゃ　に　はいります。
おとうさん　と　わたし　は　ほんだ　が　すき　です。ほん
だ　は　いい　かいしゃ　です。しけん　は
むずかしい　です　から　じゅく　が　ひつよう　です。

Okaasan: *Kono yasumi, Kazuko chan wa juku ga hitsuyoo desu. Sono shiken no ato de Kazuko chan wa ii kaisha ni hairimasu. Otoosan to watashi wa Honda ga suki desu. Honda wa ii kaisha desu. Shiken wa muzukashii desu kara juku ga hitsuyoo desu.*

しつもん
1   かずこ　さん　は　その　しけん　の　あと　で　なに　を　します
か。
2   じゅく　が　ひつよう　です。なぜ　です　か。
3   ほんだ　は　どんな　かいしゃ　です　か。

Shitsumon
1   *Kazuko san wa sono shiken no ato de nani o shimasu ka.*
2   *Juku ga hitsuyoo desu. Naze desu ka.*
3   *Honda wa donna kaisha desu ka.*

Part Two
Familiarize yourself with the new words.

NEW WORDS

まいつき	*maitsuki*	every month
つかれます　つかれる	*tsukaremasu* (*tsukareru*)	be tired
つかれて	*tsukarete*	*te* form of *tsukaremasu*
ごご	*gogo*	afternoon
さんぽ	*sanpo*	a walk
どの　ぐらい　です　か	*dono gurai desu ka*	How long/How far/ How much is it?
に　ききます　に　きく	*ni kikimasu (ni kiku)*	ask
に　きいて	*ni kiite*	*te* form of *ni kikimasu*
からだ	*karada*	body/health
ほんとう（に）	*hontoo (ni)*	honestly/truthfully
うんどう	*undoo*	exercise

かずこ　でも　おかあさん、やすみ　も　たいせつ　です。たいへん
つかれました。うんどう　も　ひつよう　です。
からだ　に　いい　です。

おかあさん　じゅく　は　くじ　から　じゅうにじ　まで　です。ごご　は
しゅくだい　が　あります。よる　スポーツ　を　して、
ともだち　と　いっしょ　に　あそんで、テレビ　を　みて、
ほん　と　ざっし　を　よみます。しゅうまつは　ともだち
と　いっしょ　に　いなか　へ　キャンプ　に　いって、つり
を　して、さんぽ　に　いきます。いい　やすみ　でしょう。

Kazuko:　*Demo okaasan . . . Yasumi mo taisetsu desu. Taihen tsukaremashita. Undoo mo hitsuyoo desu. Karada ni ii desu.*

Okaasan:　*Juku wa kuji kara juuniji made desu. Gogo wa shukudai ga arimasu. Yoru SUPOOTSU o shite, tomodachi to issho ni asonde, TEREBI o mite, hon to zasshi o yomimasu. Shuumatsu wa tomodachi to issho ni inaka e KYANPU ni itte, tsuri o shite, sanpo ni ikimasu. Ii yasumi deshoo.*

しつもん
1　かずこ　さん　は　なに　が　ひつよう　です　か。
2　やすみ　の　じゅく　は　いつ　から　いつ　まで　です　か。
3　どこ　に　キャンプ　に　いきます　か。
4　だれ　と　キャンプ　に　いきます　か。
5　いなか　で　なに　を　します　か。

Shitsumon
1　*Kazuko san wa nani ga hitsuyoo desu ka.*
2　*Yasumi no juku wa itsu kara itsu made desu ka.*
According to Kazuko's mother's ideas:
3　*Doko ni KYANPU ni ikimasu ka.*
4　*Dare to KYANPU ni ikimasu ka.*
5　*Inaka de nani o shimasu ka.*

あと で……

かずこ　　　じゅく は いくら です か。

おかあさん　まいつき ろくまんさんぜん えん です。

かずこ　　　おかあさん…… おとうさん は あたらしい くるま が
　　　　　　ほしい です。あたらしい くるま が いります。
　　　　　　わたし は うち で よく べんきょう します。
　　　　　　ほんとう に よく べんきょう します。
　　　　　　その じゅく は たいへん たかい です。
　　　　　　くるま は きゅうじゅうまん えん ぐらい でしょう ね。

おかあさん　じゃ、おとうさん に ききます。

Ato de:
Kazuko: *Juku wa ikura desu ka.*
Okaasan: *Maitsuki rokumansanzen en desu.*
Kazuko: *Okaasan . . . Otoosan wa atarashii kuruma ga hoshii desu.*
            Atarashii kuruma ga irimasu. Watashi wa uchi de yoku benkyoo
            shimasu. Hontoo ni yoku benkyoo shimasu. Sono juku wa taihen
            takai desu. Kuruma wa kyuujuuman en gurai deshoo ne.
Okaasan: *Ja . . . Otoosan ni kikimasu.*

しつもん
1　おとうさん は なに が ほしい です か。
2　かずこ さん は どこ で べんきょう します か。

Shitsumon
1　*Otoosan wa nani ga hoshii desu ka.*
2　*Kazuko san wa doko de benkyoo shimasu ka.*

STUDY

● Look carefully at the use of *tsukaremashita*. Just as you found with *nodo ga kawakimashita* and *onaka ga sukimashita*, by the time you comment on your tiredness you have already become tired, so you use the past tense of the verb.

"I am tired" means, therefore, "I have already become tired at some time in the past and therefore I am tired now."

ACTIVITIES

● Using the words in the new word list to help you, write the conversation of either Part One or Part Two in natural English in your notebook.
After you have finished, compare your version with the one on p. 175.

● Ask a friend if you may do something; e.g.,
Anata no hon o yonde mo ii desu ka.
The friend refuses you and gives you an alternative. Don't say what you are going to ask ahead of time, just offer your request. Your friend will listen and then make his/her own answer.

STUDY

• For those of you who have noticed a pattern emerging with some time words, they are explained below for your interest. Absorb them as quickly as you can.

The prefixes *rai* (next) and *mai* (every) and *kon* (this) are used in several time words:

raishuu next week, *raigetsu* next month, *rainen* next year; *mainichi* every day, *maishuu* every week, *maitsuki* every month, *maitoshi* every year. (Don't get caught expecting all of them to follow the same pattern as the line above!)

Another set uses the prefix *kon*:

konnichi (this) day/good day, *konshuu* this week, *kongetsu* this month, **but** *kotoshi* this year. (There are two words for year – *nen* and *toshi*.)

English version of the conversation
Part One:
K: The summer holiday begins tomorrow. May I play sports from morning until night every day?
O: But Kazuko, you won't have time.
K: Why?
O: Next year you've got an important exam. Next Monday you'll be going to cram school.
K: Mom, that's terrible. This year I'm really studying. I'm a good student. I don't need cram school.
O: This vacation you need cram school. After that exam you'll get into a good company. Your father and I like Honda. It's a good company. You'll need cram school because the exam is difficult.

Part Two
K: But Mom, vacation is important, too. I'm very tired. I need exercise, too. It's good for the health.
O: Cram School will be from nine o'clock until twelve. In the afternoons there will be homework. In the evenings (you will) play sports, relax with your friends, watch TV, read books and magazines. On the weekends go camping in the country, go fishing and go for walks with your friends. It will probably be a good vacation.
K: How much does cram school cost?
O: Sixty three thousand yen a month.
K: Mom . . . Dad wants a new car. He needs a new car. I'll study well at home. Really, I will study hard.
That cram school's very expensive. . . .
A car will probably be about nine hundred thousand yen, won't it?
O: Well . . . I'll ask your father.

Now answer the following questions:
1   What does the passage tell you about life for Japanese students?
2   What do you learn from the passage that you are not actually told?
3   Why did the mother use Kazuko's name when talking directly to her?

STUDY

- *ni kikimasu* "ask." This verb must be learned very carefully so that every time you see *ni kikimasu* you remember that it means "ask" not "listen."

  The **te** form is **ni kiite**. If mother was asking father at that moment, Kazuko would say to her friends: *Ima haha wa chichi ni kiite imasu.* "Mom is asking Dad at this minute."

  Note carefully: If *kikimasu* meaning "listen/hear" is intended, as in the sentence "I'll listen to records" it has to be *REKOODO o kikimasu.* Another example:

  "I'll listen to Jon." *JON san no hanashi o kikimasu.*

  Note that it is necessary to say *JON san **no hanashi** o kikimasu.* If you think about it you can't actually listen to Jon himself, you can only listen to the words he speaks, so logically you listen to Jon's talk or speech (*hanashi*).

Check your understanding

How would you say the following using *ni kikimasu*?

1   I asked my father.
2   I'll ask my mother tomorrow.
3   Ask the teacher, please.
4   I didn't ask my older brother.
5   Will you ask your friend?
6   Shall we ask Grandmother?

How would you say the following using *kikimasu*?

1   I'll listen to the radio. (*RAJIO*)
2   I listened to the teacher. (Remember the note above?)
3   Henry listens to records.
4   Let's listen to the tape with Sue.
5   Miki did not listen to the news. (*NYUUSU*)

ACTIVITY

In pairs make up five questions of your own in Japanese about the passage and write them in *kana* in your notebook. Under each question write a correct answer.

Be prepared to offer one of your questions to the class. Don't read it. Say it. Listen carefully to the answer to see if it is correct in fact. Be prepared to accept a slightly different way of putting the answer if the facts are correct. Your teacher will be the judge. How many different questions did you make up between you?

STUDY

- **Gogo** "afternoon" (p.m.).

  Usually you will use *gogo* in a phrase like: "at two o'clock in the afternoon . . .". Together, make sentences like the following:

  "At five o'clock in the afternoon I went to the pool."

  Gogo goji ni PUURU ni ikimashita.

  "May I watch that video at three o'clock this afternoon?"

  Gogo (no) sanji ni sono BIDEO o mite mo ii desu ka.

  "What time is the game?"

  GEEMU wa nanji desu ka.

  "It's four o'clock in the afternoon."

  Gogo yoji desu.

- **Sentence order:** (Time/topic – object or place – verb)

  Note that you usually place the time first or following the topic. Although it is acceptable to put it the other way around, it is less common, because Japanese people like to get the most important part of the message across first, and usually a particular time needs to be noted carefully. The "safe" way to construct your sentences is to put either the topic or the time first. That way you don't get into problems over which particle to use; e.g.,

  Watashi wa gogo yoji ni tsukimasu.

  "I'll arrive at four p.m."

  Gogo yoji ni watashi wa tsukimasu.

  "At four p.m. I'll arrive."

  It is possible to say:

  "You may watch a video at three-thirty this afternoon."

  (Anata wa) BIDEO o gogo sanjihan ni mite mo ii desu.

  but it has a different emphasis, suggesting that "you," but only you, may watch at that time. Or the video has to become the topic: "Talking about the video," *BIDEO wa sanjihan ni mite mo ii desu* "You may watch it at three-thirty."

  Think about and discuss these different ways of emphasizing what you want to say. We do it in English too, by changing the position of words and phrases within a sentence. In Japanese if you change positions, you have the problem of deciding which is the appropriate particle. So play safe!

ACTIVITY

Divide into small groups.

1   Each person prepares five questions that could be answered with a time in the afternoon. Make the questions relevant to the lives of people in your group.

Randomly choose partners and ask each other your questions. Change partners and ask your questions again until you have all questioned each other.

2   Write down the questions you have been asked, after you have checked that they are correct, and write your own answers to them in *kana*.

Writing practice

- Review **HO**   ホ
  and write **BO** and **PO**.   ボ   ポ

- Learn **KU**   ク

From *KU* make **GU**   グ

- Write   *KURASU*   クラス
           KEEKI   ケーキ
           SUKII   スキー
           HOKKEE   ホッケー
           FUTTOBOORU   フットボール

- Which sports are listed below?
  1   サッカー
  2   スキー
  3   バスケットボール
  4   フットボール
  5   テニス
  6   バレーボール

Unit 4

あなた の しゅみ は なん です か
anata no shumi wa nan desu ka
What is your hobby?

NEW WORDS

しゅみ	*shumi*	hobby
もちます　もつ	*mochimasu (motsu)*	have/hold
もって	*motte*	te form of *mochimasu*
ペット　を　かって います	*PETTO o katte imasu*	I've got a pet
つくります　つくる	*tsukurimasu (tsukuru)*	make
つくって	*tsukutte*	te form of *tsukurimasu*
あまり　あんまり	*amari/anmari*	not very/not many/ not much
Review		
いけばな	*ikebana*	flower arranging
つり　を　します	*tsuri o shimasu*	fishing
りょうり　を　します	*ryoori o shimasu*	cook
さんぽ	*sanpo*	a walk
Interest		
どくしょ	*dokusho*	reading
コンピューター　ゲーム	*KONPYUUTAA GEEMU*	computer games
たこ	*tako*	kite
プラモデル	*PURAMODERU*	plastic models
だけ	*dake*	only
あつめます　あつめる	*atsumemasu (atsumeru)*	collect/gather
あつめて	*atsumete*	te form of *atsumemasu*
きって	*kitte*	stamps
など	*nado*	et cetera (etc)

There are many, many hobbies, and you would probably feel a bit over-whelmed if a larger selection were included in those you must learn. A few extras are included as interest words above, but if your own hobby has not been mentioned, ask your teacher for it as a special item for you alone.

Sports are not strictly hobbies, but come into a different area of information that you can give about yourself. However, it is an area of possible argument, and most people would accept that the question "What's your hobby?" could be answered with a sport.

けんじ　　あなた　の　しゅみ　は　なん　です　か。

まりこ　　きって　を　あつめて　います。

け　　　　たくさん　もって　います　か。

ま　　　　いいえ、あまり　もって　いません。
　　　　　ことし　この　しゅみ　を　もちました。

け　　　　そう　です　か。

ま　　　　アメリカ　や　イギリス　や　フランス　や　イタリア　や
　　　　　スペイン　や　にほん　など　から　あつめました。

け　　　　わたし　は　ニュージーランド　の　ともだち　が　います。
　　　　　ときどき　わたし　に　てがみ　を　かきます。ニュージーランド
　　　　　の　きって　が　ほしい　です　か。

ま　　　　はい、ありがとう　ございます。

Kenji: *Anata no shumi wa nan desu ka.*
Mariko: *Kitte o atsumete imasu.*
K: *Takusan motte imasu ka.*
M: *Iie, amari motte imasen.*
            Kotoshi kono shumi o mochimashita.
K: *Soo desu ka.*
M: *AMERIKA ya IGIRISU ya FURANSU ya ITARIA ya SUPEIN ya Nihon
            nado kara atsumemashita.*
K: *Watashi wa NYUUJIIRANDO no tomodachi ga imasu.*
            Tokidoki watashi ni tegami o kakimasu.
            NYUUJIIRANDO no kitte ga hoshii desu ka.
M: *Hai. Arigatoo gozaimasu.*

Check your understanding of the conversation.
K: What's your hobby?
M: I collect stamps.
K: Have you got a lot?
M: No, not very many.
      I've only done it this year.
K: Oh, I see.
M: I have collected from America, England, France, Italy, Spain, and
      Japan, etc.
K: I have a New Zealand friend. He sometimes writes to me.
      Do you want New Zealand stamps?
M: Yes. Thank you.

STUDY

- In response to *Shumi wa nan desu ka*, you could say *Kitte desu*, but it's
  better to use the correct verb for that activity.

- **Amari** not very (much/many)
  Amari (sometimes *anmari* in conversation) usually goes in front of a
  negative verb. Only use it that way at this stage of your study. Because

it is a quantity word, like *takusan* and numbers, it is placed right in front of the verb.

e.g.: *Taroo san wa amari suki dewa arimasen*. I don't like Taroo very much.

Manga wa amari yomimasen. I don't read comics much.

Haha wa amari tabemasen. Mom doesn't eat much.

Kono hon wa amari yokunai desu. This book is not very good.

Practice together making more sentences with *amari*. Write some examples into your notebook to remind you always to use *amari* for "**not very**" and always to use a negative right after it.

**PETTO o katte imasu (top)
Ryoori o shimasu (lower left)
TENISU o shimasu (lower right)**

- **Mochimasu** (*mottsu*) is a very useful word. Now you have the possibility of saying that you own something. Until now we have skirted around the business of ownership using *arimasu* to say that things exist but never quite saying that we **have** something – that we **own** or **hold** something.

Mochimasu is usually used in the **te** form, because if you **have** something or **own** something, it is usually a continuing process. You had it a while ago, even if only a short while, and will continue to own it a bit longer. In the future you may lose it or give it away, but until that happens, it is a continuing state of ownership; e.g.,

KAMERA o motte imasu I have a camera.

Kasa o motte imasu She is holding an umbrella.

If you are describing pictures, it is very useful to be able to say, for example: "He has a bicycle." *Jitensha o motte imasu* or "He is holding a bicycle." *Jitensha o motte imasu*, instead of "There is a bicycle/a bicycle exists" *Jitensha ga arimasu*.

If you were describing a person in a picture or you were trying to identify someone, it would be useful to be able to say:

"She is carrying a bag" *Kaban o motte imasu*.

The context will usually make clear the version to choose. If you have pets though, you can't use *mochimasu* for ownership. In that case you must use *PETTO o katte imasu* "I keep a pet." Again, it is a continuous process, so use the **te** form.

If you had a pet, it will have been something that continued over a period of time, so you will use *PETTO o katte imashita* "I had a pet/I was keeping a pet."

If you ever see *PETTO (Inu, neko, uma) o katte imasu*, it means "I **keep** a pet/I have a pet" (dog, cat, horse). If you are describing a picture in which someone is holding a pet, you can say: *PETTO o motte imasu*.

Put all of this in the back of your mind and let it slowly but thoroughly percolate. We'll return to it later.

ACTIVITIES

* Using the illustration, describe the park and say what each person is holding or doing.

* Draw your own sketches and describe the people and their activities to a partner or a small group while showing them the picture. Your listeners should all be prepared to ask you one question to show that they have been listening and want to know more. Develop the questioning into a genuine conversation if possible.

EXTENSION

* **dake** "only" is used after the thing you are talking about instead of in front as in English. *Dake* takes the place of other particles; e.g.,
  I write only hiragana.
  Hiragana dake kakimasu.
  I eat only Japanese food.
  Washoku dake tabemasu.
  I drink only water.
  Mizu dake nomimasu.
  Mr. Brown speaks only English.
  BURAUN san wa eigo dake hanashimasu.

  Together make ten sentences to illustrate the use of *dake* and write them in your book in *kana*.

* **nado** means "etcetera" or "and the like" and may be used following a list of nouns that have been joined with **ya**; e.g.,
  Watashi wa JUUSU ya MIRUKU ya KOKA KOORA nado o nomimasu.
  I drink juice, milk, Coke, etcetera.

Check your understanding

1

Photocopy the box so that each student has a copy. The following are all replies that could be made to the question:
Shumi wa nan desu ka.

On the right is a list of names. As you listen to the information, your aim is to match the information to the correct person. Read them through before the reading begins. Close your books while the teacher reads.

1	*Dokusho ga suki desu*	*Rieko*
2	*Kitte o atsumete imasu*	*Junji*
3	*Shumi wa ikebana desu*	*Ryuuichi*
4	*Ryoori o shimasu*	*Saki*
5	*Tako o tsukurimasu*	*Haruko*
6	*PURAMODERU o tsukurimasu*	*Yukiko*
7	*Bonsai dake shimasu*	*Kumiko*
8	*Shodoo o renshuu shimasu*	*Tsutomu*
9	*PETTO o katte imasu*	*Junji*
10	*Watashi no shumi wa SUPOOTSU dake desu*	*Watashi*

Listen to the following information. (Your teacher will pause briefly between items to give you time to match the person with the activity on your sheet.)

わたし の ともだち は しゅみ が たくさん あります。
ゆきこ ちゃん は いつも いけばな を します。いつも うち で
れんしゅう します。

はるこ ちゃん は いぬ と ねこ と さかな を かって います。
まいにち いぬ と こうえん で さんぽ を します。どようび は
いぬ を あらいます。りょうり も します。

くみこ ちゃん は しょどう が すき です。じょうず です。

つとむ くん は まいにち がっこう の あと で スポーツ だけ
します。どようび の ごご と にちようび は ゲーム を します。

りゅういち くん は きって を あつめて います。きって を
たくさん もって います。

さき くん は ぼんさい が すき です。いつも ぼんさい の ほん
を よみます。

りえこ ちゃん は にほん の りょうり を します。にほん の
りょうり は わしょく です。

じゅんじ　くん　は　プラモデル　の　ひこうき　と　たこ　を　つくりま
す。

わたし　の　しゅみ　は　どくしょ　です。

Watashi no tomodachi wa shumi ga takusan arimasu.
Yukiko chan wa itsumo ikebana o shimasu. Itsumo uchi de renshuu shimasu.

Haruko chan wa inu to neko to sakana o katte imasu. Mainichi inu to kooen de
sanpo o shimasu. Doyoobi wa inu o araimasu.
Ryoori mo shimasu.

Kumiko chan wa shodoo ga suki desu. Joozu desu.

Tsutomu kun wa mainichi gakkoo no ato de SUPOOTSU dake shimasu.
Doyoobi no gogo to nichiyoobi wa GEEMU o shimasu.

Ryuuichi kun wa kitte o atsumete imasu. Kitte o takusan motte imasu.

Saki kun wa bonsai ga suki desu. Itsumo bonsai no hon o yomimasu.

Rieko chan wa nihon no ryoori o shimasu. Nihon no ryoori wa washoku desu.

Junji kun wa PURAMODERU no hikooki to tako o tsukurimasu.

Watashi no shumi wa dokusho desu.

2
Use the question *Shumi wa nan desu ka*. Look back at the word list for words
to use and tell a partner what you and your friends or family do for a hobby;
e.g., "I make model airplanes" *PURAMODERU no hikooki o tsukurimasu*. In
this situation you can use the *masu* form, because the action will be broken
from time to time as you finish one model and before you begin another. In
collection type hobbies it is a continuing process, so you use the **te** form.
Therefore if you collect model planes you would say *atsumete imasu* (collect),
rather than *tsukurimasu* (make).
    If you are in the process of making them, use:
PURAMODERU no hikooki o tsukutte imasu.
But it is usual for a continuing hobby to be spoken of using the **te** form; e.g.,
"I collect butterflies" *Choochoo o atsumete imasu.*

    After you have asked for your partner's hobby, ask about the hobbies
practiced by members of his/her family; e.g.,
What is your older sister's hobby?
Oneesan no shumi wa nan desu ka.
My older sister collects stamps.
Ane wa kitte o atsumete imasu.

Copy the following chart in your notebook.

> **しゅみ**
>
>   の　しゅみ　は
> おとうさん　の　しゅみ　は
> おかあさん　の　しゅみ　は
> おにいさん
> おねえさん
> おとうとさん
> いもうとさん

3

Using *Shumi wa nan desu ka* or (Member of family) *no shumi wa nan desu ka*, make a survey of the hobbies or leisure activities practiced by class members and their families. Find out which are the most popular within that sample. Fill in the names of the class members you approach, and when you speak to them, remember to add "noises" like *omoshiroi desu ne! . . soo desu ka . . soo desu ne . . . . .*

Copy the following chart to use in your survey.

どうきゅうせい　の　しゅみ
　　(Name)

4

In pairs, using the information that was read to you (p. 184), take turns asking each other the following questions. (Note: you will use **san**, because they are not your friends.)

1 *Yukiko san no shumi wa nan desu ka.*
2 *Yukiko san wa doko de shumi o shimasu ka.*
3 *Haruko san wa PETTO o katte imasu ka.*
4 *Haruko san wa doko de sanpo o shimasu ka.*
5 *Haruko san wa nanyoobi ni inu o araimasu ka.*
6 *Kumiko san wa shodoo ga joozu desu ka heta desu ka.*
7 *Tsutomu san wa SUPOOTSU o shimasu ka.*
8 *Tsutomu san wa itsu GEEMU o shimasu ka.*
9 *Ryuuichi san no shumi wa nan desu ka.*
10 *Saki san wa nani o yomimasu ka.*

5

How would you say in Japanese:

1 May I make a kite?
2 May I collect stamps?
3 What is your hobby?
4 Do you have a hobby? (careful with this)
5 Do you have a pet? (another to be careful with)
6 My little sister collects insects. (*mushi*)
7 I am collecting cars.
8 I collected nine models.
9 My hobby is computer games.
10 Your hobby is interesting.

ACTIVITIES

- You will need a list of class members' names.

  Make a chart of the hobbies practiced by people in your group. Move around the group asking: *Shumi wa nan desu ka*. Make a note of the hobby by each name. Count the replies that are the same in Japanese numbers. Make your chart.

- Make posters to advertise a hobby. Make them sound interesting. Say where the club (*KURABU*) meets and when.

- In groups of five make up a role play in which an interviewer on a TV game asks the following questions to help you to choose a partner for a day out at the expense of the TV studio.

  Your characters are: the host, talking with one participant, who cannot see the three participants from whom to choose.

    Greetings followed by questions like:
  Onamae wa nan desu ka.
  Nansai desu ka.
  Doko no kata desu ka.
  Doko ni sunde imasu ka.
  Kazoku wa nannin imasu ka.
  Anata no shumi wa nan desu ka.
    Follow up questions on the hobby; for example,
  Itsu sono shumi o shimasu ka.
  Shumi ga takusan arimasu ka.
  Shumi wa hitotsu dake desu ka.
  Shumi wa doko de shimasu ka.
  (And any other questions you'd like to ask.)
    The participant may then ask one or two questions of each of the hidden players to find out as much as possible about them as quickly as possible. As always confine yourself to words that everyone can be expected to know.

- Groups report to the class on who was chosen from each group, introduce the chosen person and say a little about each one and his/her interests in Japanese.

- Imagine that they have had their day out. Either write or tell the story of their day together in Japanese (about ten sentences).

  Name the people. Say where and when they went, what they did. Was it interesting/boring? What was the weather like? etc. Will they meet again? If so, when and where?

Extension

Remember **sukina** means "liked (thing)" and **kiraina** "disliked (thing)" **Ichiban** means "Number One." Therefore:

Ichiban sukina tabemono wa nan desu ka. "What's your favorite food?"
Ichiban kiraina SUPOOTSU wa nan desu ka. "What's your most disliked sport?"

You could ask about favorite country, sport, film, book, etc. Use *Ichiban ookii* "biggest," *ichiban omoshiroi* "most interesting," etc.

Writing practice

- Review **TA** and **DA** タ ダ
  Review **PI** and **YU** ピ ユ

- Learn **PYU** ピュ

- Learn **MO** モ

- Learn **ME** メ

Write   *MODERU*   モデル
         AMERIKA   アメリカ

- Identify the *katakana* in the puzzle below. How many of each syllable can you find?

サ	ダ	ル	ム	バ	パ	ザ	ハ	イ
ザ	セ	ム	ル	ノ	イ	パ	ハ	ニ
ニ	バ	サ	ル	ス	オ	ハ	パ	イ
ラ	ス	ル	セ	ノ	ニ	ハ	ニ	パ
ム	ル	ヘ	ヘ	サ	ハ	ニ	イ	タ
ル	ム	オ	ノ	ハ	セ	ニ	テ	オ
ラ	テ	ノ	ハ	フ	フ	サ	フ	フ
ラ	ノ	ハ	フ	フ	オ	タ	セ	テ
ラ	ハ	ノ	ニ	テ	ヘ	テ	オ	サ
ハ	ラ	ニ	ダ	ノ	タ	ヘ	ヘ	ヘ
ラ	ラ	ダ	ダ	タ	ノ	タ	ヘ	タ

SONG
ちょうちょう

ちょうちょう
ちょうちょう
なのはに　　とまれ
なのはに　　あいたら
さくらに　　とまれ
さくらの　　はなの
はなから　　はなへ
とまれよ　　あそべ
あそべよ　　とまれ

Choochoo

Choochoo
Choochoo
nano ha ni　　*tomare*
nano ha ni　　*aitara*
sakura ni　　*tomare*
sakura no　　*hana no*
hana kara　　*hana e*
tomare yo　　*asobe*
asobe yo　　*tomare*

Unit 5

あした は ひま です
ashita wa hima desu
Tomorrow is a free day

NEW WORDS

ひ	*hi*	day/sun
ひま な	*hima (na)*	free time
ステレオ	*SUTEREO*	stereo
むずかしい	*muzukashii*	difficult
おそい	*osoi*	late/slow (adjective)
はやい	*hayai*	fast/early (adjective)
おそく	*osoku*	adverbial form of *osoi*: slow/late
はやく	*hayaku*	adverbial form of *hayai*
ねん	*nen*	year
ごねん かん	*gonenkan*	for five years
ピクニック を します	*PIKUNIKKU o shimasu*	have a picnic
すこし	*sukoshi*	a little/somewhat/a moment/a little way
にじ まで に	*niji made ni*	by two o'clock
わかりました	*wakarimashita!*	I know!

Interest

ちょうちょう	*choochoo*	butterfly
コンサート	*KONSAATO*	concert
すばらしい	*subarashii*	wonderful/marvelous

Note: in Japan you don't eat a picnic or go for a picnic but do a picnic!

1   Read the Japanese passage that follows by yourself first, or listen while your teacher reads it to see how much you can understand.
2   Next read it aloud as if you are Betty talking to herself. Concentrate hard in order to avoid sounding as if you are reading it. Think about your pronunciation.
3   Listen to your teacher read the passage, and take note of the sound and intonation.
4   Read it aloud again, trying to improve the sound you produce.
5   If you have a tape recorder, record your own reading and offer it to the teacher for help in improving your pronunciation.

Here is the translation of the passage:
"Tomorrow is a free day. All day long I'm free! . . . I won't go to school. I

won't study. I won't go to cram school . . .

I won't do piano practice . . .

What shall I do? . . .

First . . . shall I get up late or get up early?

It's difficult, isn't it! . . .

Shall I do a hobby? But what kind of hobby shall I do? . . . I want a new hobby. My present hobby is ikebana, but it's boring . . . I've done ikebana for five years . . . What kind of hobbies do I like? . . .

Perhaps stamps . . . But stamps are a winter hobby.

What is a summer hobby? . . . I know, I'll collect butterflies!

Tomorrow I'll collect butterflies with my friend in the countryside . . . We'll go by bike to the country . . . It's a good hobby. It's probably cheap.

But what time shall I get up? . . . Probably nine o'clock . . .

In the morning I'll read books and magazines in bed and I'll listen to the stereo, and then before lunch I'll do some shopping in the shops close by . . . After lunch we'll go by bike to the country . . . Today I'll phone my friend.

How much (What) time shall we spend (be) in the country? . . .

I'll leave home at one o'clock . . . I'll meet my friend in front of the school at about one fifteen . . .

How far (about how long) is it to the country? . . .

It's not far. We'll arrive in the country by two o'clock. We'll collect butterflies in the forest. We'll have a picnic and return home . . . It'll probably be five o'clock. Then . . . shall we go to the movies or to a concert or to a coffee bar? . . .

Tomorrow there's a pop concert in town. It'll probably be good.

It's not expensive . . . We'll go to the pop concert.

The concert will finish at ten o'clock.

After the concert I'll go to bed early.

It'll be a wonderful day!"

Now read the Japanese passage section by section and understand.

あした　ひま　です。いちにちじゅう　ひま　です。がっこう　に
いきません。べんきょう　しません。じゅく　に　いきません。ピアノ
の　れんしゅう　を　しません。なに　を　しましょう　か。
はじめ　に　おそく　おきましょう　か　はやく　おきましょう　か。
むずかしい　ね。

Ashita hima desu. Ichinichijuu hima desu. Gakkoo ni ikimasen.
Benkyoo shimasen. Juku ni ikimasen. PIANO no renshuu o shimasen.
Nani o shimashoo ka.
Hajime ni osoku okimashoo ka hayaku okimashoo ka.
Muzukashii ne!

しゅみ　を　しましょう　か。でも　どんな　しゅみ　を　しましょう
か。あたらしい　しゅみ　が　ほしい　です。いま　わたし　の
しゅみ　は　いけばな　です　が　つまらない　です。いけばな　は
ごねんかん　しました。どんな　しゅみ　が　すき　です　か。

*Shumi o shimashoo ka. Demo donna shumi o shimashoo ka. Atarashii shumi
ga hoshii desu. Ima watashi no shumi wa ikebana desu ga tsumaranai desu.
Ikebana wa gonenkan shimashita. Donna shumi ga suki desu ka.*

きって　を　あつめましょう　か。……でも　きって　は　ふゆ　の
しゅみ　です。なつ　の　しゅみ　は　なん　です　か。
わかりました！ちょうちょう　を　あつめます。あした　ともだち　と
いなか　で　ちょうちょう　を　あつめます。じてんしゃ　で　いなか
に　いきます。いい　しゅみ　です。やすい　でしょう。

*Kitte o atsumemashoo ka. Demo kitte wa fuyu no shumi desu. Natsu no shumi
wa nan desu ka. Wakarimashita! Choochoo o atsumemasu!
Ashita tomodachi to inaka de choochoo o atsumemasu. Jitensha de inaka ni
ikimasu. Ii shumi desu. Yasui deshoo.*

でも　なんじ　に　おきましょう　か。……くじ　でしょう。あさ　は
ベッド　で　ほん　と　ざっし　を　よみます。ステレオ　を　ききます。
ひるごはん　の　まえ　に　この　ちかく　の　みせ　で　かいもの　を
すこし　します。ひるごはん　の　あと　で　じてんしゃ　で　いなか　に
いきます。

*Demo nanji ni okimashoo ka. Kuji deshoo. Asa wa BEDDO de hon to zasshi o
yomimasu. SUTEREO o kikimasu.
Hirugohan no mae ni kono chikaku no mise de kaimono o sukoshi shimasu.
Hirugohan no ato de jitensha de inaka ni ikimasu.*

きょう　わたし　の　ともだち　に　でんわ　します。
なんじ　から　なんじ　まで　いなか　に　います　か。……
いちじ　に　うち　を　でます。いちじ　じゅうごふん　ごろ　がっこう
の　まえ　で　ともだち　に　あいます。……

*Kyoo watashi no tomodachi ni denwa shimasu.
Nanji kara nanji made inaka ni imasu ka.
Ichiji ni uchi o demasu. Ichiji juugofun goro gakkoo no mae de tomodachi ni
aimasu.*

いなか　まで　どの　ぐらい　です　か。……
とおくない　です。にじ　まで　に　いなか　に　つきます。もり　で
ちょうちょう　を　あつめます。ピクニック　を　して、うち　に
かえります。……ごじ　でしょう。

*Inaka made dono gurai desu ka . . .
Tookunai desu. Niji made ni inaka ni tsukimasu. Mori de choochoo o
atsumemasu. PIKUNIKKU o shite, uchi ni kaerimasu. Goji deshoo.*

そして　えいが　に　いきましょう　か　コンサート　に　いきましょう
か。きっさてん　に　いきましょう　か。
あした　まち　で　ポップ　コンサート　が　あります。いい　でしょう。
たかくない　です。……ポップ　コンサート　に　いきます。

……コンサート は じゅうじ に おわります。コンサート の あと
で はやく ねます。
すばらしい ひ でしょう。

Soshite eiga ni ikimashoo ka KONSAATO ni ikimashoo ka.
Kissaten ni ikimashoo ka.
Ashita machi de POPPU KONSAATO ga arimasu. Ii deshoo. Takakunai desu.
POPPU KONSAATO ni ikimasu. KONSAATO wa juuji ni owarimasu.
KONSAATO no ato de hayaku nemasu.
Subarashii hi deshoo.

STUDY

- In the passage Betty talks about a summer hobby. In Japan people don't distinguish between summer and winter hobbies when speaking.

- *niji made ni* "by two o'clock." Learn this just as a phrase for the moment, adapting it for your own purposes to be able to say "I'll finish by a certain time" or "I'll arrive by a certain time."
  e.g.: *Sanji made ni kono shigoto o owarimasu.*
  "I'll finish this job by three o'clock". Remember, *made* means "up to, until, as far as," so you can probably work out the logic of the phrase.

- *Dono gurai desu ka* "How far is it?/How long will it be?" Learn this phrase just as it is. It doesn't actually translate directly.

- *Wakarimashita* is often used in Japanese where in English we would use "know" rather than "understand."
  When you want to say "I know," more often than not you will need to use *wakarimashita*.

- **Adverbs**
  You are very familiar with ways to use adjectives. A new way to use the words you know is to give them a different ending and turn them into adverbs. Adverbs modify, tell you more about, a verb. They answer the question **how** something is done,
  e.g., He ran **fast**. I went **slowly** down the road.
  Often their English form takes "ly" as an ending:
  quickly, easily, superbly, badly, comfortably, beautifully. Sometimes they don't; e.g., "He walked fast." "Fast" is still telling you how he walked.
  In English adverbs usually go after the verb:
  "She walked quickly." "He talked fast." "They did it beautifully." "She sat down comfortably." "He wrote furiously." "They walked slowly." "He studied well." etc.
  In Japanese, to make an adverb, take off the *i* of the adjective and add *ku*; e.g.,
  hayai (fast/early) *hayaku*
  osoi (late/slow) *osoku*
  Hayaku okimashita. He got up early.

Hayaku tabemashita. She ate early/fast.
(The context will tell you which meaning is appropriate, though some-times in single sentences it's hard to know.)
Osoku nemashita. He went to bed late.
Osoku arukimashita. They walked slowly.
Hon o hayaku yomimashita. She read the book quickly.
GEEMU wa osoku shimashita. They played the game slowly.
Hayaku ikimasu. I'll go quickly.
Hayaku kakimasen. I don't write quickly.
Hayaku kite kudasai. Please come quickly.
Osoku tabete mo ii desu ka. Please may I eat slowly?
Hayaku kaette kudasai. Please return quickly.

Note that in Japanese the adverb usually goes directly in front of the verb.

- A word that you already know that is also in fact an adverb is **yoku**, "well." You remember *yoku dekimashita* "Well done!" "Well" is a word that you may not immediately recognize as an adverb, but when you look at it now it will be obvious that it tells more about the verb; e.g., *yoku shimasu* "I'll do it well" *yoku yomimashita* "I read it well" *yoku benkyoo shimashita* "They studied well."

  Yoku comes from the word "good," that, as you will remember, has two forms – **ii** and **yoi**. *Yoku comes from yoi.*

  Yoku, in another sense used earlier, means "often."

- **gonenkan shimashita.** The **kan** on the end of *gonen* states a period of time, so means "I did it for five years." Look at the following examples:
  ichinenkan – "one year's **time**" or "for one year"
  ninenkan – "two years' time" or "for two years"
  KEN san wa TENISU o ninenkan shimashita.
  Ken has played tennis for two years.
  Watashi wa kitte o ichinenkan atsumete imasu.
  I've been collecting stamps for one year.

  The length of time goes in front of the verb without any particles between.

  More on the use of *kan* will be dealt with later. For the present put it into the back of your head and let it gradually be assimilated.

ACTIVITIES

- With a partner. (You are only allowed to use Japanese, and you are not allowed to write the sentences down first!)

  Only using *hayaku, osoku,* and *yoku,* see how many different sentences you can make with the verbs and verb forms you know; e.g., *Kooen de GEEMU o hayaku shimashita.* "They played the game quickly in the park."

- Written work. Have a class competition to see how many different, correct sentences each person can make in five minutes using *hayaku* and *osoku.*

- Extend the previous activity by reading sentences around the class. Keep a record of the sentences given. If you have a sentence identical with one read, you should delete it from your list. When you have exhausted all the sentences, add up the total of different sentences.

- What would you do with a free day if money was no object? In small groups each tell your story. Don't write it down first. If you run out of things to say, that's fine; just stop and let the others ask you questions (in Japanese, of course).

Writing practice

- Review **TO**   ト

    and learn **DO**   ド
- Learn **MI**   ミ

- Learn **RO**   ロ

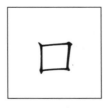

- Learn **MYO**   ミ ョ
- Learn **MYU**   ミ ュ

    Write   *DORU*   ドル
             MIRUKU   ミルク
             REKOODO   レコード
             PIKUNIKKU   ピクニック
             SUMISU   スミス
             ROSHIA   ロシア
             INDO   インド

Unit 6

あした つり に いきたい です
ashita tsuri ni ikitai desu
Tomorrow I want to go fishing

NEW WORDS

いきたい　です	*ikitai desu*	want to/would like to go
したい　です	*shitai desu*	want to do/have

Interest

かんがえ	*kangae*	idea
おべんとう	*Obentoo*	packed lunch

Review

そして	*soshite*	and then

Fishing in fishing ponds is a popular activity for many Japanese people. A student is thinking about his free day and what he wants to do.

しげ　　　　きょう、しゅくだい は おわりました。そして あした
は ひま です。あした つり に いきたい です。きょう
は いい おてんき です から あした は いい
おてんき でしょう。

おかあさん　ひとり で いきたい です か。

しげ　　　　いいえ、トムくん と いきたい です。いって も いい
です か。

おかあさん　はい。いい おてんき です から いい かんがえ です。
ピクニック が したい です か。
おべんとう を もって いきたい です か。

しげ　　　　はい、もって いきたい です。

Shige:	*Kyoo, shukudai wa owarimashita. Soshite ashita wa hima desu.*
	Ashita tsuri ni ikitai desu.
	Kyoo wa ii Otenki desu kara ashita wa ii Otenki deshoo.
Okaasan:	*Hitori de ikitai desu ka.*
Shige:	*Iie. TOMU kun to ikitai desu. Itte mo ii desu ka.*
Okaasan:	*Hai. Ii Otenki desu kara ii kangae desu.*
	PIKUNIKKU ga shitai desu ka.
	Obentoo o motte ikitai desu ka.
Shige:	*Hai, motte ikitai desu.*

S: Today I finished my homework and so tomorrow will be free. I would like to go fishing tomorrow.
      As it's nice today it will probably be a nice day tomorrow.
O: Do you want to go by yourself?
S: No, I want to go with Tom. May I go?
O: Yes. Because the weather's nice, it's a good idea.
      Do you want to have a picnic?
      Would you like to take a packed lunch?
S: Yes, I'd like to take one.

STUDY

• The *tai desu* form of verbs.
  This new verb form gives you the ability to say you would **like** to do something or **want** to do something.

  In English these two phrases have a slightly different politeness level. In Japanese they are interchangeable without a social difference.

  Making the new construction is easy: take off the *masu* from any verb and add *tai desu*. Examples:
  Tabetai desu. I want to eat/I'd like to eat.
  Nomitai desu. I want a drink/I'd like a drink.
  Hanashitai desu. I want to talk/I'd like to talk, etc.

  You will usually use **ga** with the **tai desu** form, because again you are focusing on one particular thing out of many possibilities. Nowadays you will hear some Japanese people use particle **o** if choice is not available and you are only asking about one possibility. You are always safe to use **ga** and gradually you will come to know when you could use **o** instead.

  Together brainstorm all the verbs you now know and change each one into the *tai desu* form. Just as you discovered with adjectives, the *desu* on the end never changes.

• To make the negative: "I don't want to . . .," **from the *tai desu* form take off the *i* and add *kunai*. Does that sound familiar?!
  Gakkoo ni ikitakunai desu. I don't want to go to school.
  Sushi wa tabetakunai desu. I don't want to eat sushi.
  JUUSU wa nomitakunai desu. I don't want to drink juice.

  Be careful to remember that you are taking off the *i* from the **tai desu** form. It means that you will always have **ta** in the middle of your verb after your usual stem.

  To make the other tenses of this construction, the endings behave in exactly the same way as adjectives.
  Ikitai desu. I want to go.
  Ikitakunai desu. I don't want to go.
  *Ika**katta** desu*. I wanted to go.
  *Ika**kunakatta** desu*. I did not want to go.

  This construction opens up incredible new horizons for your communication. Previously you learned how to say that you wanted an **object** with **ga hoshii desu**. That was only usable for **things**. This **tai desu** structure gives you the freedom to talk about **actions** you would like.

Check your understanding

How would you say the following?
1   I want to eat sushi today.
2   I don't want to go to the park.
3   I wanted to see a temple.
4   I did not want to drink sake.
5   I want to read a Japanese book.
6   I don't want to use your umbrella.
7   I did not want to swim in the sea, because the water was cold.

Some of those were difficult. How did you score? Did you remember *tsumetai* for "cold water" and *tsukaimasu* for "use"?

Practice these new structures together with all the verbs you know.

STUDY

- ***(kai) ni ikimasu*** (A new structure)
  kai ni ikimasu "go to buy"
  mi ni ikimasu "go to see"
  tabe ni ikimasu "go to eat"
  nomi ni ikimasu "go to drink," etc.
  Use the stem of the verb followed by ***ni*** and usually ***ikimasu, kimasu***, or ***kaerimasu***; e.g.,
  RESUTORAN ni tabe ni ikimasu. I'll go to eat at a restaurant.
  Toshokan ni hon o yomi ni ikimasu. I'll go to read in the library.
  BIDEO o mi ni kaerimasu. I'll return to watch a video.
      This structure can be combined with . . . ***tai desu*** to enable you to say:
  "I want to go to see a car." *Kuruma ga mi ni ikitai desu.*
  "I would like to go to eat some tempura." *Tenpura ga tabe ni ikitai desu.*
  etc.
      Practice this new structure with the *tai desu* form.

Writing practice

- Review ***KI*** and learn ***GI***   ギ

- Review ***KO*** and learn ***GO***   ゴ

- Learn **NA** ナ

- Learn **NE** ネ

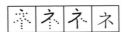

- Learn **U** ウ

- Write the following:
GITAA	ギター
GORUFU	ゴルフ
NEKUTAI	ネクタイ
KANADA	カナダ
BURAUN	ブラウン

Unit 7

けんどう が できます か
kendoo ga dekimasu ka
Can you do kendo?

NEW WORDS

できます できる	*dekimasu (dekiru)*	can do/able to do
ならいます ならう	*naraimasu (narau)*	learn
ならって	*naratte*	*te* form of *naraimasu*

Review
もちろん	*mochiron*	of course
と いっしょ に	*to issho ni*	together with
けんどう	*kendoo*	a martial art

Shigeharu has come to stay with Masao for a couple of days.

まさお　きょう の ごご けんどう の れんしゅう を します。

しげはる　わたし は けんどう は できません。むずかしい です。
みて も いい です か。

まさお　もちろん。むずかしい です が おもしろい です。けんどう
は わたし の いちばん すきな しゅみ です。
まいにち れんしゅう します。おとうと も けんどう が
できます。ときどき おとうと と いっしょ に れんしゅう
します。
ひるごはん の まえ に けんどう の ビデオ を
みましょう か。

しげはる　それ は いい です ね。けんどう が ならいたい です。

Masao:	*Kyoo no gogo kendoo no renshuu o shimasu.*
Shigeharu:	*Watashi wa kendoo wa dekimasen. Muzukashii desu.*
	Mite mo ii desu ka.
Masao:	*Mochiron. Muzukashii desu ga omoshiroi desu. Kendoo wa watashi no ichiban sukina shumi desu. Mainichi renshuu shimasu. Otooto mo kendoo ga dekimasu.*
	Tokidoki otooto to issho ni renshuu shimasu.
	Hirugohan no mae ni kendoo no BIDEO o mimashoo ka.
Shigeharu:	*Sore wa ii desu ne.*
	Kendoo ga naraitai desu.

STUDY

- ***Dekimasu*** is a verb of ability: "**can** do" or "**able** to do." It always take ***ga***, like *miemasu* "can see" and *wakarimasu* "understand." Use it when telling someone what you do or play and when asking what other people play or do.

  If you have **learned** to do something like playing tennis or karate, as opposed to doing something naturally, use *dekimasu*; e.g.,
  TENISU ga dekimasu. I play tennis.
  GORUFU ga dekimasu ka. Do you play golf?
  But if you are about to play a game of tennis, use *TENISU o shimasu*, in the same way that you have always done.

- If you want to say that you speak a foreign language, *dekimasu* is the verb you should use. You will remember that when you learned *hanashimasu*, the point was made that *hanashimasu* is used for your native language. Now with *dekimasu* you can say "I speak Japanese/I can do Japanese." Being strictly realistic, it will be a long time before you can speak Japanese as well as a native speaker, so you must say "I can speak Japanese," which people will understand means "as a learned language."

  It would probably be better to say:
  Nihongo ga sukoshi dekimasu. "I can do (speak) a little Japanese."

  The negative is straightforward, but of course takes **wa** as its particle; e.g.,
  Kendoo wa dekimasen. I can't do kendo.
  Juudoo wa dekimasen deshita ga konogoro renshuu shite imasu. I couldn't do judo, but these days I'm practicing.

- You may sometimes be asked simply: *Dekimasu ka?* "Can I/you do it?" "Is it possible?" Your answer would be either:
  Ee, dekimasu. Yes, I/you can/It's possible.
  or *Iie, dekimasen*. No, I can't/It's not possible.

  The translation of the last would usually only refer to yourself, because you can't really answer for someone else's **ability**; otherwise, you'll appear impolite. If your friend is trying to make a model, for example, and is having trouble, you can't politely say "You can't do it!" You could say either *Dekimasu ka*. "Can you do it?" "Are you able to do it?" or *Dekimasen ka* "Can't you do it?"

  In English we sometimes use "can't do" in a different way. If the situation was, for example, a parent telling a child "you can't do it," meaning that the child is not allowed to do it, then you need a totally different structure.

Check your understanding of the conversation.

Masao: This afternoon I'll practice kendo.
Shigeharu: I can't do kendo. It's difficult.
            May I watch?
Masao: Of course. It's difficult but it's interesting.
            Kendo is my favorite hobby. I practice every day.

My younger brother does it, too. Sometimes we practice together.
Shall we watch a kendo video before lunch?

Shigeharu: That would be good. I want to learn kendo.

ACTIVITIES

- Interview five people each to find out what they can and can't do, using *dekimasu* and *dekimasen*. Your questions will be *Nani ga dekimasu ka* or *(TENISU) ga dekimasu ka*.

- Write a report which states the name of each person interviewed and the results of your questioning.

- Imagine the school dance is coming up soon and there will be ballroom dancing as well as your usual dancing. You want to find a partner who can dance, so you go around the room greeting everyone and asking them the vital question – "Can you dance?" They will understand that you mean the more formal variety!
  DANSU ga dekimasu ka.
  Hai, DANSU ga dekimasu/Iie, DANSU wa dekimasen.
  Keep a record of those who claim to be able to do it.

- Imagine that you have been invited to make up a ski team to compete against another school in the national school ski *(SUKII)* championship. Go around the class questioning to sort out your team.

- When you have found the potential partners or team, find out if they are available on the date in question:
  (particular date) . . . *ii desu ka.*
       Arrange a meeting place and time and transportation. Write yourself a note for your diary to remind you of the arrangements.

Writing practice

- Review **SU** and learn **ZU**   ズ

- Review **SE** and learn **ZE**   ゼ

- Learn **WA**   ワ

- Learn **NYU**   ニュ

- Write the following
TAIWAN	タイワン
ZERO	ゼロ
ZUUMURENZU	ズームレンズ
NYUUYOOKU	ニューヨーク

ア	ウ	エ	オ	セ	ー	ル	イ	ギ	リ	ス
メ	コ	ー	ヒ	ー	ヒ	フ	レ	プ	ー	ル
リ	カ	キ	ナ	ニ	タ	バ	チ	ツ	テ	テ
カ	キ	ウ	イ	ー	マ	ス	ー	パ	ー	レ
ア	ユ	ヨ	ロ	ン	レ	ス	ト	ラ	ン	ビ
イ	ラ	モ	ノ	ー	ト	プ	テ	デ	ラ	ヘ
カ	ン	ガ	ル	ー	ケ	ノ	ニ	ポ	ト	ゴ
ナ	ア	ペ	イ	マ	ミ	ゴ	ス	キ	ー	ミ
ダ	フ	ッ	ト	ボ	ー	ル	ム	ナ	リ	ル
ヤ	コ	ト	ン	オ	パ	フ	ゴ	リ	ラ	ク
ロ	ド	ン	ト	プ	バ	ー	ケ	ン	チ	ズ
ブ	ス	ポ	ー	ツ	ヌ	ケ	ア	パ	ー	ト

- **Wordsearch.** Find the following words.

AMERIKA	SUPOOTSU	BAAGEN	KANGARUU
SEERU	NOOTO	BASU	RESUTORAN
TEREBI	GORUFU	IGIRISU	PUURU
KANADA	SUUPAA	PETTO	FUTTOBOORU
MIRUKU	GORIRA	APAATO	
KOOHII	SUKII	TENISU	

- Find out from the puzzle which sports are played by whom. Make a list. Practice writing these names, especially the ones which you or your friends play.

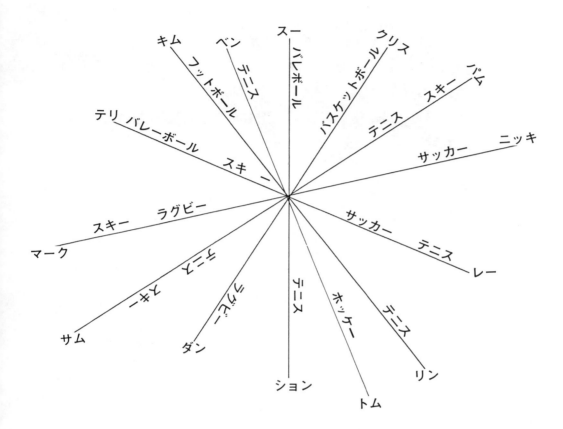

Unit 8

ピアノ と ギター を ひいて、
ポップ の うた を うたいます
PIANO to GITAA o hiite, POPPU no uta
o utaimasu
**I play the piano and guitar, and I sing
pop songs**

NEW WORDS

ポピュラー　おんがく	*POPYURAA ongaku*	pop music
ポップ	*POPPU*	pop music
クラシック　おんがく	*KURASHIKKU ongaku*	classical music
おんがく	*ongaku*	music
ひきます　ひく	*hikimasu (hiku)*	pluck/play a stringed instrument
ひいて	*hiite*	te form of *hikimasu*
おしえます　おしえる	*oshiemasu (oshieru)*	teach/show someone how to do something
おしえて	*oshiete*	te form of *oshiemasu*

Interest

きみ	*kimi*	you (used only by males)
うた	*uta*	song
うたいます　うたう	*utaimasu (utau)*	sing
うたって	*utatte*	te form of *utaimasu*

Tadao is finding out about the interests of a new student in his class.

ただお　おんがく が すき です か。

さぶろう　ええ、すき です。ポピュラー おんがく が たいへん
　　　　　すき です。きみ は。

ただお　わたし は クラシック おんがく が すき です。
　　　　　ピアノ と ギター を ひきます。

さぶろう　クラシック おんがく は すきじゃない です。
　　　　　ポップ の ギター が できます。おんがく は
　　　　　じゅうねん かん ならって います。うた は
　　　　　ポップ だけ うたいます。

ただお　　おもしろい　です。わたし　は　ときどき　ポップ　を
　　　　　ひきます。あした　の　よる　は　わたし　の　うち　に　きて
　　　　　ください。わたし　と　いっしょ　に　おんがく　を
　　　　　ひきましょう。

さぶろう　ありがとう　ございます。あした　の　はちじ　に　あいましょ
　　　　　う。どこ　に　すんで　います　か。

ただお　　わたし　の　うち　は　がっこう　の　うしろ　に　あります。
　　　　　おしえます。……ここ　に　きて　ください。……
　　　　　あの　たかい　き　が　みえます　か。

さぶろう　はい、　みえます。

ただお　　うち　は　その　き　の　うしろ　に　あります。

さぶろう　わかりました。

ただお　　あした　また。　はちじ　に　あいましょう。

Tadao: *Ongaku ga suki desu ka.*
Saburoo: *Ee, suki desu. POPYURAA ongaku ga taihen suki desu.*
            Kimi wa?
Tadao: *Watashi wa KURASHIKKU ongaku ga suki desu.*
            PIANO to GITAA o hikimasu.
Saburoo: *KURASHIKKU ongaku wa sukijanai desu.*
            POPPU no GITAA ga dekimasu. Ongaku wa juunenkan naratte
            imasu. Uta wa POPPU dake utaimasu.
Tadao: *Omoshiroi desu. Watashi wa tokidoki POPPU o hikimasu.*
            Ashita no yoru wa watashi no uchi ni kite kudasai.
            Watashi to issho ni ongaku o hikimashoo.
Saburoo: *Arigatoo gozaimasu. Ashita no hachiji ni aimashoo.*
            Doko ni sunde imasu ka.
Tadao: *Watashi no uchi wa gakkoo no ushiro ni arimasu . . .*
            Oshiemasu . . . Koko ni kite kudasai . . .
            Ano takai ki ga miemasu ka.
Saburoo: *Hai, miemasu.*
Tadao: *Uchi wa sono ki no ushiro ni arimasu.*
Saburoo: *Wakarimashita.*
Tadao: *Ashita mata. Hachiji ni aimashoo.*

From this point on the English version of many of the passages will not be presented. You will be using different strategies to check your understanding.

STUDY

- *Hikimasu*: to pluck or play a stringed instrument.
  In English we usually only use the word "play," but in Japanese it is necessary to use different verbs for different instrument actions. A piano makes sound because its strings are in fact plucked by the hammer as the player strikes the keys. *Hikimasu* is used for violins *(BAIORIN)*, too.

  (It may seem strange, but the verb for catching a cold: "plucking a cold out of the air" is also *hikimasu!* So to say you have caught a cold, you say *Kaze o hikimashita.*)

- If you play a flute or recorder the verb is **fukimasu** "blow." The **te** form is **fuite imasu**. This is not essential information unless you want to be able to tell people that you play an instrument like a recorder, flute or saxophone that you play by blowing.

- **Kimi wa** is an expression that means "How about you?" *Kimi* is only used by males.

- **Oshiemasu**, the verb "to teach" is used in Japanese in many situations where in English we would say "show"; e.g., "Show me how to do it . . . Show me the way . . . ." In other words, "teach me."

  In any situation where you would like a person to "show" you how to do something (not merely letting you look at an object as in shopping), use *Oshiemasu* "I will show you" or, e.g., *Michi o oshiete kudasai*. Please show me (teach me) the way.

  Note that the number of years Saburoo has been learning is placed directly in front of the verb, with no particle between, in just the same way as other numbers and quantities.

ACTIVITIES

- Make lists of all the **te** forms of the verbs you know, grouped by pattern; e.g., all the ones with:

te	ending
tte	ending
iite	ending
nde	ending
uite	ending
uide	ending
oide	ending

  Look in the vocabulary lists at the back of the book to find them all.

- Have a team competition to see how many leisure activities you can list in Japanese.

- Around the class or in small groups, each person says which musical instruments he plays and doesn't play, how long he has played (one year, two years, etc) and whether he prefers pop or classical music. Extend yourselves by giving the names of your favorite pop groups or musicians, where you saw them (at a concert or on TV), etc. Make sure that you add comments on each other's information with: *Soo desu ne, Omoshiroi desu ne*, etc, and ask questions to find out more information.

- Imagine that a small group of you have been out together and are now telling a friend in the hospital what he/she missed.

  Describe the evening out with friends where people played instruments, sang songs, listened to a stereo, tapes or records, watched a video, sang to *KARAOKE* videos, ate different foods, drank a variety of beverages, danced and enjoyed themselves.

The sick person can join in by asking questions to find out things that he/she wants to know.

Listen carefully to each other so you don't keep repeating information.

Reading practice

• What sort of music do the people in the following puzzle enjoy, or what instruments do they play?

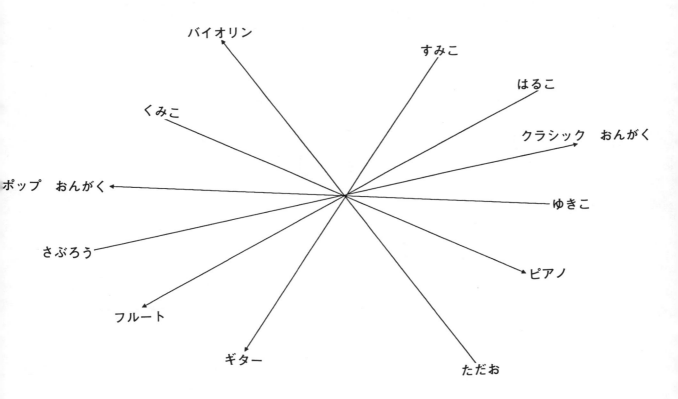

SONG
しきのうた

1   はるをあいするひとは　　こころきよきひと
    すみれのはなのような　　ぼくのともだち

2   なつをあいするひとは　　こころつよきひと
    いわをくだくなみのような　　ぼくのちちおや

3   あきをあいするひとは　　こころふかきひと
    あいをかたるハイネのような　　ぼくのこいびと

4   ふゆをあいするひとは　　こころひろきひと
    ゆきをとかすだいちのような　　ぼくのははおや

Shiki no uta
1   *Haru o ai suru hito wa kokoro kiyoki hito*
    sumire no hana no yoo na Boku no tomodachi

2   *Natsu o ai suru hito wa kokoro tsuyoki hito*
    iwa o kudakunami no yoo na Boku no chichi oya

3   *Aki o ai suru hito wa kokoro fukaki hito*
    ai o kataru HAINE no yoo na Boku no koibito

4   *Fuyu o aisuru hito wa kokoro hiroki hito*
    yuki o tokasu daichi no yoo na Boku no haha oya

Unit 9

やまのぼり が すき ですか
yamanobori ga suki desu ka
Do you like mountain climbing?

NEW WORDS

もう	*moo*	already
やまのぼり	*yamanobori*	mountain climbing
のぼります　のぼる	*noborimasu (noboru)*	climb
のぼって	*nobotte*	te form of *noborimasu*
まだ　です	*mada desu*	not yet
まえ　に	*mae ni*	before this

Interest
あぶない	*abunai*	dangerous (adjective)

Review
しゅうまつ	*shuumatsu*	weekend
さんぽ	*sanpo*	walk
つり	*tsuri*	fishing
やま	*yama*	mountains

ダン　しゅうまつ に なに を します か。

ニール　わかりません。なぜ です か。

ダン　あに は やまのぼり が すき です。ちかく の やま に いきます。あに と いっしょ に いきましょう か。

ニール　わかりません。やまのぼり は できません。まえ に しません でした。あぶない でしょう。やま に は もう のぼりました か。

ダン　いいえ、まだ です。わたし は き だけ のぼりました！

ニール　おにいさん と やま に いきましょう。きれい です。でも やま は のぼりません。やま に さんぽ に いって、つり を しましょう。

ダン　そう しましょう。いい かんがえ です。

Dan:　*Shuumatsu ni nani o shimasu ka.*
Neil:　*Wakarimasen. Naze desu ka.*
Dan:　*Ani wa yamanobori ga suki desu. Chikaku no yama ni ikimasu. Ani to issho ni ikimashoo ka.*
Neil:　*Wakarimasen. Yamanobori wa dekimasen. Mae ni shimasen deshita. Abunai deshoo. Yama ni wa moo noborimashita ka.*

Dan: *Iie, mada desu.*
       Watashi wa ki dake noborimashita!
Neil: *Oniisan to yama ni ikimashoo. Kirei desu. Demo yama wa*
       noborimasen. Yama ni sanpo ni itte, tsuri o shimashoo.
Dan: *Soo shimashoo. Ii kangae desu.*

STUDY

* **moo** "already/yet."
  mada desu "not yet."
  Study the following sentences. Note the position of *moo* within the sentence:

Moo gohan o tabemashita ka.	Have you eaten a meal yet?
Hai/ee, tabemashita.	Yes, I have.
Iie, mada desu.	No, I haven't (eaten) yet.
Moo toshokan ni ikimashita ka.	Have you been to the library yet?
Ee, moo ikimashita.	Yes, I have.
Iie, mada desu.	No, I haven't been yet/not yet.
Moo sore ga dekimasu ka.	Can you do it/that thing yet?
Mada desu.	Not yet.

  Practice together making sentences with *moo* and *mada*.

* Remember that *sanpo ni ikimasu* means "to go for a walk" while *sanpo o shimasu* means "to take a walk" or "to stroll.")
  Likewise, *tsuri ni ikimasu* means "to go fishing" while *tsuri o shimasu* means "to fish."

ACTIVITY

Work in pairs to understand the conversation. What are they talking about? Discuss it with another pair and see if you agree on the general idea and whether you picked up the details.

Unit 10

あなた の あかい ブラウス を
きて も いい です か
anata no akai BURAUSU o kite mo ii desu ka
May I wear your red blouse?

NEW WORDS

せいふく	*seifuku*	school uniform
ブラウス	*BURAUSU*	blouse
ティーシャツ	*TII-SHATSU*	T-shirt
セーター	*SEETAA*	sweater
シャツ	*SHATSU*	shirt
きます　きる	*kimasu (kiru)*	wear on upper half of body
きて	*kite*	*te* form of *kimasu*
きもの	*kimono*	Japanese national dress
ワイシャツ	*WAISHATSU*	white shirt/business shirt
コート	*KOOTO*	coat
Interest		
ジャケット	*JAKETTO*	jacket
ドレス	*DORESU*	dress
ゆかた	*yukata*	cotton kimono

Mariko is going to a concert and wants to borrow her sister's blouse.

まりこ　すみこ　ちゃん、きょう　コンサート　に　いきます。
　　　　あなた　の　あかい　ブラウス　を　きて　も　いい　です　か。

すみこ　いいえ。まりこ　ちゃん　は　ブラウス　を　たくさん　もって
　　　　います。

まりこ　でも　あかい　ブラウス　は　もって　いません。

すみこ　じゃ　わかりました。わたし　の　あかい
　　　　ブラウス　を　きて　も　いい　です。

まりこ　いい　おねえさん　です　ね。ありがとう　ございます。

Mariko: *Sumiko chan, kyoo KONSAATO ni ikimasu. Anata no akai*
          BURAUSU o kite mo ii desu ka.
Sumiko: *Iie. Mariko chan wa BURAUSU o takusan motte imasu.*
Mariko: *Demo akai BURAUSU wa motte imasen.*
Sumiko: *Ja wakarimashita. Watashi no akai BURAUSU o kite mo ii desu.*
Mariko: *Ii oneesan desu ne. Arigatoo gozaimasu.*

With a friend read the conversation and get the general understanding without worrying about detail.

Check your understanding of the conversation.
Mariko: Sumiko, I'm going to a concert today. Please may I wear your red
          blouse?
Sumiko: No. You've got a lot of blouses.
Mariko: But, I don't own a red blouse/haven't got a red blouse.
Sumiko: Well then . . . it's OK. You may wear my red blouse.
Mariko: You're a good older sister. Thank you very much.

STUDY

● *Kimasu* "wear." This verb looks and sounds like *kimasu* "come," but it
  means "to wear on the upper part of the body." In the *kanji* it is totally
  different. For any clothes that hang on the shoulders use this verb.
      There are different verbs to use for other clothing, which will be
  covered in the following units.

come　来

wear　着

ACTIVITY

Working in pairs, imagine that the two of you are going out or have had a special evening out:

1 Practice using **kimasu** with the new words for this unit.
2 Practice saying what you want to wear, don't want to wear and when or why (**kitai desu** "want to wear").
3 Practice using "May I wear this . . .?"
4 Practice using "Please wear. . . ."
5 Practice saying what you did not wear and why.
6 Practice saying what you did not want to wear but (wore).
7 If you have learned *te wa ikemasen*, practice saying you may not wear (my . . . that . . . this . . . your . . .).

Check your understanding

1   *Yamada san ga kimashita.*
2   *HANNA chan wa BURAUSU o kite imasu.*
3   *Nani o kite imasu ka.*
4   *Dare ga kite imasu ka.*
5   *Akai DORESU o kimashita ka.*
6   *Ano aoi SEETAA o kimasen deshita.*
7   *Watashi no atarashii TII-SHATSU o kimasu.*
8   *Kaisha ni WAISHATSU o kimasu.*
9   *WAISHATSU o kite imasu ka.*
10 *Samui desu kara KOOTO o kimasu.*

ACTIVITIES

● Make a chart that shows all the clothing for which you use the verb **kimasu** (use magazine illustrations if you wish).

● In small groups (ten minutes for planning the outline, then just let it happen) role play a situation in which: you plan an outing; decide what each of you is going to wear; and, if necessary, borrow from each other.

In scene two of your play, comment on the clothes people are wearing; go off to your chosen activity and say what you think it will be like.

In scene three, chat as you leave the activity: comment on whether it was interesting or boring; say what you plan to do next; and organize a date, day, time, and place to meet again.

Show your role play to the class.

Writing practice

- Review **TII**　ティー
  and **JI**　ジ

- Learn **JA**　ジャ

- Learn **SHA**　シャ

- Practice the *katakana* words in this unit:

BURAUSU	ブラウス
SHATSU	シャツ
TII-SHATSU	ティーシャツ
WAISHATSU	ワイシャツ
SEETAA	セーター
KOOTO	コート
JAKETTO	ジャケット
DORESU	ドレス

Unit 11

くろい ジーンズ を はきます
kuroi JIINZU o hakimasu
I'll wear black jeans

NEW WORDS

はきます　はく	*hakimasu (haku)*	wear on the legs and feet
はいて	*haite*	*te* form of *hakimasu*
くろい	*kuroi*	black
くつ	*kutsu*	shoes
スカート	*SUKAATO*	skirt
ピンク の	*PINKU no*	pink
みどり いろ の	*midori (iro) no*	green
ズボン	*ZUBON*	trousers
はんズボン	*hanZUBON*	shorts/short trousers

Interest

ジーンズ	*JIINZU*	jeans
ショーツ	*SHOOTSU*	shorts
もも いろ の	*momo iro no*	peach pink
ねずみ いろ の	*nezumi iro no*	grey (mouse color)
むらさき いろ の	*murasaki iro no*	purple
だいだい いろ の	*daidai iro no*	orange
ちゃ いろ の	*cha iro no*	brown (tea color)

Osamu comes to call on Masatsugi.

まさつぎ　きょう は パーティー に いきます か。
　　　　　くろい ジーンズ を はきます か。

おさむ　　はい。くろい ジーンズ と くろい くつ を はいて、
　　　　　くろい ティーシャツ を きます。きみ は。

まさつぎ　いつも くろい ようふく を きます ね。
　　　　　わたし は くろい ジーンズ を はいて、むらさき いろ
　　　　　の シャツ を きます。
　　　　　きのう あたらしい シャツ を かいました。
　　　　　たかかった です が たいへん すき です。

おさむ　　みて　も　いい　です　か。

まさつぎ　はい。わたし　の　へや　に　きて　ください。シャツ　は
　　　　　とだな　の　なか　に　あります。………

おさむ　　いい　シャツ　です　ね。いくら　でした　か。

まさつぎ　ななせんごじゅうえん　でした。

おさむ　　たいへん　たかかった　です　ね。

Masatsugi: *Kyoo wa PAATII ni ikimasu ka.*
             Kuroi JIINZU o hakimasu ka.
Osamu: *Hai. Kuroi JIINZU to kuroi kutsu o haite, kuroi TII-SHATSU o*
             kimasu. Kimi wa?
Masatsugi: *Itsumo kuroi yoofuku o kimasu ne!*
             Watashi wa kuroi JIINZU o haite, murasaki iro no SHATSU o
             kimasu.
             Kinoo atarashii SHATSU o kaimashita. Takakatta desu ga taihen
             suki desu.
Osamu: *Mite mo ii desu ka.*
Masatsugi: *Hai. Watashi no heya ni kite kudasai. SHATSU wa todana no*
             naka ni arimasu . . . .
Osamu: *Ii SHATSU desu ne. Ikura deshita ka.*
Masatsugi: *Nanasengojuuen deshita.*
Osamu: *Taihen takakatta desu ne!*

STUDY

- In Japanese some colors are ordinary adjectives and some are color nouns; e.g., *midori iro* "green color" and *daidai iro* "orange color." The word **iro** means color. *Iro* on the end of a color name means it is a color noun not an adjective. (*Iroiro* means "many colors" or "various.")

    Color nouns always need to have the package **iro no** after them.

    The adjectives **akai, shiroi, kuroi, aoi** and **kiiroi** are just used as ordinary adjectives:

Akai DORESU o kite imasu. I'm wearing a red dress.
SUKAATO wa akakunai desu. The skirt is not red.
ZUBON wa akakatta desu. The trousers were red.
BURAUSU wa akakunakatta desu. The blouse was not red.

(Note: *kiiroi* is sometimes to be seen as *ki iro*. If *ki iro* is used, it behaves as a color noun as below.)

    The color nouns are different from adjectives. Please learn them carefully.

Rule: (in front of a noun)

If the color has **iro** on the end it must always have the particle **no** following it. **No** is the beginning of the word **noun**. "In front of a noun use **no**" may be a way to help you to remember.

Kuroi JIINZU o hakimasu

- **Midori** (green) has two forms: *midori iro no* and just *midori no*. But it is a color noun and always behaves like one whether it has the word *iro* with it or not; e.g.,
Midori no DORESU o kimasu. I'll wear a green (color) dress.
Midori iro no SUKAATO o hakimasu. I'll wear a green (color) skirt.
Murasaki iro no SHATSU o kimasu. He'll wear a purple (color) shirt.
Cha iro no ZUBON o hakimasu. She'll wear brown (color) trousers.
    However, in front of *desu*, use *midori* or *midori iro*:
DORESU wa midori (iro) desu. The dress is green.
SUKAATO wa midori (iro) dewa arimasen/janai desu. The skirt is not green.
BURAUSU wa midori (iro) deshita. The blouse was green.
SUKAATO wa midori (iro) dewa arimasen/janai desu. The skirt is not green.
    Practice together using color adjectives and color nouns and keep the two carefully separated in your mind.

ACTIVITIES

- Role play. After each mini role play change partners, make sure you don't talk with the same partner twice! (Use vocabulary from the last unit as well, and try to remember what you *kimasu* and what you *hakimasu*!)
    Using the conversation on p. 218 as a pattern, have a conversation with a partner: Greet each other appropriately and ask each other what you are going to wear for a particular activity; e.g.,
KONSAATO ni wa nani o hakimasu ka/nani o kimasu ka.
"Talking about going to the concert, what are you going to wear?"
    Don't forget that, depending on the verb you use and the first reply, you may need to ask the second question to find out what they plan to wear on the other half of their body. Use the following situations:
1 Going to a concert next Friday.
2 Going to the park to play a game on Sunday.
3 Going to a party next Wednesday.
4 Going to the movies on Monday.
5 Going to the beach on Saturday.

- Fill in the appropriate verb.
1 *Kutsu o* ....
2 *JIINZU o* ....
3 *TII-SHATSU o* ....
4 *BURAUSU o* ....
5 *DORESU o* ....
6 *SEETAA o* ....
7 *WAISHATSU o* ....
8 *Seifuku o* ....
9 *SUKAATO o* ....
10 *JAKETTO o* ....

- As a class or in small groups, collect illustrations of clothing from magazines. Have a discussion on what you would choose to wear, telling each other in Japanese what you like or dislike.

- Do a survey to see which color or style is most popular in your group. If you have the prices, you can comment on those, too. Report to the whole class on the survey you made.
  Nani iro ga suki desu ka. (What color . . .?)
  Donna SUTAIRU ga suki desu ka. (What style . . .?)

- Work in pairs. Price each item. Allow each person a specified amount of money. Which items of clothing would they choose? Try to give some reasons for your choice.
  You may like to write your decisions down in your notebook.

Writing practice

- Review **SHA**   シャ

- Learn **SHU**   シュ

- Learn **SHO**   ショ

- Practice the *katakana* words for this unit:
  SHOOTSU   ショーツ
  JIINZU   ジーンズ
  SUKAATO   スカート
  PINKU   ピンク
  ZUBON   ズボン

- Make a list of the clothes you are wearing at the moment. Draw a sketch of yourself and label it appropriately.

Unit 12

ネクタイ を しましょう か
NEKUTAI o shimashoo ka
Shall I wear a tie?

NEW WORDS

ネクタイ	*NEKUTAI*	tie/necktie
Interest		
ベルト	*BERUTO*	belt
イヤリング	*IYARINGU*	earrings
ぼうし	*booshi*	hat, cap
スカーフ	*SUKAAFU*	scarf
Extension		
かぶります	*kaburimasu*	wear on the head
かぶる	*(kaburu)*	
かぶって	*kabutte*	*te* form of *kaburimasu*

STUDY

- Ties, belts, scarves, jewelry all use the word **shimasu** to express "wear."
  Look at the examples:
  NEKUTAI o shimasu. I'll wear a tie.
  BERUTO o shimasu. I'll wear a belt.
  IYARINGU o shimasu. I'll wear earrings.

- Until recently, girls who had their ears pierced were considered rebels. The same was considered true of girls who had their hair permed or boys who had crew cuts or wore their hair longer than the standard set by Japanese schools. In fact policemen were issued with lists of non-conformist behavior like those and kept a special eye on people who disobeyed convention.
  Even now it is unusual to see a boy with earrings, and many parents would be horrified if their daughter had her ears pierced.

- You may remember that for wearing glasses (spectacles), the verb to use is **kakemasu** (*kakeru*) and the **te** form is *kakete imasu*; e.g.,
  She wears glasses. *Megane o kakemasu*.
  He is wearing glasses. *Megane o kakete imasu*.
  I don't wear/He doesn't wear glasses. *Megane o kakemasen*.
  He is not wearing glasses. *Megane o kakete imasen*.

- Extension

  Kaburimasu (*kaburu*) (*kabutte imasu*) is the verb to use for things that you wear on your head; e.g.,

  Booshi o kabutte imasu. He is wearing a hat.

ACTIVITIES

- In pairs, using the illustrations on p. 224, practice asking your partner:

  The name of the person.

  Physical characteristics.

  What each person is wearing.

     Take turns asking each other questions and answering.

- Play "Who's my friend?" *Tomodachi wa dare desu ka*.

  Photocopy the illustrations on p. 224. Glue the sheets on cardboard and, if you wish, cover them with plastic. Cut them up into cards. You need one set for each person.

     Set the cards out in rows on your desk. Choose one of your cards as the person you are thinking about. Don't tell your partner who you've chosen (and don't cheat by changing people half-way through the game!). Take turns asking your partner questions about the pictures; e.g.,

  Tomodachi wa hana ga ookii desu ka.

  Is the friend's nose big?

  Tomodachi wa megane o kakete imasu ka.

  Is the friend wearing glasses?

  Tomodachi wa onna no hito desu ka, otoko no hito desu ka.

  Is the friend male or female?

  Tomodachi wa me ga chiisai desu ka.

  Are the friend's eyes small?

  DORESU o kite imasu ka.

  Is she wearing a dress?

     You will be able to think up many questions to give you the most profitable answers.

     When you receive a reply, turn over all the cards that have been eliminated by that answer. For example, if the answer was "Yes, the person has big ears," turn over all the pictures of people with small ears. Gradually eliminate all the cards until you are able to name the person chosen by your opponent.

Writing practice

- Learn **JU**   ジュ

- Learn **JO**   ジョ

- Learn **JE**   ジェ

- Learn **CHA**   チャ

JAPLISH

One of the interesting aspects of young people's clothing and accessories in Japan is the use or misuse of other languages as decoration. Often the messages they are putting across are amusing to nationals of the language concerned.

This sort of language is often referred to as "Japlish"!

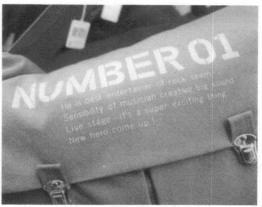

• Identify the following names.

1	リチャード	9	ジェーソン
2	ジョン	10	ジャン
3	カイル	11	ジェームス
4	ニール	12	ティム
5	ブライアン	13	チャーリ
6	ジェーン	14	ジェーク
7	クリス	15	サイモン
8	マンディー	16	リン

Unit 13

とも だち に でんわ を して
も いい です か
tomodachi ni denwa o shite mo
ii desu ka
May I phone my friend?

NEW WORDS

しります しる	*shirimasu (shiru)*	know
しって	*shitte*	*te* form of *shirimasu*
こたえます こたえる	*kotaemasu (kotaeru)*	answer
こたえて	*kotaete*	*te* form of *kotaemasu*

Interest
でんわ ばんごう	*denwa bangoo*	telephone number
もしもし	*moshimoshi*	Hello (on the telephone)

Review
でんわ を します	*denwa o shimasu*	make a telephone call

Reading in pairs. With a partner, read through the following conversations. If you have any difficulty, try to work out the meaning between yourselves.

Haruko and her friend Yukiko are planning a shopping outing and decide to invite another friend.
Haruko asks Yukiko's mother if she may use the phone.

はるこ   すみません が、ともだち に でんわ を して も いい
です か。

おかあさん はい。だれ に でんわ を します か。

はるこ   すみこ ちゃん に………

おかあさん そう………でんわ ばんごう を しって います か。

はるこ   はい。ありがとう。

She tries the number.
もしもし……はるこ です。
すみこ さん は うち に います か。

Sumiko's little sister answers:

いもうとさん すみこ は うち に いません が すぐ かえります。

はるこ ありがとう。あと で また でんわ を します。

Haruko: *Sumimasen ga tomodachi ni denwa o shite mo ii desu ka.*
Okaasan: *Hai. Dare ni denwa o shimasu ka.*
Haruko: *Sumiko chan ni . . .*
Okaasan: *Soo . . . Denwa bangoo o shitte imasu ka.*
Haruko: *Hai. Arigatoo.*
She tries the number.
            Moshimoshi . . . Haruko desu.
            Sumiko san wa uchi ni imasu ka.
(Sumikosan no imootosan wa kotaemashita.)
Imootosan: *Sumiko wa uchi ni imasen ga sugu kaerimasu.*
Haruko: *Arigatoo. Ato de mata denwa o shimasu.*

STUDY

- **Moshimoshi.**

  Moshimoshi is the standard way to open a telephone conversation, and the caller usually speaks first. It means "Excuse me" but can only be used on the telephone or if **you are standing behind someone** and want to get their attention. It is an easy phrase to mispronounce. If you say *mushi mushi*, as so many people do, you are actually talking about worms or insects! It's very important, therefore, to get the sound correct!

  For "Excuse me" in other situations, use *sumimasen ga . . .*

- **Shitte imasu** is used in the **te** form for "know," because something you know is a continuing state in your mind, you knew it before, know it now, and will probably still know it in the future. (Note how careful you have to be in the pronunciation of *shitte* "know," and *shite* "do.")

  In English we say we "are **going to do** something,") or "are **doing** something,") meaning future action, not that we are doing it at that moment or that it is a continuing action. Remember that in Japanese the **te** form is only used for continuing action or something that is happening now; e.g., *KOOHII o nonde imasu.* He is drinking coffee.

  Haruko returns to Yukiko and they start planning what they will wear.

NEW WORDS

なおります　なおる	*naorimasu (naoru)*	heal/get better
もって　いきます	*motte ikimasu*	take
もって　いく	*(motte iku)*	
もって　いって	*motte itte*	*te* form of *motte ikimasu*
にきび	*nikibi*	pimples

Review
ほんとう　に　　　　　　　　*hontoo ni*　　　　　　　　honestly, truly

はるこ　すみこ　ちゃん　は　うち　に　いません。あと　で　また　でんわ　を　します。

ゆきこ　あした　なに　を　きます　か。

はるこ　ねずみ　いろ　の　ドレス　を　きて、あかい　くつ　を　はきます。　あなた　は。

ゆきこ　その　しろい　ブラウス　を　きて、ジーンズ　と　しろい　くつ　を　はきます。

はるこ　いい　です　ね。

The phone rings, and Yukiko goes to answer it.

ゆきこ　もしもし、ゆきこ　です。すみこ　ちゃん　です　か。
あした　はるこ　ちゃん　と　まち　に　いきます。わたし　たち　と　いっしょ　に　いきません　か。
ジョン　さん　と　ジョン　さん　の　ともだち　に　あいます。

すみこ　ありがとう。でも　わたし　は　いきません。

ゆきこ　なぜ　です　か。ジョン　さん　が　すき　です　ね。

すみこ　はい。でも　きょう　にきび　が　あります。
たいへん　いや　です。

ゆきこ　それ　は　いけません　ね。　わかりました。　にきび　は　いや　ですね。

すみこ　そう　です　ね。くすりや　で　にきび　の　くすり　を　かいました。

ゆきこ　じゃ……　その　にきび　は　すぐ　なおります。
げつようび　に　でんわ　を　します。

すみこ　ありがとう。でんわ　を　して　ください。　じゃ　また。

Yukiko returns to her room, and she and Haruko continue their planning.

はるこ　すみこ　ちゃん　でした　か。

ゆきこ　はい　そう　です。すみこ　ちゃん　は　にきび　が　たくさん　あります　から　わたしたち　と　いきません。

She starts brushing her hair.

にきび　は　いや　です　ね。にきび　が　たいへん　きらい　です。

はるこ　わたし　も　にきび　が　きらい　です。ほんとう　に　いや　です。

Yukiko continues to do her hair.

ゆきこ　……あした　さむい　でしょう　か。
コート　を　もって　いきましょう　か。

はるこ　はい。……もう　ごじはん　です　か。

ゆきこ　はい、そう　です。

はるこ　おそい　です　から　そろそろ　しつれい　します。
あした　また。
くじはん　に　えき　の　まえ　で　あいましょう。

ゆきこ　はい。じゃ　また。

Haruko:　*Sumiko chan wa uchi ni imasen. Ato de mata denwa o shimasu.*
Yukiko:　*Ashita nani o kimasu ka.*
Haruko:　*Nezumi iro no DORESU o kite, akai kutsu o hakimasu. Anata wa?*
Yukiko:　*Sono shiroi BURAUSU o kite, JIINZU to shiroi kutsu o hakimasu.*
Haruko:　*Ii desu ne.* (The phone rings downstairs, and Yukiko goes to answer it.)
Yukiko:　*Moshimoshi, Yukiko desu.*
Sumiko chan desu ka.
Ashita Haruko chan to machi
ni ikimasu. Watashitachi to issho ni ikimasen ka.
JON san to JON.san no tomodachi ni aimasu.
Sumiko:　*Arigatoo. Demo watashi wa ikimasen.*
Yukiko:　*Naze desu ka. JON san ga suki desu ne.*
Sumiko:　*Hai. Demo kyoo nikibi ga arimasu.*
Taihen iya desu.
Yukiko:　*Sore wa ikemasen ne. Wakarimashita. Nikibi wa iya desu ne.*
Sumiko:　*Soo desu ne. Kusuriya de nikibi no kusuri o kaimashita.*
Yukiko:　*Ja . . . sono nikibi wa sugu naorimasu.*
Getsuyoobi ni denwa o shimasu.
Sumiko:　*Arigatoo. Denwa o shite kudasai. Ja mata.*
Yukiko returns to her room, and they continue their planning.

Haruko:　*Sumiko chan deshita ka.*
Yukiko:　*Hai, soo desu. Sumiko chan wa nikibi ga takusan arimasu kara watashitachi to ikimasen.*

She starts brushing her hair.

Yukiko:　*Nikibi wa iya desu ne. Nikibi ga taihen kirai desu.*
Haruko:　*Watashi mo nikibi ga kirai desu. Hontoo ni iya desu.*
Yukiko continues doing her hair.
Yukiko:　*. . . Ashita samui deshoo ka.*
KOOTO o motte ikimashoo ka.
Haruko:　*Hai . . . Moo gojihan desu ka.*
Yukiko:　*Hai, soo desu.*

Haruko: *Osoi desu kara sorosoro shitsurei shimasu.*
           Ashita mata.
           Kujihan ni eki no mae de aimashoo.
Yukiko: *Hai. Ja mata.*

STUDY

- Study the new verb
  motte ikimasu take (literally hold and go)
  motte ikimasen won't take
  motte ikimashita took
  motte ikimasen deshita did not take
  motte itte kudasai please take
  motte ikimashoo let's take
  motte itte mo ii desu ka May I take
  motte ikitai desu (I) want to take

  Motte ikimasu "take" may only be used for **things.**
  Motte ikimasu means "hold and go" – in English we say "take."
  Motte kimasu "bring" is also only used for **things.**
  Motte kimasu means "hold and come" – in English we say "bring."
  The Japanese use these double or triple verbs a great deal to be more precise about the actions that need to be gone through; e.g., *Katte kimasu* "I'll buy it and come."
  Itte katte kaette kudasai "Go and buy it and come home again."
  Notice how careful you have to be with your pronunciation if you want to get the correct message across.
  Motte ikimasu cannot be used for taking an animal or a person with you. There is another verb *(tsurete ikimasu)* used for taking something that is dependent on you, like a child or your dog. If you'd like to learn it, that's fine. If you have enough to do remembering *motte ikimasu* and *motte kimasu*, leave it till later, but remember that *motte ikimasu* and *motte kimasu* are only used for things.

- Previously you have only used **kara** "because" with *desu*; e.g., *ame desu kara* "because it is raining . . .," etc. In this unit it is used after *arimasu*. It may in fact be used after any verb to say "because." Study the following examples:
  JUUSU o nomimashita kara nodo wa kawaite imasen.
  Because I had (drank) some juice, I'm not thirsty.
  SANDOITCHI o tabemashita kara onaka wa suite imasen.
  Because I had (ate) a sandwich, I'm not hungry.
  Hayaku ikimashita kara kaimono o shimashita.
  Because I went early, I did some shopping.
  Nihongo o benkyoo shite imasu kara wakarimasu.
  Because I am studying Japanese, I understand.
  There is another way to express "because" that you will learn later, but this way is useful for the moment. Remember: the reason in Japanese always goes first.
  (Remember too – in English we often say "had" a sandwich, etc, when we mean "ate." The Japanese are more precise. Every time you want to

say "had," ask yourself what you really mean. Is it eat? Or drink? Went for? etc, and use the precise word for the action.)

Learn how to say you are not hungry, not thirsty.

Check your understanding

With a partner, ask each other questions. Take alternate questions. Suggested answers are given in brackets.

1 Ask what your partner had for lunch. *(HANBAAGAA)*
2 Ask if your partner is hungry. (No)
3 Ask if your partner is thirsty. (Yes)
4 Ask if your partner has had dinner already. (No)
5 Ask if your partner has seen that video already. (Yes)
6 Ask if your partner has read that book yet. (Yes)
7 Ask if your partner had had medicine today. (No, not yet)
8 Ask if your partner has had a walk today. (Yes)
9 Ask if your partner will have lunch with you. (Yes)
10 Ask if your partner will have a cup of coffee. (No, thank you)

Change partners again. Take turns answering. How would you say the following in Japanese? (Take care with the adjectives.)

1 Because it was cold, I took a coat.
2 Because I had an exam, I studied hard (well).
3 I went to town because I needed a book.
4 The water was cold, so they didn't want to swim.
5 The coffee was hot, so they didn't drink it.
6 Because I hadn't read it, I didn't understand.
7 I didn't need a coat, because it was hot.
8 I don't want to go to town, because my friend is coming today.
9 He won't read the book, because it is difficult.
10 We don't want to go to the movies, because we have seen that film.

ACTIVITIES

• Role play, in a group of three or five, a situation in which friends meet or telephone each other to decide on a leisure activity for this weekend.

They will need to know what they are going to do so that they can decide:

what to take with them;

what to wear;

how much money they will need;

how they'll travel.

(Don't plan it in English!)

After the greetings and comments on the weather now and the probable weather over the weekend, someone suggests an activity (in Japanese). The rest of you are free to agree or disagree, or to suggest an alternative. Let the conversation flow on from one person to another as it does in natural conversation, but please try to make a contribution of some sort.

● The real thing!
Try out your Japanese on a Japanese national if you have the opportunity to meet one. You may be fortunate enough to find someone looking puzzled about which way to go, or someone waiting for a bus who has obviously got time to talk!

Check that he/she is Japanese first by asking:
Sumimasen ga Nihonjin desu ka, as sometimes the "Japanese" person you've found turns out to be Chinese or Taiwanese! Don't be embarrassed if that happens; it's an easy mistake to make.

You are able to say so much now in Japanese; e.g., Introduce yourself. Tell her or him you are studying Japanese. Say you like to practice your Japanese (*Nihongo no renshuu ga suki desu*). Ask if you may speak with him. And here are some of the things you could talk about:
Ask if he has time to talk to you.
Talk about the weather.
Ask if he is on vacation.
Ask if he likes your town.
Tell him something about your town.
Ask where she lives in Japan/here.
Tell her what you are studying at school.
Tell her what your hobbies are.
If she has time to talk to you, she will contribute too, and the conversation will take its own direction.

Here are some useful phrases in case you can't immediately understand:
Yukkuri itte kudasai. Please say it/speak slowly.
Hakkiri itte kudasai. Please say it/speak clearly.
Moo ichido itte kudasai. Please repeat that.
Don't forget to say thank you, and bow before you say goodbye.

Practice asking these sorts of things with a friend, or talk to yourself in the privacy of your room if it will help you to feel more confident.

If you go up to Japanese people and say hello and then get shy, don't worry. If you are genuinely interested in speaking to them and in finding out a little bit about them, you will try to put them at ease, and your own shyness will probably melt away. If everything you wanted to say goes out of your head, just smile in a friendly way and say goodbye. You have communicated, and next time it will be easier.

Many people find that they feel shy speaking Japanese in their own country but feel more comfortable when in Japan with Japanese all around them, even though they know they may be making mistakes. Unfortunately, it's not possible for most of us to have much time in Japan, so we have to learn to overcome these problems and get practice whenever we can. Remember the rules: Don't think about yourself and how you sound or look or whether your sentences are correct. Help the other person to feel comfortable.

You will probably be surprised how much and how easily you can communicate as you try to help them to find their way, ask questions politely, or tell them about yourself. Don't worry about mistakes – the important thing is to get the message across.

If they are living near you, you and your family may make new friends. Many Japanese outside Japan find it very hard to get to know people or to visit people in their homes and are often quite lonely. They usually want to improve their English too, so you can be helpful to each other. So give it a try!

Vocabulary checklist (Topic Thirteen)

Introduction

あいきどう	*aikidoo*	martial art
けんどう	*kendoo*	martial art
じゅうどう	*juudoo*	martial art
からて	*karate*	martial art
きゅうどう	*kyuudoo*	archery
やぶさめ	*yabusame*	Japanese horseback archery
ぼんさい	*bonsai*	miniature tree cultivation
いけばな	*ikebana*	flower arranging
しょどう	*shodoo*	calligraphy
ふで	*fude*	paintbrush
こと	*koto*	Japanese harp
しゃみせん	*shamisen*	three stringed long lute
しゃくはち	*shakuhachi*	vertical flute
おりがみ	*origami*	paper folding
カラオケ	*KARAOKE*	sing along with tape
むし	*mushi*	insects/worms
いろは　カルタ	*iroha KARUTA*	hiragana card game
えんか	*enka*	Japanese popular songs
こおろぎ	*koorogi*	cricket (insect)

Unit 1 and 2

The *masu* form of each verb is followed by its dictionary form and its *te* form.

いって　も　いい　です　か	*itte mo ii desu ka*	May I go?
もちろん	*mochiron*	of course
おわります	*owarimasu*	finish
おわる	*owaru*	
おわって	*owatte*	
すぐ	*sugu*	soon
つかいます	*tsukaimasu*	use
つかう	*tsukau*	
つかって	*tsukatte*	
つまらない	*tsumaranai*	boring/worthless
りか	*rika*	science
しゅくだい	*shukudai*	homework
らいしゅう	*raishuu*	next week
いつ	*itsu*	when
たちます	*tachimasu*	stand
たつ	*tatsu*	
たって	*tatte*	
すわります	*suwarimasu*	sit
すわる	*suwaru*	
すわって	*suwatte*	
かいます	*kaimasu*	buy
かう	*kau*	
かって	*katte*	

よみます	*yomimasu*	read
よむ	*yomu*	
よんで	*yonde*	
だめ　です	*dame desu*	It's no good
だめ　な	*dame na*	no good (Q noun)
あと	*ato*	after
まえ	*mae*	before
なぜ	*naze*	why?
キャンプ　に　いきます	*KYANPU ni ikimasu*	go to camp
いなか	*inaka*	countryside
クラス	*KURASU*	class
どんな	*donna*	what kind of (Q noun)

Unit 3 (Part 1)

ばん	*ban*	evening/night
やすみ	*yasumi*	holiday/rest
らいねん	*rainen*	next year
しけん	*shiken*	examination
ことし	*kotoshi*	this year
かいしゃ	*kaisha*	company/business
なつ	*natsu*	summer
たいせつ　な	*taisetsu na*	important (Q noun)
ひつよう　な	*hitsuyoo na*	necessary (Q noun)

(Part 2)

まいつき	*maitsuki*	every month
に　ききます	*ni kikimasu*	ask
に　きく	*ni kiku*	
に　きいて	*ni kiite*	
ほんとう　に	*hontoo ni*	truly/really/honestly
つかれます	*tsukaremasu*	be tired
つかれる	*tsukareru*	
つかれて	*tsukarete*	
からだ	*karada*	health/body
どの　ぐらい　です　か	*dono gurai desu ka*	How far/how long/ how much is it?
うんどう	*undoo*	exercise
ごご	*gogo*	afternoon/p.m.
さんぽ	*sanpo*	a walk
しつもん	*shitsumon*	question

Unit 4

しゅみ	*shumi*	hobby
もちます	*mochimasu*	have/hold
もつ	*motsu*	
もって	*motte*	
ペット　を　かって　います	*PETTO o katte imasu*	keep a pet
つくります	*tsukurimasu*	make
つくる	*tsukuru*	
つくって	*tsukutte*	
あまり　あんまり	*amari/anmari*	not very/not many/ not much

いけばな	ikebana	flower arranging
つり を します	tsuri o shimasu	to fish
りょうり を します	ryoori o shimasu	do cooking

Interest

どくしょ	dokusho	reading
コンピューター ゲーム	KONPYUUTAA GEEMU	computer games
たこ	tako	kite
プラモデル	PURAMODERU	plastic models
だけ	dake	only
あつめます	atsumemasu	collect
あつめる	atsumeru	
あつめて	atsumete	
きって	kitte	postage stamps
など	nado	etcetera

Unit 5

ひ	hi	day/sun
ひまな	hima (na)	free time
ステレオ	SUTEREO	stereo
むずかしい	muzukashii	difficult
おそい	osoi	late/slow
はやい	hayai	early/fast
おそく	osoku	adverbial form of osoi
はやく	hayaku	adverbial form of hayai
ねん	nen	year
ごねんかん	gonenkan	five years' time/ for five years
ピクニック を します	PIKUNIKKU o shimasu	have a picnic
すこし	sukoshi	a little/a bit
にじ まで に	niji made ni	by two o'clock
わかりました	wakarimashita!	I know!

Interest

ちょうちょう	choochoo	butterfly
コンサート	KONSAATO	concert
すばらしい	subarashii	wonderful

Unit 6

いきたい です	ikitai desu	want to go
したい です	shitai desu	want to do/have
そして	soshite	and then

Interest

| かんがえ | kangae | idea |
| おべんとう | Obentoo | packed lunch |

Unit 7

| できます | dekimasu | able to do/can do |
| できる | dekiru | |

ならいます	naraimasu	learn
ならう	narau	
ならって	naratte	

Unit 8

ポピュラー おんがく	POPYURAA ongaku	pop music
ポップ	POPPU	pop music
クラシック おんがく	KURASHIKKU ongaku	classical music
おんがく	ongaku	music
ひきます	hikimasu	pluck/play a stringed instrument
ひく	hiku	
ひいて	hiite	
うた	uta	song
おしえます	oshiemasu	teach/show how to do something
おしえる	oshieru	
おしえて	oshiete	
うたいます	utaimasu	sing
うたう	utau	
うたって	utatte	

Interest

きみ	kimi	you (used only by males)
ふきます	fukimasu	blow (play flute, etc)
ふく	fuku	
ふいて	fuite	

Unit 9

やまのぼり	yamanobori	mountain climbing
のぼります	noborimasu	climb
のぼる	noboru	
のぼって	nobotte	
まだ です	mada desu	not yet
もう	moo	already/more
まえ に	mae ni	before this

Interest

| あぶない | abunai | dangerous |

Unit 10

せいふく	seifuku	uniform
ブラウス	BURAUSU	blouse
ティーシャツ	TII-SHATSU	T-shirt
セーター	SEETAA	sweater/jumper
シャツ	SHATSU	shirt
きます	kimasu	wear on upper half of body
きる	kiru	
きて	kite	

きもの	*kimono*	Japanese national dress
ワイシャツ	*WAISHATSU*	white shirt/business shirt
コート	*KOOTO*	coat

Interest

ジャケット	*JAKETTO*	jacket
ドレス	*DORESU*	dress
ゆかた	*yukata*	cotton kimono

Unit 11

はきます	*hakimasu*	wear on feet and legs
はく	*haku*	
はいて	*haite*	
くろい	*kuroi*	black (adj)
くつ	*kutsu*	shoes
スカート	*SUKAATO*	skirt
ピンク の	*PINKU no*	pink
みどり いろ の	*midori iro no*	green
ズボン	*ZUBON*	trousers
はんズボン	*hanZUBON*	short trousers/shorts

Interest

ジーンズ	*JIINZU*	jeans
ショーツ	*SHOOTSU*	shorts
もも いろ の	*momo iro no*	peach pink
ねずみ いろ の	*nezumi iro no*	grey
むらさき いろ の	*murasaki iro no*	purple
だいだい いろ の	*daidai iro no*	orange
ちゃ いろ の	*chairo no*	brown

Unit 12

| ネクタイ | *NEKUTAI* | (neck) tie |

Interest

ベルト	*BERUTO*	belt
イヤリング	*IYARINGU*	earrings
ぼうし	*booshi*	cap/hat
スカーフ	*SUKAAFU*	scarf
かぶります	*kaburimasu*	wear on the head
かぶる	*kaburu*	
かぶって	*kabutte*	
めがね を かけます	*megane o kakemasu*	wear glasses
かける	*kakeru*	
かけて	*kakete*	

Unit 13 (Part 1)

| しります | *shirimasu* | know |
| しる | *shiru* | |

しって	*shitte*	
こたえます	*kotaemasu*	answer
こたえる	*kotaeru*	
こたえて	*kotaete*	

Interest

でんわ　ばんごう	*denwa bangoo*	telephone number
もしもし	*moshimoshi*	Hello (on phone only)

Unit 13 (Part 2)

なおります	*naorimasu*	heal/get better
なおる	*naoru*	
もって　いきます	*motte ikimasu*	take
もって　いく	*motte iku*	
もって　いって	*motte itte*	
にきび	*nikibi*	pimple

TOPIC FOURTEEN
travel

Introduction

ACHIEVEMENTS

By the end of this topic you will be able to:
- Talk about a trip you are going to make or have made.
- Describe where you go and the things you do there.
- Describe how you go.
- Talk about what you like to do during holidays.
- Learn the rest of the *katakana* combined sounds.

Topic Fourteen begins the story of a young student, Mandy, who visits Japan on a scholarship to improve her Japanese and lives with a family in Shibuya (Tokyo). She has been doing well at school and is considered a good student but has only learned a little about life in Japan. Her teacher has been most careful to tell her how to behave in a Japanese home so she doesn't offend, but has not had time to prepare her fully. She gets a few surprises! (Later she will have the chance to visit other parts of the country on a special tour.)

It is suggested that the passages in this topic be used each time for listening comprehension as a continuing story of Mandy's experiences in Japan. Students will be listening for a general understanding of the passage. Reading the passages in pairs or alone after the listening will consolidate the understanding.

Topic Fourteen consolidates structures and vocabulary learned earlier in the course, refreshes your memory and helps you to feel more confident. There are no new structures, which will enable you to spend time on learning and reviewing vocabulary, and using and understanding the Japanese you know.

Travel

The traveler who goes to Japan with a sense of adventure and a real curiosity about Japanese life, places and customs will have enviable experiences that will deepen his or her own awareness of life and provide much food for thought.

If you have studied Japanese, you'll have the pleasure of being able to communicate with Japanese people, and your confidence will be boosted by being able to find your way around unaided, and by knowing that you understand a little more about the life of the country than ordinary tourists.

You may not like or agree with all that you see. But everything that you see and think about has value in helping you to evaluate your life in comparison with other people's lives. Is the surface the truth? What lies behind the lives of the people? What sacrifices do individuals have to make towards the smooth running of the lives of the majority?

If you are an "armchair traveler," gaining your impressions of the country from books, films and photographs, you will still be enriched by the information you are accumulating. It will color your thinking and be valuable in helping you in your own life. Use your library. The more you find out about the country, the more fascinated you will become as the strands of knowledge start to weave themselves into a more complex appreciation. If you then have the opportunity to visit, the pleasure you will obtain from the experience will be great, because your background knowledge and understanding will direct you towards sights, sounds, and experiences that will truly come alive for you.

Arriving in Japan

When passengers arrive at Narita (Tokyo's International Airport), signs direct them towards passport control and luggage collection in English as well as Japanese.

At passport control, there are many control booths for returning Japanese but only two or three for visitors. These used to be labeled "Aliens" until the Japanese realized that "Foreign passports" might be more appropriate!

Passengers line up to present their passports and immigration forms, which have been filled in on the plane. Once these have been inspected carefully, part of the immigration form is torn off and stapled to the inside of the passport. It must be left there or passengers will have complications when they try to leave the country.

Downstairs from passport control are the luggage carousels and carts. After picking up their luggage, passengers proceed to customs officers, who want to know if they are carrying alcohol, tobacco or prohibited items. These officers are able to ask their questions in English and are always very helpful to visitors – especially to those who tell the truth! They are not worried about the small presents vacationing passengers may be carrying for homestay families or friends in Japan. They are more careful with people who are staying in Japan for long periods.

From the customs control to the exit is only a few yards. Passengers walk through exit doors displaying the **Deguchi** (exit) sign. (The *kanji* for *deguchi* and *iriguchi* [entrance] are shown.) They are confronted by a crowd of people waiting to meet friends, some holding up signs with names or messages of welcome. Passengers are now in the main pedestrian thoroughfare of the airport, from which they can take buses to local places, and Tokyo. There are counters in this hall where English is spoken, at which tickets can be bought and information sought about hotels, transportation and general needs, money changed, food bought, and luggage lockers found. If people choose to eat at the airport or have to wait for someone to meet them, the coin operated luggage lockers (*KOIN ROKKA*) leave them free to wander around unhampered.

出口
でぐち

入口
いりぐち

Some domestic flights leave from this same hallway at Narita, but most depart from Haneda airport, which is about an hour's travel across the city.

When travelers return home, they will leave from Narita, having remembered to save the appropriate amount in yen for their departure tax.

When entering or exiting the airport area, visitors will be surprised by the security measures in place. When the airport was built over twenty years ago, local farmers, in what was then a small farming community, had to give up their land to make way for the airport. They were extremely angry about giving up the land and about the level of compensation that they were offered. It meant the loss of a way of life as well as the loss of their land. Most had to change from farming to other activities, maybe moving to another part of the country to find work and homes they could afford. It disrupted their families' lives and most importantly took them away from their ancestral areas in many cases.

Through the years since the airport was built, they have never given up their protests. Travelers leaving the airport, therefore, still have to pass through complex security screens where armed security men are on alert twenty-four hours a day in case the farmers protest again. The government of the time may have been better advised to pay very large compensation to the farmers! Now the security checks have become part of the normal airport security system.

Vehicles entering the airport area are very carefully searched. Though tourist buses receive less attention, passports are checked and security police inspect the interior of the bus before permission is given to enter the airport.

Once past the security checks, all the excitement, fascination and difference of Japan awaits you. In this topic you will be introduced to a taste of traveling in Japan.

Immigration lounge (left)
Information counter (right)

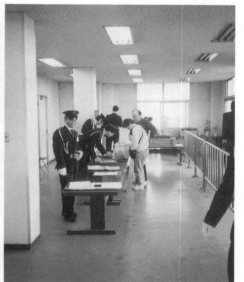

Passport check (top left)
Airport security officer (top right)
In the customs lounge (center left)
Main concourse – ticket counter
(lower left)
Departure security check (lower
right)

Unit 1

マンディーさんは にほんに つきます
MANDII san wa Nihon ni tsukimasu
Mandy arrives in Japan

NEW WORDS

(Note: from Topic Fourteen onwards, in the *kana* text particles are linked to the preceding words. However, in the word lists they are still separated for clarity and ease of understanding.)

くうこう	*kuukoo*	airport
しんぱい します する	*shinpai shimasu (suru)*	to be worried/anxious
しんぱい して	*shinpai shite*	*te* form of above
しゃしん	*shashin*	photo
たいへん です ね	*taihen desu ne*	may also mean "It's serious, isn't it?"
おきます おく	*okimasu (oku)*	put
おいて	*oite*	*te* form of *okimasu*
にもつ	*nimotsu*	luggage
おもい	*omoi*	heavy (adj)
おもかった です	*omokatta desu*	was heavy
どう です か	*. . . doo desu ka*	how about/what do you think about . . . ?
たかい ビル	*takai BIRU*	tall buildings
いりぐち	*iriguchi*	entrance
でぐち	*deguchi*	exit

Interest

パスポート	*PASUPOOTO*	passport
サイン	*SAIN*	sign
ターンテーブル	*TAANTEEBURU*	luggage carousel
コントロール	*KONTOROORU*	control
トローリー	*TOROORII*	trolley, cart
ふつう	*futsuu*	ordinary/usual

Close your book and listen to the story of Mandy's arrival in Japan. Concentrate to understand as much as possible from the reading. Then open your book and read it on your own. When you come to a word you don't know, don't stop, don't look at the word list, just read on and see what you can gather. (In a real situation people will often use words you don't know, and you have to try to get the message without turning to a dictionary.)

あさ　はやく　マンディー　さんは　なりた　くうこうに　つきました。
ひとが　たくさん　いました。パスポート　の　ひとに　パスポートを
みせました。
その　ひとは　マンディーさんの　かお　を　よく　みました。
そして　マンディーさんの　しゃしん　を　よく　みました。
たいへん　ですね。
あとで　にもつの　ターンテーブルに　いって　じゅっぷん　ぐらい
まって　いました。
そして　その　にもつを　みました。にもつは　おもかった　ですから
トローリーの　うえに　おきました。
コントロールの　あとで　でぐちに　あるきました。
しんぱい　して　いました。

Asa hayaku MANDII san wa Narita kuukoo ni tsukimashita. Hito ga takusan imashita. PASUPOOTO no hito ni PASUPOOTO o misemashita.
Sono hito wa MANDII san no kao o yoku mimashita. Soshite MANDII san no shashin o yoku mimashita.
Taihen desu ne.
Ato de nimotsu no TAANTEEBURU ni itte, juppun gurai matte imashita.
Soshite sono nimotsu o mimashita. Nimotsu wa omokatta desu kara TOROORII no ue ni okimashita.
KONTOROORU no ato de deguchi ni arukimashita. Shinpai shite imashita.

Work with a partner. Tell your partner what you understood – and see if your opinions differ.

STUDY

- ***Okimasu*** is a new verb. It sounds the same, and in *hiragana* looks the same, as **okimasu** (get up) but means "put." Learn it carefully and re-member that each time you see *okimasu* you'll have to decide which verb it is according to the context.

  The **te** forms are different because the dictionary forms are different:
  oku okimasu **oite** put
  okiru okimasu **okite** get up/wake up
  Learn them carefully, too.

- Learn the following two phrases and get used to using them in your role plays and stories.
  asa hayaku is a phrase to learn for "early in the morning."
  yoru osoku means "late at night/late in the evening."

- Look at the position of **takusan** and **juppun gurai** in the passage. Be-cause they refer to numbers or quantities, they are placed before the verb.

- **Ni** is used in the passage to say "to" someone or "to" a place, e.g., *Hito ni misemashita . . . TAANTEEBURU ni itte.*
  Make some sentences together using different verbs, which will give you practice with these.

- Remember to use **de** particle when you talk about doing an activity in a particular place.

ACTIVITIES
- Role Play

  Imagine that you have just arrived at an airport early in the morning and are waiting in a line to complete the formalities: Decide what time you left home yesterday. Find out who has had the longest journey. Go around the room asking each other *Kinoo no nanji ni uchi o demashita ka*, to find your positions in the line, from earliest start to latest.

  When everyone is in position, call out your start time one after the other and, if necessary, adjust your place in the line. You will then be in a line ready for the next activity.

- Role play in pairs. Stand in a long line chatting, and in turn, hand your papers to a "passport control officer," then move towards the exit, where each couple in turn say goodbye to each other and look for the people who are meeting them. Appoint a passport control officer or two.

  Here is a sample conversation. Read it through, then use it as a base for your own role play.

  1 *Ohayoo gozaimasu. Hayai desu ne. Doko no kata desu ka.*
  2 *OOSUTORARIAjin desu. Anata wa?*
  1 *AMERIKAjin desu.*
  2 *Soo desu ka. Yasumi desu ka.*
  1 *Iie, Nihon no gakkoo de benkyoo shimasu. Tookyoo ni ikimasu. Anata wa?*
  2 *Yasumi desu. Kyooto to Hiroshima ni ikimasu.*
  1 *Watashi mo Hiroshima ni ikimasu.*
  2 *Soo desu ka. Hiroshima wa omoshiroi deshoo ne.*
  1 *Hai. Itsu Hiroshima ni ikimasu ka.*
  2 *Raishuu ikimasu.* (Passport is handed over to passport officer) *Doozo.*
  Passport officer looks at it carefully and asks:
  P *Nihon de benkyoo shimasu ka.*
  2 *Hai soo desu.*
  (The passport is stamped and handed back.)
  Arigatoo.
  (Second passenger goes through passport control. They say goodbye.)

  You will be able to make some excellent relevant conversations using your imagination and your store of Japanese.

- Write a conversation for others to role play similar to the sample above, and enjoy watching them act it out.

- Explain each photo on p. 242 and 243 to a partner or explain the route from the plane to the exit using the photos as a guide.

- Pairwork. Imagine that one of you has just arrived from Japan and is being questioned by a friend who has not yet been there, on what the airport procedures are. Make the conversation more natural by asking questions like *Shinpai shimashita ka. Nimotsu wa omokatta desu ka*, etc.

- Write the story of your arrival at Narita (five to ten sentences). Say when you arrived, what you had to do, what happened, where you were going, who was meeting you, etc. (Write it in the present, past or future – your choice.)

- Let's start discussing things in Japanese. At this time your discussion may be limited and hampered by lack of vocabulary, but please confine yourself to words you've learned in the course. This way, others will understand, and you will get more practice with essential words.

  You will gradually improve your discussion skills in activities like the ones that follow, which are tightly guided.

  Work in groups of three or four people. (Any other comments in Japanese should also be recorded if you think of more to say on the subject.) Report to the other groups.

  Photocopy the box below. One copy for each group is required. Each person's response (which will of course be a complete sentence!) should be recorded with a check, word, or phrase. Take turns to ask the questions. When finished, report your information to the group. Count the replies with *hitori, futari, sannin*, etc.

Ryokoo Travel

Yoku ryokoo o shimasu ka.	Hai Iie
Ryokoo ga suki desu ka.	Hai Iie
Doko e ryokoo o shimashita ka.	Kuni (Country):
Kotoshi ryokoo o shimashita ka.	Hai Iie
Kyonen ryokoo o shimashita ka.	Hai Iie
Nani o shinpai shimashita ka.	?
Nani ga muzukashikatta desu ka.	?
Nimotsu wa doo deshita ka.	Omokatta desu.
	Karukatta desu. (was light)
	Ookikatta desu.
Takusan arimashita ka.	Hai Iie
PASUPOOTO no hito wa doo deshita ka.	Taisetsu na hito deshita.
	Warui hito deshita.
	Ii hito deshita.
	Omoshiroi hito deshita.
Nihon ni ikimashita ka.	Hai Iie

Check your understanding

A

How would you say the following in Japanese?

1   Put the book on top of the desk, please.
2   Put your shoes over there, please.
3   I won't put my shoes in the living room.
4   Where did you put the umbrella?
5   I put it beside your bed.
6   I got up early in the morning.
7   I went to bed late.
8   How long did you wait?
9   I waited five minutes.
10 He left early in the evening.
11 The magazine is in the living room.
12 James is in the kitchen.
13 How was yesterday's party?
14 What did you think of the movie?

Did you remember to use *imasu* and *arimasu* in the correct places?
Did you remember when to use *ni* and when to use *de*?
Did you remember that some sentences would not have particles at all?

B

Match the English sentences in **A** with their Japanese equivalents below.

a   *Anata no BEDDO no soba ni okimashita.*
b   *Dono gurai machimashita ka.*
c   *Yoru hayaku demashita.*
d   *Anata no kutsu o soko ni oite kudasai.*
e   *Kinoo no PAATII wa doo deshita ka.*
f   *Kasa wa doko ni okimashita ka.*
g   *Eiga wa doo deshita ka.*
h   *Ima no naka ni wa watashi no kutsu o okimasen.*
i   *JEMUSU san wa daidokoro ni imasu.*
j   *Asa hayaku okimashita.*
k   *Hon wa tsukue no ue ni oite kudasai.*
l   *Osoku nemashita.*
m   *Gofun machimashita.*
n   *Zasshi wa ima ni arimasu.*

Writing practice

- Review **HO** ホ
          BO ボ
          PO ポ

  Remember that in *katakana* you double consonants with a half-size
  TSU: ッ
  You double vowels with a long bar: —

- Practice writing the following words. Next, sketch some of them and label
  them in Japanese.

トローリー	*TOROORII*
ターンテーブル	*TAANTEEBURU*
パスポート	*PASUPOOTO*
パスポート　コントロール	*PASUPOOTO KONTOROORU*
パスポート　の　ひと	*PASUPOOTO no hito*
でぐち　の　サイン	*Deguchi no SAIN*

Unit 2

じゅんじさんは そこに いますか
Junji san wa soko ni imasu ka
Will Junji be there?

Mandy, pushing her luggage trolley, walks through the exit doors. *Hon o tojite kudasai. Hanashi o yoku kiite kudasai.* (Close your book and listen carefully to the story.) Then listen to the questions that follow each section. (The story is presented in four sections.) Check that your understanding was correct by answering the questions on p. 251 and 252. After that, look up any words you were not sure about.

   Later you may like to follow up by writing the answers to the questions.

でぐち　の　そとで　ひとが　たくさん　まっていました。
にほんじんは　たくさん　いました……だれが　じゅんじさん　でしょうか。
はじめに　マンディーさんは　じゅんじさんが　みえませんでした。
むずかしかった　です。じゅんじさんは　どこに　いましたか。
マンディーさんは　ちょっと　しんぱいしました。

しつもん
1　でぐちの　そとで　だれが　まっていましたか。
2　ひとは　どこの　かた　でしたか。
3　はじめに　マンディーさんは　じゅんじさんが　みえましたか。
4　マンディーさんは　しんぱいしましたか。

Deguchi no soto de hito ga takusan matte imashita.
Nihonjin wa takusan imashita . . . Dare ga Junji san deshoo ka.
Hajime ni MANDII san wa Junji san ga miemasen deshita.
Muzukashikatta desu. Junji san wa doko ni imashita ka.
MANDII san wa chotto shinpai shimashita.

Shitsumon (Questions)
1　*Deguchi no soto de dare ga matte imashita ka.*
2　*Hito wa doko no kata deshita ka.*
3　*Hajime ni MANDII san wa Junji san ga miemashita ka.*
4　*MANDII san wa shinpai shimashita ka.*

（また　きいて　ください。）
いっぷん　あとで　マンディーさんは　じゅんじさんを　みました。
おおきい　かみを　うえに　もっていました。かみ　のうえに
"MANDY"　が　みえました。
マンディーさんは　あんしんしました。じゅんじさんは　まっていました。
マンディーさんは　じゅんじさん　の　かおを　みました。ハンサムな
おとこの　こ　です。

しつもん
1　マンディーさんは　じゅんじさんを　みましたか。
2　じゅんじさんは　なにを　しましたか。
3　かみの　うえに　なにが　ありましたか。
4　マンディーさんは　しんぱいしましたか　あんしんしましたか。

(Mata kiite kudasai)
Ippun ato de MANDII san wa Junji san o mimashita. Ookii kami o ue ni motte imashita. Kami no ue ni "MANDY" ga miemashita.
MANDII san wa anshin shimashita. Junji san wa matte imashita!
MANDII san wa Junji san no kao o mimashita. HANSAMU na otoko no ko desu! . . .

Shitsumon (Questions)
1　*MANDII san wa Junji san o mimashita ka.*
2　*Junji san wa nani o shimashita ka.*
3　*Kami no ue ni nani ga arimashita ka.*
4　*MANDII san wa shinpai shimashita ka anshin shimashita ka.*

（また　きいて　ください。）
　　　　じゅんじさんは　おじぎを　しました。「マンディーさん　ですか。」
マ　　「はい、わたしは　マンディー　です。」
じゅ　「はじめまして、わたしは　じゅんじ　です。あなたの　にもつ
　　　　ですか。」
マ　　「はい、そう　です。……すみません。……おもい　です。」
じゅ　「だいじょうぶ　です。こちらへ　どうぞ。……
　　　　ちちと　はは　は　くるまで　まって　います。」

しつもん
1　じゅんじさんは　はじめに　なにを　しましたか。
2　にもつは　おもかった　ですか。
3　おかあさん　と　おとうさんは　どこに　いましたか。

(Mata kiite kudasai)
Junji san wa Ojigi o shimashita. "MANDII san desu ka . . ."
M:　*Hai, watashi wa MANDII desu.*
J:　*Hajimemashite . . . watashi wa Junji desu.*
　　Anata no nimotsu desu ka.
M:　*Hai, soo desu . . . Sumimasen . . . omoi desu.*
J:　*Daijoobu desu. Kochira e doozo . . . chichi to haha wa kuruma de matte imasu.*

Shitsumon (Questions)
1　*Junji san wa hajime ni nani o shimashita ka.*
2　*Nimotsu wa omokatta desu ka.*
3　*Okaasan to otoosan wa doko ni imashita ka.*

Hon o akete kudasai.
How much did you understand?
1　Why was Mandy a bit worried when she went out the exit doors?

2   Who was supposed to meet her?
3   Who did meet her?
4   How did she know which person had come to meet her?
5   What did he do before speaking?
6   What were Mandy's first impressions of Junji?
7   Where were his parents?

Exit from the main concourse (left)
Main concourse in the North Wing at Narita (right)

ACTIVITIES

- Role play the situation in the passage, using your own ideas. Show your role plays to the class.

- Write a similar meeting conversation of your own. Give a little bit of general information telling where you are and when the action is taking place (in Japanese), and then launch into the conversation.

- In small groups, discuss meetings at airports in Japanese. Write down the general consensus of opinion in Japanese and report to the class after ten minutes.

    Here are the questions to ask each other:
Kuukoo ga suki desu ka.
Kuukoo ni itte, shinpai shimasu ka.
Aisatsu (greetings) *wa muzukashii desu ka.*
Itsu aisatsu wa muzukashii desu ka.
Nimotsu wa doo desu ka.

Unit 3

マンディーさんは　とうきょうに
いきます
MANDII san wa Tookyoo ni ikimasu
Mandy goes to Tokyo

NEW WORDS

いそがしい	*isogashii*	busy (adj)
うるさい	*urusai*	noisy (adj)
かんこうバス	*kankoo BASU*	tourist bus
こみます　こむ	*komimasu (komu)*	be crowded
こんで　います	*konde imasu*	*te* form of *komimasu*
こんで　いました	*konde imashita*	was crowded
こうそくどうろ	*koosokudooro*	freeway/expressway

Review
べんり　な	*benri (na)*	convenient
つぎ	*tsugi*	next
こたえ	*kotae*	answer

Interest
かべ	*kabe*	wall
やね	*yane*	roof
だけ	*dake*	only
わたります　わたる	*watarimasu (wataru)*	cross over
わたって	*watatte*	*te* form of *watarimasu*
トラック	*TORAKKU*	truck
しぶや	*Shibuya*	district of Tokyo
カーテン	*KAATEN*	curtain
シート　カバー	*SHIITO KABAA*	seat cover
とじます　とじる	*tojimasu (tojiru)*	shut, close (books)
とじて	*tojite*	*te* form of *tojimasu*

(Junji makes his way through the crowds of people waiting for buses, with Mandy following behind.)

（ほん　を　とじて　ください。
はなし　を　きいて　ください。）

マンディーさんは　じゅんじさんと　いっしょに　くうこうを　でました。
くうこうの　そとで　じゅんじさんの　おとうさん　と　おかあさんは
くるまの　なかで　まっていました。じゅんじさんは　にもつを　もって、

みちを　わたりました。かんこうバス　と　ふつうの　バスが　たくさん
ありました。うるさかった　です。

こたえて　ください：
1　おかあさん　と　おとうさんは　どこで　まっていましたか。
2　だれが　にもつを　もっていましたか。

(Hon o tojite kudasai.
Hanashi o kiite kudasai.)

MANDII san wa Junji san to issho ni kuukoo o demashita.
Kuukoo no soto de Junji san no otoosan to okaasan wa kuruma no naka de
matte imashita. Junji san wa nimotsu o motte, michi o watarimashita.
Kankoo BASU to futsuu no BASU ga takusan arimashita. Urusakatta desu.

(Kotaete kudasai.)
1　*Okaasan to otoosan wa doko de matte imashita ka.*
2　*Dare ga nimotsu o motte imashita ka.*

**Leaving the airport
(left)
Limousine Bus to
Tokyo (right)**

（また　きいて　ください。）

おとうさん　と　おかあさんは　くるまの　なかで　すわって　いました。
マンディーさんに　あいました。そして　くるまで　とうきょうの　しぶや
に　いきました。こうそくどうろは　おもしろかった　です。
こうそくどうろは　うるさい　です　から　たかい　かべが　みちの
そばに　ありました。こうそくどうろ　から　あまり　みえません
でした。ときどき　かべ　だけ　みえました。ときどき　うちの　やね
だけ　みえました。あおい　やねが　たくさん　ありました。
いなかは　あまり　ありません。ときどき　たかい　ビルが　みえました。
その　たかい　ビルの　うえに　かんじと　カタカナの　サインが
ありました。マンディーさんは　その　カタカナの　サインを　よみました
が　かんじの　サインは　むずかしかった　です。ときどき　Tolls　が
ありました。

しつもん
1　おかあさんと　おとうさんは　どこで　まっていましたか。
2　しぶやには　なんで　いきましたか。
3　かべは　どこに　ありましたか。
4　こうそくどうろ　から　なにが　みえましたか。
5　やねは　なに　いろ　でしたか。
6　いなかが　ありましたか。
7　ビルの　うえに　なにが　ありましたか。
8　マンディーさんは　カタカナの　サインを　よみましたか。
9　かんじの　サインは　どう　でしたか。

(Mata kiite kudasai)
Otoosan to okaasan wa kuruma no naka de suwatte imashita. MANDII san ni aimashita. Soshite kuruma de Tookyoo no Shibuya ni ikimashita.
Koosokudooro wa omoshirokatta desu. Koosokudooro wa urusai desu kara takai kabe ga michi no soba ni arimashita.
Koosokudooro kara amari miemasen deshita. Tokidoki kabe dake miemashita. Tokidoki uchi no yane dake miemashita. Aoi yane ga takusan arimashita. Inaka wa amari arimasen. Tokidoki takai BIRU ga miemashita. Sono takai BIRU no ue ni kanji to KATAKANA no SAIN ga arimashita.
MANDII san wa sono KATAKANA no SAIN o yomimashita ga kanji no SAIN wa muzukashikatta desu. Tokidoki "TOLLS" ga arimashita.

(Many expressways in Japan are privately owned and tolls have to be paid to use them.)

Shitsumon
1　*Okaasan to otoosan wa doko de matte imashita ka.*
2　*Shibuya ni wa nan de ikimashita ka.*
3　*Kabe wa doko ni arimashita ka.*
4　*Koosokudooro kara nani ga miemashita ka.*
5　*Yane wa nani iro deshita ka.*
6　*Inaka ga arimashita ka.*
7　*BIRU no ue ni nani ga arimashita ka.*
8　*MANDII san wa KATAKANA no SAIN o yomimashita ka.*
9　*Kanji no SAIN wa doo deshita ka.*

おかあさんは　ときどき　マンディーさんに　はなしましたが
マンディーさんは　わかりません　でした。おとうさんと
じゅんじさんは　はなしません　でした。
こうそくどうろの　ドライブは　たいへん　たかい　です。でも　べんり
です　から　たいへん　こんで　いました。くるまと　トラックは
たくさん　ありました。くるまは　ぜんぶ　あたらしかった　です。
くるまの　なかに　ときどき　カーテン　と　シート　カバー　が
ありました。おもしろかった　です。

しつもん
1　マンディーさんは　おかあさんの　はなし　が　わかりましたか。

2　こうそくどうろの　ドライブは　たかい　ですか　やすい　ですか。
3　こうそくどうろは　こんでいましたか。
4　くるまの　なかには　なにが　ありましたか。

Okaasan wa tokidoki MANDII san ni hanashimashita ga MANDII san wa wakarimasen deshita.
Otoosan to Junji san wa hanashimasen deshita.
Koosokudooro no DORAIBU wa taihen takai desu. Demo benri desu kara taihen konde imashita. Kuruma to TORAKKU wa takusan arimashita.
Kuruma wa zenbu atarashikatta desu. Kuruma no naka ni tokidoki KAATEN to SHIITO KABAA ga arimashita.
Omoshirokatta desu.

Shitsumon
1　*MANDII san wa Okaasan no hanashi ga wakarimashita ka.*
2　*Koosokudooro no DORAIBU wa takai desu ka yasui desu ka.*
3　*Koosokudooro wa konde imashita ka.*
4　*Kuruma no naka ni wa nani ga arimashita ka.*

（また　はなしを　きいて　ください。）
にじかんの　あとで　おおきい　かわを　みました。えどがわ　でした。
えどは　まえに　とうきょうの　なまえ　でした。マンディーさんは　めが
いそがしかった　です。いつも　まど　から　みていました。たくさん
みました。はなしませんでした。
なぜ　でしたか。
これは　マンディーさんの　こたえ　です。
「わたしの　にほんごが　へた　です　から　はなしませんでした。
つかれました。ちょっと　しんぱいしました。」

(Mata hanashi o kiite kudasai.)

On the expressway (left)
Toll gate (right)

Nijikan no ato de ookii kawa o mimashita. Edogawa deshita.
Edo wa mae ni Tookyoo no namae deshita. MANDII san wa me ga isogashikatta desu. Itsumo mado kara mite imashita. Takusan mimashita. Hanashimasen deshita.

Naze deshita ka.
Kore wa MANDII san no kotae desu:
"Watashi no nihongo ga heta desu kara hanashimasen deshita.
Tsukaremashita. Chotto shinpai shimashita."

(Hon o akete kudasai)

Car curtains and seat covers (top left)
View from the expressway (top right and lower)

Check your understanding

Answer as many of the questions as possible in Japanese, preferably in complete sentences. Use the passage to help you. At the end of each sentence it is suggested which language you should try to use – Japanese or English.

1   Where did Mandy meet the homestay parents? (J)
2   Explain to someone who doesn't know Japanese what you know about Japanese expressways and what you might see driving from the airport into Tokyo. (E)

3 Did she find it easy to communicate? (J)
4 How did she occupy herself in the car? (J)
5 How much did she speak on the way to Tokyo? (J)
6 Who spoke to her? (J)
7 Did she understand? (J)
8 What was Tokyo's name long ago? (J)
9 What was the traffic flow like? (J)
10 Why do you think it was difficult for all of them? (E)

STUDY

- During this unit it is suggested that you do a thorough review of the following:
  adjectives in the present and past tenses;
  the present and past tenses of qualitative nouns (*na* words);
  te forms and joining sentences with *te* forms;
  the use of position words and phrases.

  Brainstorm together all of the above, group by group, to bring them all back into productive use. If there are some you had forgotten or don't even remember seeing before, work out a plan to learn them thoroughly. Try consciously learning five a day until you know them all.

  Make sentences together to reinforce your understanding of the vocabulary, structures and particles.

- **Kuukoo o demashita.** Remember that the place you leave is the "thing" you're leaving and takes the particle **o**. This applies to getting off buses, trains, etc. Remember too that the point at which you change direction or the place you pass through is also marked with particle o, e.g.,
  Kado o magatte kudasai. "Please turn at the corner."

Make some sentences together for review. Use the places and verbs given. In front of that information, state a time or day. Vary the verb form that you use.
. . . *masu . . . mashita . . . te mo ii desu ka . . . te kudasai*
kooen toshokan gakkoo chuugakkoo kootoogakkoo
PUURU machi yama inaka eiga eki BASUnoriba
DEPAATO kado demasu magarimasu

ACTIVITIES

- In groups of four, role play the situation in the car when Mandy and the parents are introduced to each other for the first time. Ask polite questions about health and Mandy's journey (*Hikooki wa doo deshita ka*).

- Mandy wrote a postcard in Japanese to her classmates to tell them about her arrival. Write Mandy's card.
  Read your card to a partner or to the class. Display the cards on the wall for everyone to read.

- Have a discussion about traveling. It will of course be limited by the vocabulary and structures you have, but you may be surprised how much you can actually say. (Discuss in Japanese.)

The teacher may start it off by asking the class a question; e.g., *KANADA (MEKISHIKO/FURANSU*, etc.) *ni ikimashita ka.* (Distant town) *ni ikimashita ka.* Answers could range from "Yes" and "No" to comments on what you saw, ate, liked, disliked, where you went, what you saw or did that was the same as someone else's experience, or what was different.

It will probably amaze you how much genuine discussion takes place. Don't stop to discuss structures. This is communication time and understanding each other is your aim.

Listen to the comments made by others, and you can agree or disagree (remember particle **mo**) and ask further questions or give extra information.

STUDY TIPS

Don't worry if the questions don't flow very logically at this point. Do your best to keep it logical, but offering a contribution of some sort is more important at this point than strict logic or accuracy, so try to join in, no matter how briefly.

Remember the cardinal rule in discussion: everyone has the right to be heard and has something to contribute, and no one ever gets put down for what they say.

Learn to appreciate each other's effort, and realize how much everyone else is contributing to your own advancement in the language. When you start to recognize the mistakes that you and others make, you have really made progress.

Apart from it being the principle that you adhere to in your everyday lives, it is even more necessary when you are dealing with Japanese people to be tactful and a good listener. These discussion activities are intended to prepare you for the real situation, and in Japan politeness and kindness are essential.

Try to join in and say at least one thing, but if you just can't, don't get upset. Don't feel that "everyone else" can manage but you can't. It may just be that other people have said the only thing that came into your mind before you had a chance! Be a good listener, understand well what is going on, and next time make a real effort to become actively involved! If you manage to contribute one item this time, it will be easier next time.

You may like to take a few minutes to discuss the points above (in English!).

Unit 4

マンディーさんは じゅんじさんの うちに つきます
MANDII san wa Junji san no uchi ni tsukimasu
Mandy arrives at Junji's home

NEW WORDS

おります	おりる	orimasu (oriru)	get off/get out of
おりて		orite	te form of orimasu
ぬぎます	ぬぐ	nugimasu (nugu)	take off clothes/undress
ぬいで		nuide	te form of nugimasu
さきます	さく	sakimasu (saku)	bloom/blossom
さいて		saite	te form of sakimasu
ガレージ		GAREEJI	house garage

Interest

かいだん	kaidan	stairs/stairway
もん	mon	gate
いっかい	ikkai	first floor
にかい	nikai	second floor

（ほん を とじて ください。はなし を きいて ください。）

くじはんに じゅんじさんの うちに つきました。じゅんじさんは
しぶやに すんで、しぶやの こうとうがっこうで べんきょう しています。
はじめに じゅんじさんは くるまを おりました。もんを あけま
した。そして じゅんじさんは がっこうに はしって いきました。

しつもん
1 なんじに うちに つきましたか。
2 うちは どこ です か。
3 じゅんじさんの こうとうがっこうは どこ ですか。
4 じゅんじさんは なにを しました か。
5 じゅんじさんは どこに いきましたか。

(Hon o tojite kudasai. Hanashi o kiite kudasai.)

Kuji han ni Junji san no uchi ni tsukimashita. Junji san wa Shibuya ni sunde, Shibuya no kootoogakkoo de benkoo shite imasu. Hajime ni Junji san wa kuruma o orimashita. Mon o akemashita.
Soshite Junji san wa gakkoo ni hashitte ikimashita.

Shitsumon
1 *Nanji ni uchi ni tsukimashita ka.*
2 *Uchi wa doko desu ka.*
3 *Junji san no kootoogakkoo wa doko desu ka.*
4 *Junji san wa nani o shimashita ka.*
5 *Junji san wa doko ni ikimashita ka.*

（また　はなしを　きいて　ください。）

にかい　の　うち　でした。うちの　そとに　ちいさい　にわが　ありまし
た。にわには　あかい　はなが　さいていました。ちいさい　ガレージが
ありました。ドアは　ありませんでした。じゅんじさんの　おかあさんは
ドアを　あけて、うちに　はいりました。マンディーさんは　くるまを
おりました。かばんと　カメラを　もって　げんかんに　はいりました。
おかあさんを　みました。おかあさんは　くつを　ぬぎました。
スリッパを　はきました。
マンディーさんも　くつを　ぬぎました。そして　スリッパを　はきました。
おもしろかった　です。

（ほんを　あけて　ください。）

**View from the back of Junji's house (top
right)**
Genkan **(top center)**
Junji's house (top right)
**The light in Mandy's house may be turned off
by pulling the cord (lower left)**

(Mata hanashi o kiite kudasai.)

Nikai no uchi deshita. Uchi no soto ni chiisai niwa ga arimashita.
Niwa ni wa akai hana ga saite imashita. Chiisai GAREEJI ga arimashita. DOA wa arimasen deshita. Junji san no okaasan wa DOA o akete, uchi ni hairimashita. MANDII san wa kuruma o orimashita. Kaban to KAMERA o motte, genkan ni hairimashita. Okaasan o mimashita. Okaasan wa kutsu o nugimashita.
SURIPPA o hakimashita.
MANDII san mo kutsu o nugimashita, soshite SURIPPA o hakimashita.
Omoshirokatta desu!

(HON o akete kudasai.)

In pairs, take turns asking each other questions about the house and, of course, answer in Japanese. (Complete sentences if possible.) Make up your own or use the ones given below. Try not to use the passage, but if you can't remember, find the relevant sentence and work out your answer.

1   うちの　そとに　なにが　ありますか。
2   にわは　おおきい　ですか　ちいさい　ですか。
3   ガレージは　おおきい　ですか　ちいさい　ですか。
4   ガレージは　ドアが　ありますか。
5   マンディーさんは　なにを　もっていましたか。
6   みなさんは　げんかんで　なにを　しましたか。

1   *Uchi no soto ni nani ga arimasu ka.*
2   *Niwa wa ookii desu ka chiisai desu ka.*
3   *GAREEJI wa ookii desu ka chiisai desu ka.*
4   *GAREEJI wa DOA ga arimasu ka.*
5   *MANDII san wa, nani o motte imashita ka.*
6   *Minasan wa genkan de nani o shimashita ka.*

（ほんを　とじて　ください。
また　はなしを　きいて　ください。）

おかあさんは　マンディーさんと　にかいに　いきました。おかあさんは
スリッパを　ぬぎました。それから　マンディーさんは　スリッパを
ぬいで、へやの　そとに　おきました。おかあさんと　しんしつに　はい
りました。ちいさい　たたみの　へや　でした。ベッドは　ありません
でした！
しんしつの　なかには　ほんばこ　だけ　ありました。へん　でしたね！
マンディーさんは　ほんばこの　うえに　カメラを　おきました。
ほんばこの　そばに　かばんを　おきました。コートを　かばんの
うえに　おきました。それから　かいだんの　したに　いきました。
かいだんは　たいへん　せまかった　です。

(Hon o tojite kudasai.
Mata hanashi o kiite kudasai.)

Okaasan wa MANDII san to nikai ni ikimashita. Okaasan wa SURIPPA o nugimashita. Sorekara MANDII san wa SURIPPA o nuide, heya no soto ni okimashita. Okaasan to shinshitsu ni hairimashita.
Chiisai tatami no heya deshita. BEDDO wa arimasen deshita!
Shinshitsu no naka ni wa honbako dake arimashita. Hen deshita ne!
MANDII san wa honbako no ue ni KAMERA o okimashita. Honbako no soba ni kaban o okimashita. KOOTO o kaban no ue ni okimashita.
Sorekara kaidan no shita ni ikimashita. Kaidan wa taihen semakatta desu.

Write or say:
In your own words tell the story in English of what happened and what was surprising to Mandy.

STUDY

- Remember that you take the tense of a sentence from the tense of the final verb.

- Counting floors of a building starts in Japan with the ground floor being called the first floor. The counter **kai** is used and is simply *ikkai, nikai, sankai, yonkai*, etc. You will find it useful later when asking for the floors on which goods are sold in department stores.

ACTIVITY

Here is a plan of Junji's house and surroundings.

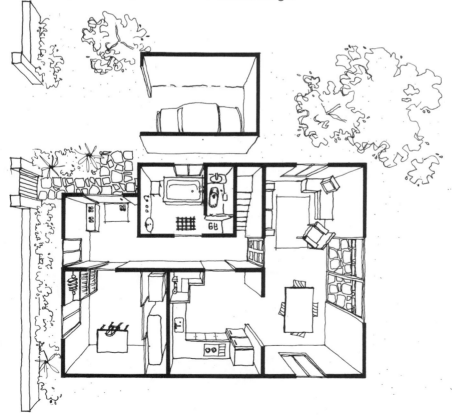
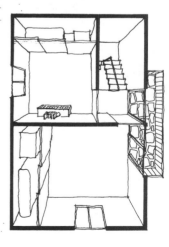

Mandy is very good at remembering to keep her friends and family in touch with what she is doing in Japan. She really appreciates having the opportunity to be there and feels very much like a Japanese in wanting to share her experiences with the people left at home. She also realizes that it is actually the little things that are often of most interest. She wants to share everything!

Mandy wrote a letter home to her Japanese teacher and class, to describe the house in which she is staying. Write Mandy's letter or make a tape recording.

Unit 5

おなかが すきましたか
Onaka ga sukimashita ka
Are you hungry?

NEW WORDS

ひくい	*hikui*	low (adj)(short in height)
ざぶとん	*zabuton*	cushions
ぜんぜん	*zenzen*	nothing at all
どこの へや です か	*doko no heya desu ka*	Which room is it?
どう します か	*doo shimasu ka*	How will it be?/ How will we get on/how will we manage?
いえ	*ie*	house
Interest		
そら	*sora*	sky
ニュース	*NYUUSU*	news
と いいました	*to iimashita*	he/she said (reported speech)
はたけ	*hatake*	vegetable garden/field

The story of Mandy's experiences continues. (Use this passage for listening or reading comprehension. For listening purposes it has been split into four sections. After listening to each section take turns with a partner, asking each other the questions.)

（ほんを とじて ください。はなしを きいて ください。）
マンディーさんは しんしつ から いまに いきました。いまには
ひくい テーブル と ざぶとんが ありました。まどの そばには
テレビが ありました。まど から はたけ（やさいの にわ）
と いえ が みえました。そらは ねずみいろ でした。

しつもん
1 マンディーさんは どこ から どこに いきましたか。
2 テレビは いまの どこに ありましたか。
3 まど から なにが みえましたか。
4 どんな おてんき でしたか。

(Hon o tojite kudasai.
Hanashi o kiite kudasai.)

MANDII san wa shinshitsu kara ima ni ikimashita. Ima ni wa hikui TEEBURU to zabuton ga arimashita. Mado no soba ni wa TEREBI ga arimashita. Mado kara hatake (yasai no niwa) to ie ga miemashita. Sora wa nezumi iro deshita.

Shitsumon
1   *MANDII san wa doko kara doko ni ikimashita ka.*
2   *TEREBI wa ima no doko ni arimashita ka.*
3   *Mado kara nani ga miemashita ka.*
4   *Donna Otenki deshita ka.*

（ほんを　とじて　ください。はなしを　きいて　ください。）

テレビで　ニュースを　みましたが　テレビの　ひとは　はやく
はなしました。マンディーさんは　ぜんぜん　わかりません　でした。
おてんきの　ニュースは　もっと　よかった　です。えが　ありました。
かさの　えは　あめ　でした！

（ほんを　あけて　ください。
しつもんに　こたえて　ください。）

1   マンディーさんは　テレビの　ニュースが　わかりましたか。
2   おてんきの　ニュースが　わかりましたか。
3   おてんきの　ニュースは　どんな　えが　ありましたか。

(Hon o tojite kudasai.
Hanashi o kiite kudasai.)

TEREBI de NYUUSU o mimashita ga TEREBI no hito wa hayaku hanashimashita. MANDII san wa zenzen wakarimasen deshita.
Otenki no NYUUSU wa motto yokatta desu. E ga arimashita!
Kasa no e wa ame deshita.

(Hon o akete kudasai.
Shitsumon ni kotaete kudasai.)

Shitsumon
1   *MANDII san wa TEREBI no NYUUSU ga wakarimashita ka.*
2   *Otenki no NYUUSU ga wakarimashita ka.*
3   *Otenki no NYUUSU wa donna e ga arimashita ka.*

（ほんを　とじて　ください。
はなしを　きいて　ください。）

おかあさんは　だいどころ　から　きました。
おかあさんは　「おなかが　すきましたか」　と　いいました。
マンディーさんは　わかりません　でした。おかあさんの　かおを
みました。おかあさんは　だいどころ　から　サンドイッチを　もって
きました。「どうぞ」　と　いいました。
マンディーさんは　わかりました！
「ありがとう」　と　いいました。

（ほんを　あけて　ください。
しつもんに　こたえて　ください。）

しつもん
1　おかあさんは　どこの　へや　から　きましたか。
2　おかあさんは　なん　と　いいましたか。
3　マンディーさんは　なにを　しましたか。
4　おかあさんは　だいどころ　から　なにを　もって　きましたか。

(Hon o tojite kudasai.
Hanashi o kiite kudasai.)

Okaasan wa daidokoro kara kimashita.
Okaasan wa "Onaka ga sukimashita ka" to iimashita.
MANDII san wa wakarimasen deshita. Okaasan no kao o mimashita.
Okaasan wa daidokoro kara SANDOITCHI o motte kimashita.
"Doozo" to iimashita.
MANDII san wa wakarimashita!
"Arigatoo" to iimashita.
(Hon o akete kudasai.
Shitsumon ni kotaete kudasai.)

Shitsumon
1　*Okaasan wa doko no heya kara kimashita ka.*
2　*Okaasan wa nan to iimashita ka.*
3　*MANDII san wa nani o shimashita ka.*
4　*Okaasan wa daidokoro kara nani o motte kimashita ka.*

Learn the phrase for "which room" *doko no heya (kara kimashita ka)*. It is not easy to follow a literal translation in English, so just accept it.

（また　きいて　ください。）

おかあさんと　ざぶとんに　すわって、サンドイッチを　たべました。
マンディーさんは　にほんご　は　わかりません　でした　から　ちょっと
しんぱいしました。
むずかしかった　です。
おかあさんも　ちょっと　しんぱいしました。マンディーさんは
おかあさんの　にほんごが　わかりません　でした。おかあさんは　えいごは
できません　でした。どう　します　か。

（ほんを　あけて、しつもんに　こたえて　ください。）

しつもん
1　おかあさんと　マンディーさんは　なにを　たべましたか。
2　おかあさんは　えいごが　できましたか。
3　マンディーさんは　にほんごが　じょうず　でしたか。

(Mata kiite kudasai.)

Okaasan to zabuton ni suwatte, SANDOITCHI o tabemashita.
MANDII san wa nihongo wa wakarimasen deshita kara chotto shinpai shimashita.
Muzukashikatta desu.
Okaasan mo chotto shinpai shimashita. MANDII san wa Okaasan no nihongo ga wakarimasen deshita. Okaasan wa eigo wa dekimasen deshita. Doo shimasu ka.

(Hon o akete, shitsumon ni kotaete kudasai.)

Shitsumon
1 *Okaasan to MANDII san wa nani o tabemashita ka.*
2 *Okaasan wa eigo ga dekimashita ka.*
3 *MANDII san wa nihongo ga joozu deshita ka.*

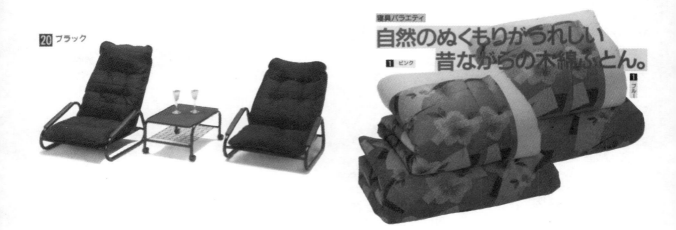

EXTENSION STUDY

- ### *to iimashita*

  The pattern for using *to iimashita* may be useful for you. The person who is speaking is usually put before what they say. It is the same principle, always used in Japanese, of directing your listener to what you are talking about before you give more information.

  e.g.: *Okaasan wa "Hai" to iimashita.* Mother said "Yes."
      MANDII san wa "Arigatoo gozaimasu" to iimashita. Mandy said "Thank you."

  Iimasu is a verb. Some people find it hard to remember its two *ii*'s and mix it up with *imasu*. To avoid that possibility just remember *to iimashita* as a phrase for "he/she/they said."

  Quotation marks in Japanese look like this: 「どうぞ」

  If the writing is being written downwards the marks are positioned like this:
  「
  ど
  う
  ぞ
  」

Check your understanding

Tell a partner in Japanese (take turns):
1   What Mandy did first.
2   What she watched.
3   What she understood and how.
4   What she could see from the window.
5   What the weather was like.
6   Where the mother was.
7   What the mother asked.
8   What Mandy's problem was.
9   How she solved her problem.
10 How the mother solved the problem.
11 Mandy's feeling and why.
12 The mother's feelings and why.
13 Where Junji was.

ACTIVITIES

• Role play the situation in threes.
  You are not allowed to read the story through again!
  Sections One and Two equal Scene One. (That's fair because there's less for the commentator to say in the first section!) Section Three is Scene Two, and Section Four is Scene Three.
     Students One and Two mime the action.
  (Mother only asks if Mandy is hungry and later says "Here you are." Mandy only answers "Thank you.")
     Student Three provides a running commentary. Each member of the group will become Student Three for one section of the story. It can be fun if the commentator really works to give a detailed commentary!
     Show your finished effort to the class. It will probably be amusing to see how different each group's version is as you comment on the actual action of your group. If you've ever played the game "Gossip," you'll know how stories can change without any intention of deviating from the original.

• Write the outline of the story in your own words.

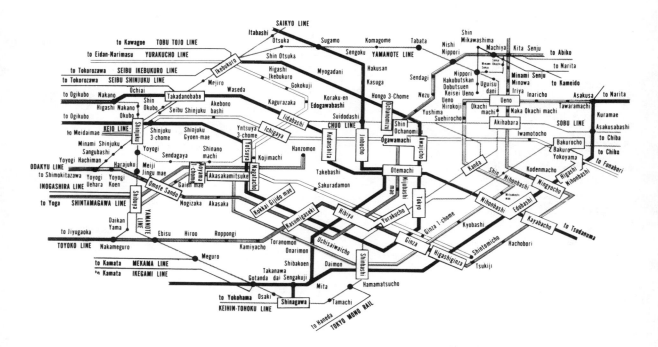

The railway and subway system in Tokyo

Unit 6

かいものを しましょうか
kaimono o shimashoo ka
Shall we do the shopping?

NEW WORDS

ひつよう な	*hitsuyoo na*	necessary
おぼえます　おぼえる	*oboemasu (oboeru)*	remember
おぼえて	*oboete*	*te* form of *oboemasu*
Interest		
さがします　さがす	*sagashimasu (sagasu)*	look for/seek
さがして	*sagashite*	*te* form of *sagashimasu*

The story continues. Read the story to yourself.

マンディーさんは　おかあさんと　サンドイッチを　たべました。あとで
おかあさんは　マンディーさんに　はなしました。
「かいものを　しましょうか」と　いいました。
マンディーさんは　わかりました！
「はい」と　いいました。
でも　おてあらい　が　ひつよう　でした。おてあらいは　どこ　でしたか。
かいものの　まえに　ひつよう　でしたが　おかあさんに
ききたくなかった　です。
おかあさんは　いまを　でました。
マンディーさんは　たって、おてあらいを　さがしに　いきました。
だいどころの　となり　でした。よかった　ですね！
にほんの　おてあらい　でした。ちょっと　むずかしかった　です　が
おもしろかった　です。マンディーさんは　おばえて　いました。
いまの　スリッパを　ぬぎます。おてあらいの　スリッパを　はきます。
それから……
スリッパを　ぬいで、ドアを　あけて、おてあらいの　スリッパを
はいて、おてあらいに　はいりました。おてあらいの　うえで
てを　あらいました。そして　マンディーさんは　おてあらいを　でて、
おてあらいの　スリッパを　ぬいで、いまの　スリッパを　はいて、
げんかんに　いきました。
げんかんで　スリッパを　ぬいで、くつを　はきました。
おかあさんと　いっしょに　かさを　もって、かいものに　いきました。

*MANDII san wa Okaasan to SANDOITCHI o tabemashita. Ato de Okaasan wa
MANDII san ni hanashimashita.*
"Kaimono o shimashoo ka" to iimashita.
MANDII san wa wakarimashita! "Hai" to iimashita!
Demo Otearai ga hitsuyoo deshita. Otearai wa doko deshita ka. Kaimono

no mae ni hitsuyoo deshita ga Okaasan ni kikitakunakatta desu. Okaasan wa ima o demashita.
MANDII san wa tatte, Otearai o sagashi ni ikimashita.
Daidokoro no tonari deshita. Yokatta desu ne!

Nihon no Otearai deshita! Chotto muzukashikatta desu ga omoshirokatta desu. MANDII san wa oboete imashita.
Ima no SURIPPA o nugimasu. Otearai no SURIPPA o hakimasu. Sorekara SURIPPA o nuide, DOA o akete, Otearai no SURIPPA o haite, Otearai ni hairimashita. Otearai no ue de te o araimashita. Soshite MANDII san wa Otearai o dete, Otearai no SURIPPA o nuide, ima no SURIPPA o haite, genkan ni ikimashita.
Genkan de SURIPPA o nuide, kutsu o hakimashita.
Okaasan to issho ni kasa o motte, kaimono ni ikimashita.

STUDY

- Note: many Japanese toilets have a handwash basin on top of the tank. (The cultural background notes for homes may be reviewed from *Level 1.*)

- *Hitsuyoo na.* A qualitative noun to add to your list. When used in front of a noun it takes **na**, as do all Q nouns; e.g., *Hitsuyoona mono* "necessary things." You will probably use it most with *desu*, as in the passage above.

- ***Kaimono ni ikimasu/kaimono o shimasu.***
  The difference between these two sentences is:
  Kaimono ni ikimasu "go to shop"
  Kaimono o shimasu "do the shopping."

- Take great care to remember the difference between *hairimasu* (**haitte**) "enter" and *hakimasu* (**haite**) "wear" (on the feet and legs).

- ***Oboemasu*** is used in the **te** form when you want to say you remember, because remembering is a continuing process; e.g., *Oboete imasu.* "I remember."

  Oboete imashita is used in the passage because Mandy was remembering what she had heard at school.

  The same principle is applied to **shirimasu** "know," which is most often encountered as **shitte imasu** "I know."

ACTIVITIES

- Write the story in natural English for the benefit of Mandy's parents.

- Divide into groups of three. Take turns asking the questions, and note everyone's comment. How would you feel in that situation? Put yourself in Mandy's place and answer the following.

  1 *Okaasan ga suki deshoo ka. (Hai/Iie)*
  2 *Anata no nihongo ga joozu deshoo ka heta deshoo ka.*
  3 *SURIPPA wa omoshiroi desu ka benri desu ka fuben desu ka.*

4   *Otearai ga hitsuyoo deshita. Okaasan ni kikimasu ka. (Hai/lie)*
5   *Hitori de Otearai o sagashimasu ka. (Hai/lie)*
6   *Tsukaremashita.*
    a) *Kaimono ni ikimasu ka.*
    b) *Uchi de yasumimasu ka.*
7   *Otearai de wa.*
    a) *Otearai no SURIPPA o hakimasu ka.*
    b) *Ima no SURIPPA o hakimasu ka.*
8   *Ichinichini nankai kutsu o nugimasu ka.* (In a day, how many times will
    she take off shoes?)

- Imagine how many times a day you'd change shoes if you lived in Japan.
  Give a number as your estimate, and at some time keep a count of the
  number of times in a day you go in or out of your house, in and out of the
  toilet, in and out of rooms that in Japan would have *tatami* mats, etc.,
  so forcing another change of shoes! Multiply your result for: a week; a
  month; a year!
  Report to the group.

- Write the next part of the story. Work it out together as a class, everyone
  offering a part, or do it individually, comparing with each other afterwards. (The textbook's episode may be found on p. 283 if you want
  another version to use for comparison.)
  You may use direct speech or tell the story in the past tense. Here are
  the guidelines:
  They walk to the shops close by. Everyone they meet greets them (it is
  by now 11 o'clock) and Mandy responds.
  The mother buys vegetables at the greengrocer's and fruit at the fruit
  shop. Mandy suddenly finds something other than "Good day" to say
  and says how expensive the fruit is. The mother agrees. Mandy also
  comments on the weather. The mother agrees.
  They return home and have lunch, then watch TV. Junji comes home
  from school and talks to Mandy in English. (*Eigo de hanashimasu.* Remember the language you use takes **de** "by means of/in (English)":
  Nihongo de kaite kudasai "Please write in Japanese," etc.) She is very
  relieved!
  Later they go up to Mandy's room, and the mother shows her a futon
  in the cupboard (*todana*), explaining what it is. Mandy does have a bed!

Writing practice

For writing practice and evaluation of your writing, write part of the story
(about ten sentences) into your book.
  Take great care with the shape of each syllable and be prepared to work
hard to re-shape letters if yours are not perfect shapes. It makes a lot
of difference in the impression you will give when writing to friends in

Japan or when you are offering your work for examination. When students get past the initial stages of learning to write, they sometimes get careless with the shapes. Don't let that happen to you!

Mandy's story

Remember, the following is only one of many ways of telling the story.

Juuichiji ni MANDII san wa Okaasan to issho ni mise ni ikimashita.

Mise wa chikakatta desu kara arukimashita. Ame dewa arimasen deshita ga kumori deshita. Yaoya ni hairimashita. Omoshirokatta desu. Okaasan wa yasai o kaimashita. Soshite kudamonoya de kudamono o kaimashita. Nihon no kudamono wa taihen takai desu kara MANDII san wa "Takai desu ne" to iimashita.

Okaasan wa "Hai, taihen takai desu" to iimashita.

Uchi ni kaerimashita. Ima de hirugohan o tabete, TEREBI o mimashita.

Yojihan ni Junjisan wa kaerimashita.

"Tadaima" to iimashita.

Okaasan wa "Okaerinasai" to iimashita.

MANDII san wa kikimashita. Omoshirokatta desu.

Junji san wa MANDII san to eigo de hanashimashita.

MANDII san wa anshin shimashita.

Ato de Okaasan wa MANDII san no shinshitsu ni ikimashita.

Todana no naka ni wa futon ga arimashita.

"Anata no BEDDO desu" to iimashita.

BEDDO ga arimashita!

Unit 7

マンディーさんは おふろばに
はいります
MANDII san wa Ofuroba ni hairimasu
Mandy enters the bathroom

NEW WORDS

Review

（お）ふろば	*(O) furoba*	Japanese bathroom
（お）ふろ	*(O) furo*	Japanese bath (tub)
シャワー を あびます	*SHAWAA o abimasu*	take a shower
よく しって います	*yoku shitte imasu*	knows well
ようふく	*yoofuku*	Western clothing
いれます　いれる	*iremasu (ireru)*	put in
いれて	*irete*	*te* form of *iremasu*
わすれます　わすれる	*wasuremasu (wasureru)*	forget
わすれて	*wasurete*	*te* form of *wasuremasu*

Interest

こと	*koto*	thing/matter/affair
カバー	*KABAA*	cover
はずかしい	*hazukashii*	(adj) embarrassed/ashamed/shy

Read this next passage together. See how much you understand before you look up anything or discuss the meaning together.

Read it in short sections and, at your teacher's direction, either ask each other questions in Japanese after each section or continue, leaving the questions until the end.

ろくじに マンディーさんは おふろばに はいりました。
おふろばは たいへん せまかった です。うちの いっかいに ありました。マンディーさんは おふろの そばに おふろの カバーを おきました。おふろに てを いれました。みずは たいへん あつかった です。
ようふくを ぬぎました。ようふくは ドアの そとに おきました。
シャワーは おふろの そばに ありました。マンディーさんは シャワーを あびました。かみのけを あらいました。おふろに はいりません でした。それから ようふくが いりました。
マンディーさんは ドアを あけましたが ようふくは ありません でした！はずかしかった です。どう しましょうか。

(*irimasu* means "need"; *iremasu* means "put in")

しつもん
1　なんじに　おふろばに　はいりましたか。
2　ようふくは　どこに　おきましたか。
3　おふろに　はいりましたか。
4　なにを　あらいましたか。
5　ようふくは　どう　しましたか。

Rokuji ni MANDII san wa Ofuroba ni hairimashita.
Ofuroba wa taihen semakatta desu. Uchi no ikkai ni arimashita.
MANDII san wa Ofuro no soba ni Ofuro no KABAA o okimashita.
Ofuro ni te o iremashita. Mizu wa taihen atsukatta desu.
Yoofuku o nugimashita. Yoofuku wa DOA no soto ni okimashita.
SHAWAA wa Ofuro no soba ni arimashita. MANDII san wa SHAWAA o abimashita. Kami no ke o araimashita. Ofuro ni hairimasen deshita.
Sorekara yoofuku ga irimashita.
MANDII san wa DOA o akemashita ga yoofuku wa arimasen deshita!
Hazukashikatta desu. Doo shimashoo ka!

Shitsumon
1　*Nanji ni Ofuroba ni hairimashita ka.*
2　*Yoofuku wa doko ni okimashita ka.*
3　*Ofuro ni hairimashita ka.*
4　*Nani o araimashita ka.*
5　*Yoofuku wa doo shimashita ka.*

ごふん　あとで　おかあさんは　おふろばの　ドアに　きました。
「だいじょうぶ　です　か」　と　いいました。「ここに　ゆかたが
あります。ゆかたを　きて　ください。マンディーさんの　ようふくを
せんたく　します。」
マンディーさんは　わかりません　でした。
おふろば　から　でません　でした。
はずかしかった　です。
どう　しましょうか。

しつもん
1　だれが　おふろばに　きました　か。
2　マンディーさんは　おかあさんの　にほんごが　わかりましたか。
3　おふろばを　でましたか。

Gofun ato de Okaasan wa Ofuroba no DOA ni kimashita.
"Daijoobu desu ka" to iimashita. "Koko ni yukata ga arimasu. Yukata o kite kudasai. MANDII san no yoofuku o sentaku shimasu."
MANDII san wa wakarimasen deshita. Ofuroba kara demasen deshita.
Hazukashikatta desu. Doo shimashoo ka.

Shitsumon
1　*Dare ga Ofuroba ni kimashita ka.*
2　*MANDII san wa Okaasan no nihongo ga wakarimashita ka.*
3　*Ofuroba o demashita ka.*

じゅんじさんは　おふろばの　ドアに　きました。じゅんじさんは
えいごで　「Mom's taken your clothes to wash. Please put on the yukata」
と　いいました。
マンディーさんは　ゆかたを　きて、いまに　はいりました。ばんごはん
を　たべました。

しつもん
1　だれが　おふろばに　きましたか。
2　じゅんじさんは　にほんごで　はなしましたか　えいごで
　　はなしましたか。
3　マンディーさんは　なにを　きましたか。

Junji san wa Ofuroba no DOA ni kimashita.
Junji san wa eigo de "Mom's taken your clothes to wash. Please put on the yukata" to iimashita.
MANDII san wa yukata o kite, ima ni hairimashita. Bangohan o tabemashita.

Shitsumon
1　*Dare ga Ofuroba ni kimashita ka.*
2　*Junji san wa nihongo de hanashimashita ka eigo de hanashimashita ka.*
3　*MANDII san wa nani o kimashita ka.*

あとで　おとうさんは　かえりました。おふろばに　はいりました。
おふろの　カバーは　おふろのうえに　ありません　でした！マンディ
ーさんは　しんぱい　しました！はずかしかった　です。

しつもん
1　なにを　おぼえていません　でしたか。
2　えいごで　こたえて　ください。マンディーさんは　はずかしかった
　　です。なぜ　でしょうか。

Ato de Otoosan wa kaerimashita. Ofuroba ni hairimashita.
Ofuro no KABAA wa Ofuro no ue ni arimasen deshita! MANDII san wa shinpai shimashita! Hazukashikatta desu!

Shitsumon
1　*Nani o oboete imasen deshita ka.*
2　*Eigo de kotaete kudasai. MANDII san wa hazukashikatta desu. Naze deshoo ka.*

ACTIVITIES
● Draw a cartoon of Mandy's face at each stage of the story, showing her thoughts in speech bubbles.

● Write the answers to the questions.

Unit 8

どこに いきたい ですか
doko ni ikitai desu ka
Where would you like to go?

NEW WORDS

Review

ねます　ねる	*nemasu (neru)*	sleep/lie down
ねて	*nete*	*te* form of *nemasu*
よく	*yoku*	well
ゆうびんきょく	*yuubinkyoku*	post office
まがります	*magarimasu*	turn
わたります	*watarimasu*	cross over
ひだりに	*hidari ni*	to the left
みぎに	*migi ni*	to the right
まっすぐ	*massugu*	straight ahead

Also review the . . . *tai desu* form.

Interest

えはがき	*ehagaki*	picture postcard
きって	*kitte*	postage stamp
はたけ	*hatake*	vegetable garden

While they are eating breakfast, Junji, her host brother, asks Mandy what she would like to do today, in Japanese, knowing that Mandy has to try to use Japanese or her visit will not be of much language value.

She is feeling much better after a good night's sleep and has got over her embarrassments of yesterday. She answers him in Japanese and is very thrilled that she understood.

(Junji speaks very slowly to help Mandy understand.)

じゅんじ　よく　ねましたか。

マ　　　はい、ありがとう。ふとんは　いい　です　ね。

じゅ　　はい、そう　です。
　　　　きょうは　どようび　です　から　ごごは　ひま　です。
　　　　ごごは　おてらに　いきたい　ですか。

マ　　　ありがとう。それは　いい　です　ね。
　　　　がっこうで　おてらの　えを　みました。おもしろかった
　　　　です。きょう　おてらに　いきたい　です。

じ　　　がっこうの　あとで　わたし　と　いっしょに　いきましょう
　　　　か。けさ　ちかくの　みせが　みたい　ですか。

マ   はい。ゆうびんきょくが　ありますか。

じゅ   はい。そう　ですね。……
        みて　ください。
        ここ　から　まっすぐ　いって、かどを　ひだりに　まがって、
        みちを　わたって、ゆうびんきょくは　はたけの
        そばに　あります。
        わかりますか。

マ   はい、わかりました。……まっすぐ　いって、ひだりに　まが
        って、みちを　わたって、ゆうびんきょくは　はたけの
        そばに　あります。

じゅ   よく　できました。にほんごが　じょうず　ですね。えんが
        ありますか。

マ   あります。えはがきを　かきました。きっては
        アメリカ　へ　いくら　でしょうか。

じゅ   わかりません。ゆうびんきょくの　ひとは　しっています。
        ひとりで　いって、だいじょうぶ　ですか。

マ   はい。だいじょうぶ　です。

Junji: *Yoku nemashita ka.*
MANDII: *Hai arigatoo. Futon wa ii desu ne.*
J: *Hai, soo desu.*
            Kyoo wa doyoobi desu kara gogo wa hima desu.
            Gogo wa Otera ni ikitai desu ka.
M: *Arigatoo. Sore wa ii desu ne.*
            Gakkoo de Otera no e o mimashita. Omoshirokatta desu.
            Kyoo Otera ni ikitai desu.
J: *Gakkoo no ato de watashi to issho ni ikimashoo ka.*
            Kesa chikaku no mise ga mitai desu ka.
M: *Hai. Yuubinkyoku ga arimasu ka.*
J: *Hai. Soo desu ne.* (He picks up paper and pencil and as he
            explains draws a sketch map) *Mite kudasai . . . .*
            *Koko kara massugu itte, kado o hidari ni magatte, michi o
            watatte, yuubinkyoku wa hatake no soba ni arimasu.*
            Wakarimasu ka.
M: *Hai. Wakarimashita . . . Massugu itte, hidari ni magatte, michi o
            watatte, yuubinkyoku wa hatake no soba ni arimasu.*
J: *Yoku dekimashita! Nihongo ga joozu desu ne.*
            En ga arimasu ka.
M: *Arimasu. Ehagaki o kakimashita. Kitte wa AMERIKA e
            ikura deshoo ka.*
J: *Wakarimasen. Yuubinkyoku no hito wa shitte imasu.*
            Hitori de itte, daijoobu desu ka.
M: *Hai, daijoobu desu.*

STUDY TIPS

Look back over your vocabulary lists frequently to remind yourself of previous vocabulary. You now have several hundred words. It is impossible to practice all of them in sentences every day, and the course keeps moving on, adding new vocabulary daily. So how do you keep them all in immediate recall?

The course keeps reminding you of previously learned vocabulary and structures, but you need to take responsibility for reminding yourself, too. Each day look through part of the vocabulary lists, not only of this book but of *Level One*, as well. When you come upon a word that you have forgotten, write it down, relearn it, and make a sentence that uses it. Five such words a day would be a sensible and manageable number. Using them in sentences helps you to keep structures fresh in your mind, if you challenge yourself to vary the structures, too.

ACTIVITIES

- Take time to have a spelling and vocabulary test. Look through your lists and compose a test of ten items for others to do. Name your test, then pass it to your neighbor, who tries to do it in his/her own book, then passes it on at a given signal to the next student, until you have each had five or ten tests. Put the original tests and answers on the wall for people to check in their own time.

- Around the class say where you would like to go or what you would like to do on the weekend.

- In pairs, find out what your partner wanted to do last weekend and what he/she actually did. Report to the group the information you gathered. Be careful with tense.

- Use **ga hoshii desu** and **tai desu** in the same mini conversations.

  Work out a statement and an action you would like. Write them on a slip of paper. Gather up all the slips of paper in a box, and take turns extracting one and reading it to the class.

  No one will know whose is being read unless you tell them, so you can put the slips in two piles (correct and incorrect) without hurting anyone's feelings. Afterwards go through any incorrect ones and together discuss why they were put in that pile.

  Here are examples:

  Kinoo KEEKI ga hoshikatta desu.
  Kyoo KEEKI ga tabetai desu.
  Kuruma ga hoshii desu.
  Ashita akai kuruma ga kaitai desu.
  Atarashii kutsu ga hoshii desu.
  Raishuu machi no kutsuya de kutsu ga kaitai desu.

- A similar activity is to write only the **hoshii** half of the pair and put them in a box. Each person draws a slip in turn, reads the statement, and makes an activity statement to follow it using **tai desu**.

- You ask your friend what he/she wants for a birthday present. You suggest things, but the friend only tells you what he/she doesn't want! Try three patterns; e.g.,
  1 *Nanika hoshii mono ga arimasu ka. Wakarimasen.*
    Is there anything you'd like? I don't know.
  2 *Nani ga hoshii desu ka. Inu wa hoshikunai desu.*
    What would you like? What do you want? I don't want a dog.
  3 *Hon ga hoshii desu ka. Iie, hon wa hoshikunai desu.*
    Do you want a book? No, I don't want a book.

- Imagine that you have received something you did not want. Tell your partner what it was and where you want to put it or use it; e.g.,
  "Ginks" no REKOODO wa hoshikunakatta desu.
  Gomibako no naka ni okitai desu.
  I didn't want a Ginks record! I want to put it in the waste basket.
  Shukudai wa hoshikunakatta desu. Shukudai wa shitakunai desu.
  I did not want homework. I don't want to do homework.

- Draw a map showing Junji's directions. Compare it with your partner's.

Writing practice

- Review **HI:** ヒ
  and **YA, YU, YO:** ヤ ユ ヨ

- Learn **HYA** ヒャ
        HYU ヒュ
        HYO ヒョ

- Learn **BYA** ビャ
        BYU ビュ
        BYO ビョ

- Learn **PYA** ピャ
  Review **PYU** ピュ
  Learn **PYO** ピョ

Unit 9

ほんとうに にほんに います
hontoo ni Nihon ni imasu!
I'm really in Japan!

NEW WORDS

ちかてつ	*chikatetsu*	subway

Interest

たまご	*tamago*	egg
サラダ	*SARADA*	salad
きって	*kitte*	postage stamps
パンダ	*PANDA*	panda

Review

トースト	*TOOSUTO*	toast
ジュース	*JUUSU*	juice
ごちそうさまでした	*Gochisoosama deshita*	Thanks for the meal
おしえます	*oshiemasu*	teach/show how

Mandy is excited and can hardly believe, after all the months of planning, that she is really in Japan and that she is managing to communicate. Her host mother, who has already discussed Mandy's day with Junji, comes to the breakfast table:

おかあさん   あさごはんは おわりましたか。

マンディー   はい。おわりました。おいしかった です。ごちそうさまでした。

お   うちの あさごはんは なん ですか。

マ   トースト と くだもの と ジュース です。

お   そう ですか。にほんの あさごはんは どう ですか。

マ   よかった です。にほんの トーストは おおきい です。おもしろい です。たまご と サラダが すき です。ジュースは おいしかった です。

お   それは いい です。きょう みせに ひとりで いきますか。

マ   はい。ゆうびんきょくに きってを かいに いきたい です。

お　みちが　わかりますか。

マ　はい。じゅんじさんが　みちを　おしえました。
　　ちずを　かきました。
　　あさごはんの　さらを　あらって　も　いい　ですか。

お　いいえ。だいじょうぶ　です。ゆうびんきょくに　いって
　　ください。

マ　ありがとう。……いって　まいります。

お　いって　いらっしゃい。

Okaasan:　Asagohan wa owarimashita ka.
MANDII:　Hai, owarimashita. Oishikatta desu. Gochisoosama deshita.
Okaasan:　Uchi no asagohan wa nan desu ka.
M:　TOOSUTO to kudamono to JUUSU desu.
O:　Soo desu ka. Nihon no asagohan wa doo desu ka.
M:　Yokatta desu. Nihon no TOOSUTO wa ookii desu.
　　Omoshiroi desu.Tamago to SARADA ga suki desu.
　　JUUSU wa oishikatta desu.
O:　Sore wa ii desu. Kyoo mise ni hitori de ikimasu ka.
M:　Hai. Yuubinkyoku ni kitte o kai ni ikitai desu.
O:　Michi ga wakarimasu ka.
M:　Hai. Junji san ga michi o oshiemashita.
　　Chizu o kakimashita.
　　Asagohan no sara o aratte mo ii desu ka.
O:　Iie. Daijoobu desu. Yuubinkyoku ni itte kudasai.
M:　Arigatoo. Itte mairimasu.
O:　Itte irasshai.

STUDY

- Here are some common expressions to become familiar with:
  Uchi is used for your own home and your own family's belongings, as well as being the word for your own house.
  e.g.: *uchi no inu* meaning "our dog."
  　　uchi no kuruma "our car."
  Gochisoosama deshita is the automatic but genuine response used to give thanks for a meal. (Mandy would have said **itadakimasu** before starting the meal.)
  Itte mairimasu. "I'm going out now."
  Itte irasshai. "Return home safely."
  Michi ga wakarimasu ka. "Do you know the way?"

ACTIVITIES

- In small groups, decide where you would like to go and what you would like to do if you were in Tokyo. You will have time to do three of the options, listed below, in one day. Decide on your first choice and what you would like to do after that. Give reasons to each other for your choices, using simple answers; e.g.,
  Omoshiroi deshoo. It'll probably be interesting.
  Omoshirokunai desu. It's not interesting.

Moo ikimashita. I've already gone.
Takai BIRU ga suki desu. I like tall buildings.
You may also choose a reason from the selection below in LIST B.

LIST A

1 *Tookyoo TAWAA* (Tokyo tower)
2 *Chikatetsu (Hachiji ni)*
3 *Eki*
4 *Kooen*
5 *Doobutsuen* (zoo)
6 *Otera*
   (Take care with pronunciation; it is easy to make it sound like *otearai*!)
7 *Honya*
8 *DEPAATO*
9 *MAKUDONARUDO*

10 *Kawa*
11 *GORUFU KOOSU*
12 *SUPOOTSU GURAUNDO*

LIST B

Keshiki (view) *ga ii desu kara.*

Konde imasu kara.
PANDA o mitai desu kara.
Sakura no ki o mi ni ikitai desu kara.
Shinkansen o mi ni ikitai desu kara.
BAAGEN SEERU ni ikitai desu kara.

Yuumeina yoofuku o mitai desu kara.
*Nihon no kodomo no hon o
kai ni ikitai desu kara.*
*GORUFU no renshuu o shitai
desu kara.*
Fune o mitai desu kara.
HANBAAGAA o tabetai desu kara.
Yakyuu o mitai desu kara.

- Use the places and reasons in the activity above to write sentences of your own, matching up appropriate places and reasons. (They are not necessarily listed in the correct order!)

Writing practice

- Learn **KYA**   キャ
        KYU   キュ
        KYO   キョ

- Learn **GYA**   ギャ
        GYU   ギュ
        GYO   ギョ

- Learn **MYA**   ミャ
        NYA   ニャ
        NYO   ニョ

Describe what Mandy saw on her walk to the post office

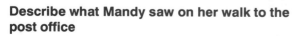

Unit 10

なにが みたい ですか
nani ga mitai desu ka
What would you like to see?

NEW WORDS

| じんじゃ | jinja | Shinto shrine |
| おてら | Otera | Buddhist temple |

Extension
| に のります | ni norimasu (ni noru) | ride on |
| に のって | ni notte | te form of norimasu |

Review
ちかてつ	chikatetsu	subway
でんしゃ	densha	train
バス	BASU	bus
じてんしゃ	jitensha	bicycle
あるきます あるく	arukimasu (aruku)	walk
あるいて	aruite	te form of arukimasu

It is Sunday and the people who organized Mandy's stay in Japan have arranged to take the whole group of exchange students out for the day together.

EXTENSION STUDY
(Optional)

Previously you learned to say how you would travel, using **de** "by means of": *BASU de ikimasu.* "I'll go by bus."

A more extended way of saying the same thing is to use the verb **norimasu**, which usually has the particle **ni** in front of it. You have learned that the Japanese like to be very precise and often use two verbs to describe an action for which only one is used in English. That is the way *ni norimasu* is used to explain how you will travel. Look at the following examples. The first uses the **te** form (**ni notte**) as a sentence joiner:

Densha ni notte, Kyooto ni ikimasu.
Riding on a train, I'll go to Kyoto.

The second puts the two verbs together to say "I'll go by train to Kyoto." (Riding on a train, I'll go to Kyoto.):

Kyooto made densha ni notte ikimasu.

It is acceptable to use *Densha de ikimasu*, but better to use *Densha ni notte ikimasu.* Put it into the back of your mind – maybe you will be able to use it in the next activity.

ACTIVITIES

Divide the class into two groups. Two thirds of the class are exchange students, waiting outside a station to be taken out by Japanese nationals for the day.

The second group (one third of the class) are Japanese people who have offered to take the tourists out for the day. The Japanese do not speak English or are too shy to try, so the tourists must all try to make themselves understood in Japanese.

The Japanese approach two tourists each and introduce themselves. They have to find out where the students would like to go, from the list of possibilities the students have with them, and tell them a little about the place.

Afterwards the "Japanese" will tell their club members where they took the visitors and what they did, and then write it up in their club "events book." (Make an "events book," if you wish, for others to read. Photos of some of these places are found in travel pamphlets, if you'd like genuine illustrations.)

The "students" will get together in groups of three, tell each other where they went and what they saw or did, and then write a letter to their Japanese classes at home telling about their day. (You too could put in pictures if you have a kindly travel agent who will provide you with some pamphlets.) Put your finished work on the wall for others to read and enjoy.

The students have a list of places they have been told are worth visiting but not what is famous about that place. It is Sunday. Here is the students' list.

Akihabara
Tokyo Tower
Asakusa
Harajuku
Yoyogi Park
Meiji Shrine
Tokyo Zoo
The Ginza
Shinjuku
The Imperial Palace Moat
Roppongi
Nihonbashi

They will ask the guides questions like:
Akihabara wa nan desu ka. What is Akihabara?
Akihabara wa yuumei desu ka. Is Akihabara famous?
Meiji Jinja wa kirei desu ka. Is the Meiji shrine beautiful?
. . . . . . *wa doo desu ka.* How about . . . . . .?
                          What's . . . . like?

Here is the guides' list:

Akihabara de	*TEREBI ya SUTEREO ya TEEPU REKOODA o kaimasu. Yasui desu.*
Tookyoo TAWAA wa	*keshiki ga ii desu. Taihen takai desu. Omoshiroi desu.*
Asakusa de	*furui Otera ga miemasu. (Namae wa Asakusa Kannon desu.) Yuumeina chiisai mise ga arimasu.*
Harajuku ni	*yuumeina yoofuku no mise ga arimasu. Omoshiroi mise ga takusan arimasu.*
Yoyogi kooen de	*nichiyoobi wa hito ga DANSU o shite, POPPU ongaku o kikimasu.*
Meiji Jinja wa	*yuumeina jinja desu. Taihen kirei desu. Shizuka* (peaceful) *desu.*
Tookyoo no doobutsuen de	*omoshiroi doobutsu ga imasu. PANDA ga imasu.*
Ginza wa	*yuumeina DEPAATO ga arimasu. Tookyoo no ichiban yuumeina michi desu.*
Shinjuku wa	*takai BIRU ga arimasu. Eki wa taihen isogashii desu. Kireina kooen ga arimasu.*
The Imperial Palace	*Furui kabe ga arimasu. Taihen ookina sakana ga imasu. Kireina kooen ga arimasu.*
Roppongi ni	*kissaten to mise ga arimasu. POPPU ongaku no hito wa Roppongi ga suki desu.*
Nihonbashi wa	*Tookyoo no ichiban furui hashi ga arimasu.*

- Pairwork or small groups. Decide what else you would like to see in Tokyo from the information given. Tell your partner what you want to see and do, and why, using the information from the last activity.

- Write a story about the things that you would like to see and do in Tokyo.

Writing practice

- Learn **RYA**   リ ャ
  RYU   リ ュ
  RYO   リ ョ

Etiquette to Be Observed When Praying at a Shrine
1. See to it that you are dressed appropriately for the occasion. Pass under the torii and walk through the "sando" or approach to the shrine.
2. Go to the hand-washing stone basin and cleanse your hands thoroughly. With a dipper, pour water into your cupped hand and then bring the water to your mouth and gargle. (Do not bring the dipper directly to your mouth.)
3. Advance before the god enshrined. Then throw some money (either paper currency or coins) into the offertory box.
4. Then bow deeply two times.
5. After that, clap your hands twice.
6. Then make a deep bow once more.

Unit 11

にほんでは なにが みたい ですか
Nihon de wa nani ga mitai desu ka
What would you like to see in Japan?

NEW WORDS

Interest

へいわ	*heiwa*	peace
こくりつ	*kokuritsu*	national
こ みずうみ	*ko/mizuumi*	lake
だいぶつ	*daibutsu*	the great Buddha
タワー	*TAWAA*	tower
ディズニーランド	*DIZUNIIRANDO*	Disneyland
しゃしん	*shashin*	photograph
さる	*saru*	monkey
へび	*hebi*	snake
むし	*mushi*	insect
にほんかい	*Nihonkai*	the Japan Sea
すごい	*sugoi*	Great! Really good! (slang)
せとないかい	*Setonaikai*	the Inland sea
すぎ	*sugi*	cedar tree

Mandy's homestay family have asked her what she wants to see in Japan. Here is what she told them:

わたし は…
おてら と じんじゃ が みたい です。
あさ えきで たくさんの ひとが みたい です。
とうきょうで あさくさの みせ と はらじゅくの みせを みに いきたいです。パチンコが みたい です。

Watashi wa . . . Otera to jinja ga mitai desu. Asa eki de takusan no hito ga mitai desu. Tookyoo de Asakusa no mise to Harajuku no mise o mi ni ikitai desu. PACHINKO ga mitai desu.

STUDY

- You already know particles **ni** and **wa**. Remember, they can be used together to say "talking about in (the)"; e.g.,
  Nihon ni wa doko de benkyoo shimasu ka.
  "Where will you study in Japan?"

- **Takusan** is an adverb and may be used in two ways:
  1) In front of the verb, following the rule of putting quantity words in front of the verb; e.g.,
     Hana ga takusan saite imashita.

"There were a lot of flowers blooming."

2) *Takusan* may be joined to a noun with **no** and put in an earlier position in the sentence; e.g.,

Takusan no hana ga saite imashita.

"Lots of flowers were blooming."

If you use *takusan* in front of a noun in this way, you must always use **no** between it and the noun it is talking about. If it is confusing to have two different ways of using *takusan*, just stick to the rule you know and always use it in front of the verb.

- **Ga** and **o** with **. . . tai desu.**

Use **ga** with . . . *tai desu* when following the rule you already know; ie, when you are focusing on a particular thing you want to do.

In practice in Japan, both **o** and **ga** are used with . . . *tai desu*, depending on the strength of the wish: **ga** is for a strong feeling and **o** for a less important feeling.

ACTIVITIES

- Mandy's family is delighted that she wants to go to those places, and they tell her something about each of them. They also talk about other places she might enjoy that they would like to take her to. (Use the list of places used in the last Unit.)

  Role play the conversation that Mandy has with them in twos, threes or fours, depending on who you decide is present for the discussion. Mandy will ask a lot of questions.

- Mandy has a long list of things to do and places to see in Japan. She doesn't expect to be able to do all of these things, but if she had the opportunity it would be great!

  How many of these things can she already cross off the list below? Read back over her experiences since she arrived in Japan, and list the things she has already done. (In Japanese)

Places to visit

ひろしまの へいわ こうえんに いきたい です。
にっこうの こくりつ こうえんに いきたい です。
ちゅうぜんじこが みたい です。
びわこに いきたい です。
きょうとに いきたい です。
ならの とうだいじの おてらに いきたい です。
とうきょう タワーに のぼりたい です。
はこねに いきたい です。
ながさきに いきたい です。

Things to do

にほんじんに あいたい です。
ふとんの うえに ねたい です。
にほんの おふろと おてあらいが みたい です。
ちかてつに のりたい です。
ディズニーランドに いきたい です。

ふじさんに のぼりたい です。
ならの だいぶつが みたい です。
にほんの さしみ と すしが たべたい です。
おさけが すこし のみたい です。
しんかんせんに のりたいです。
つりが したい です。
しゃしんを たくさん とりたい です。
にほんの たかい すぎが みたい です。
もりで にほんの さる と へび と むしが みたい です。
にほんの ながい はしが みたい です。
にほんかいに いきたい です。
たくさん ですね。

Places to visit
Hiroshima no Heiwa kooen ni ikitai desu.
Nikkoo no kokuritsu kooen ni ikitai desu.
Chuuzenji ko ga mitai desu.
Biwa ko ni ikitai desu.
Kyooto ni ikitai desu.
Nara no Toodaiji no Otera ni ikitai desu.
Tookyoo TAWAA ni noboritai desu.
Hakone ni ikitai desu.
Nagasaki ni ikitai desu.

Things to do
Nihonjin ni aitai desu.
Futon no ue ni netai desu.
Nihon no Ofuro to Otearai ga mitai desu.
Chikatetsu ni noritai desu.
DIZUNIIRANDO ni ikitai desu.
Fujisan ni noboritai desu.
Nara no daibutsu ga mitai desu.
Nihon no sashimi to sushi ga tabetai desu.
Osake ga sukoshi nomitai desu!
Shinkansen ni noritai desu.
Tsuri ga shitai desu.
Shashin o takusan toritai desu.
Nihon no takai sugi ga mitai desu. (cedar trees)
Mori de nihon no saru to hebi to mushi ga mitai desu.
Nihon no nagai hashi ga mitai desu. (Setonaikai [Inland Sea] bridges)
Nihonkai ni ikitai desu.
Takusan desu ne!

- Look at the map of Japan on p. 297. See how far Mandy would like to travel.

What Mandy wants to do and see . . .
Ride on the subway (top left)
Visit a temple (top right)
See a station at rush-hour (center left)
Go shopping in Asakusa (center right)
Visit a shrine (lower)

Go to Nikko (top left)
Visit Tokyo
Disneyland (top right)
See the dancers near
Yoyogi Park
Ride on a bullet train
(center right)
Go to the zoo (lower)

Go shopping in Ginza (top)
Visit Kyoto (center left)
Visit Todaiji in Nara (center right)
Visit Peace Park in Hiroshima
(lower)

Go to the library and find out about a particular place in Japan or an activity that people could enjoy in Japan. Alternatively, invite Japanese nationals to show you their slides or to talk about places they like. Write about it in Japanese (or English if your teacher prefers) for the benefit of others in your class. Together make a well-informed package for anyone intending to go to Japan.

Find the information and then write about it very simply. If you write in Japanese, don't get bogged down in things you can't yet say. Remember that everyone else is limited by the vocabulary and structures that you have learned and will only understand you if you stick to what you have learned in class.

After you have had time to prepare your travel information, be prepared to give a short talk on the place you chose and say why it would be good to visit.

Read everyone else's information.

- Make up a quiz in either English or Japanese after you have done the first activity (on p. 291). Work out questions to ask on places and activities to be enjoyed in Japan.

- Have a "travel agency promotion" on Japan. Set up counters in your classroom or hall advertising various aspects of Japan. Put up the information you wrote about Japan, to be easily read by "clients." Set up a real snack-bar restaurant, too.

If possible, borrow a travel film on Japan to show to your "clients" and arrange for Japanese yen to be available to spend during the "promotion." Each person changes a small amount of money (enough to buy one of your sandwiches or drinks) into Japanese yen. If you can't have real money, use counters that you have defined as particular coins, and rectangles of paper for notes.

Use the quiz questions that you made up in the last activity. Each person has to go round the booths, where some students are "travel agents," and find out the answers to the quiz by asking questions and reading the information available. Each person also buys something to eat at the cafe.

See if you can all get into the spirit of the activity and **only** speak Japanese! There will be a limited time given to the quiz and for buying something to eat and drink using your Japanese. Try to keep using only Japanese for at least half an hour.

You could maybe offer a small prize for the winner of the quiz, like a voucher for free food from your cafe, and then settle down to enjoy your film. Have fun!

Remember, in Japanese schools the students do all the cleaning – so stay in role and clean everything up before you leave!

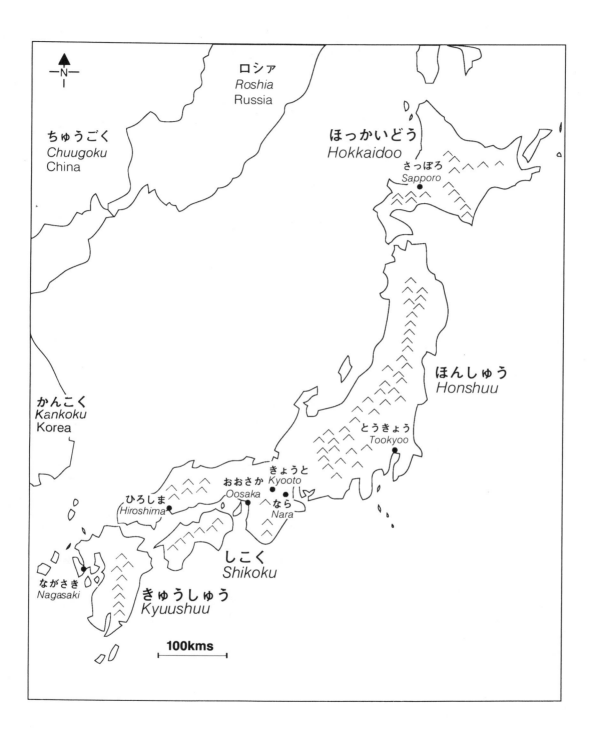

Vocabulary Checklist (Topics Ten – Fourteen)

Topic Ten

あの	*ano*	that over there
あたらしい	*atarashii*	new/fresh
だいがく	*daigaku*	university
だいがくせい	*daigakusei*	university student
だめ な	*dame (na)*	no good (Qualitative Noun)
でも	*demo*	but (beginning of sentence)
デパート	*DEPAATO*	department store
でしょう	*deshoo*	probably
どの	*dono*	which
どれ	*dore*	which out of more than two things
ドル	*DORU*	dollar
ええ と	*ee . . . to*	hesitation noise
えん	*en*	yen
ふるい	*furui*	old
が	*ga*	but
がくせい	*gakusei*	student
ごろ	*goro*	about (a time)
ははのひ	*haha no hi*	Mother's Day
はなや	*hanaya*	flower shop
はやい	*hayai*	fast/early
ほしい	*hoshii*	want (adjective)
ひゃく	*hyaku*	one hundred
にひゃく	*nihyaku*	two hundred
さんびゃく	*sanbyaku*	three hundred
よんひゃく	*yonhyaku*	four hundred
ごひゃく	*gohyaku*	five hundred
ろっぴゃく	*roppyaku*	six hundred
ななひゃく	*nanahyaku*	seven hundred
はっぴゃく	*happyaku*	eight hundred
きゅうひゃく	*kyuuhyaku*	nine hundred
いちまん	*ichiman*	ten thousand
いらっしゃいませ	*irasshaimase*	welcome
いって いらっしゃい	*itte irasshai*	come back safely, etc.
いって まいります	*itte mairimasu*	I'm going out
じてんしゃや	*jitenshaya*	bicycle shop
かいもの	*kaimono*	shopping
かいしゃいん	*kaishain*	company employee
カメラ	*KAMERA*	camera
から	*kara*	from
かって ください	*katte kudasai*	please buy
けさ	*kesa*	this morning
こんげつ	*kongetsu*	this month
この	*kono*	this
くだもの(や)	*kudamono (ya)*	fruit (stand)
くつ(や)	*kutsu (ya)*	shoe (shop)

まで	made	up to/until/as far as
まいど　ありがとう 　ございました	maido arigatoo 　gozaimashita	thank you for shopping 　here
まん	man	ten thousand (counter)
みせ	mise	shop, store
みせます/みせる	misemasu (miseru)	show
みせ　の　ひと	mise no hito	store clerk
みせて　ください	misete kudasai	please show me
ね	ne	isn't it?
にく(や)	niku (ya)	meat (butcher shop)
にまん	niman	twenty thousand, etc.
おかね	Okane	money
おきゃくさん	Okyakusan	customer
おもしろい	omoshiroi	interesting
オートバイ	OOTOBAI	motorbike, motorcycle
おつり	Otsuri	change
パン	PAN	bread
らいげつ	raigetsu	next month
さかな(や)	sakana (ya)	fish (shop)
せん	sen	thousand
いっせん	issen	one thousand
にせん	nisen	two thousand
さんぜん	sanzen	three thousand
よんせん	yonsen	four thousand
ごせん	gosen	five thousand
ろくせん	rokusen	six thousand
ななせん	nanasen	seven thousand
はっせん	hassen	eight thousand
きゅうせん	kyuusen	nine thousand
せんげつ	sengetsu	last month
セント	SENTO	cents
その	sono	that
それ　では　ありません	sore dewa arimasen	not that one
それから	sorekara	after that/then/so
スーパー　(マーケット)	SUUPAA (MAAKETTO)	supermarket
たいへん	taihen	very, extremely
たかい	takai	high/tall/expensive
とけい	tokei	watch/clock
やおや	yaoya	greengrocer
やさい	yasai	vegetables
やすい	yasui	cheap

Interest

あきはばら	Akihabara	district of Tokyo
アスピリン	ASUPIRIN	aspirin
バーゲン　セール	BAAGEN SEERU	bargain sale
バイク	BAIKU	motorbike
ぎんざ	Ginza	famous street in Tokyo
はらじゅく	Harajuku	district of Tokyo
ほしい　もの	hoshii mono	wanted thing
めいじ　じんぐう	Meiji jinguu	Meiji shrine
もの	mono	thing
なにか	nanika	something/anything
さつ	satsu	banknotes

しんじゅく	*Shinjuku*	district of Tokyo
てんいん	*ten'in*	store clerk

Topic Eleven

あちら	*achira*	that way over there
あるいて	*aruite*	*te* form of *arukimasu*
あるきます / あるく	*arukimasu (aruku)*	walk
あと　で	*ato de*	afterwards
バスてい	*BASUtei*	bus stop
ちかい	*chikai*	close/near
ちかく　に	*chikaku ni*	neighborhood/nearby
ちず	*chizu*	map
だいじょうぶ	*daijoobu (na)*	OK/all right (Qualitative Noun)
だいすき	*daisuki*	like a lot
で	*de*	particle: by means of
で	*de*	particle for location of activity
どちら　へ　いきます か	*dochira e ikimasu ka*	go which way?
えいがかん	*eigakan*	movie theater
ふん / ぷん	*fun/pun*	minutes
いっぷん	*ippun*	one minute
にふん	*nifun*	two minutes
さんぷん	*sanpun*	three minutes
よんぷん	*yonpun*	four minutes
ごふん	*gofun*	five minutes
ろっぷん	*roppun*	six minutes
ななふん	*nanafun*	seven minutes
はっぷん	*happun*	eight minutes
きゅうふん	*kyuufun*	nine minutes
じゅっぷん	*juppun*	ten minutes
じゅういっぷん	*juuippun*	eleven minutes
じゅうにふん	*juunifun*	twelve minutes
じゅうごふん	*juugofun*	fifteen minutes
にじゅっぷん	*nijuppun*	twenty minutes
ガソリン　スタンド	*GASORIN SUTANDO*	gas station
ゲーム	*GEEMU*	game
ぎんこう	*ginkoo*	bank
ぐらい	*gurai*	about (distance/length of time)
はじまります / はじまる	*hajimarimasu (hajimaru)*	be started/be begun
はじめ　に	*hajime ni*	at first/first/in the beginning
はし	*hashi*	bridge
ひだりがわ	*hidarigawa*	left-hand side
ひだり　に	*hidari ni*	to the left
ひつじ	*hitsuji*	sheep
いります / いる	*irimasu (iru)*	need
いって	*itte*	*te* form of *ikimasu*
かど	*kado*	corner
かいて	*kaite*	*te* form of *kakimasu*
かきます / かく	*kakimasu (kaku)*	write
こちら	*kochira*	this way
まちます / まつ	*machimasu (matsu)*	wait

まえ	*mae*	in front of/before/ago
まがります/まがる	*magarimasu (magaru)*	turn
まがって	*magatte*	*te* form of *magarimasu*
まっすぐ	*massugu*	straight ahead
まって	*matte*	*te* form of *machimasu*
みち	*michi*	road/street
みえます/みえる	*miemasu (mieru)*	can/able to see
みぎがわ	*migigawa*	right-hand side
みぎ　に	*migi ni*	to the right
みずうみ	*mizuumi*	lake
むちろん	*mochiron*	of course
もっと	*motto*	more
なか	*naka*	inside
のうじょう	*noojoo*	farm
おばあさん	*Obaasan*	grandmother
おぼえます/おぼえる	*oboemasu (oboeru)*	remember
おぼえて	*oboete*	*te* form of *oboemasu*
した	*shita*	under/below
して	*shite*	*te* form of *shimasu*
しゅうまつ	*shuumatsu*	weekend
そば	*soba*	beside
そちら	*sochira*	that way
そう　しましょう	*soo shimashoo*	let's do that
そして	*soshite*	and then
そと	*soto*	outside
すいえい　を　します/ 　する	*suiei o shimasu (suru)*	swim
たいせつ	*taisetsu (na)*	important (Qualitative Noun)
たくさん	*takusan*	many/a lot
（と）　いっしょ　に	*(to) issho ni*	together (with)
とおい	*tooi*	distant/far
つり　を　します/する	*tsuri o shimasu (suru)*	go fishing
うえ	*ue*	on top of/above
うま	*uma*	horse
うし	*ushi*	cow
うしろ	*ushiro*	behind
わかります/わかる	*wakarimasu (wakaru)*	understand
わたります/わたる	*watarimasu (wataru)*	cross over
わたしたち	*watashitachi*	we
わたって	*watatte*	*te* form of *watarimasu*
やま	*yama*	mountain
よく	*yoku*	well/often
ゆうびんきょく	*yuubinkyoku*	post office

Interest

かんがえ	*kangae*	thought/idea
こうさてん	*koosaten*	intersection
みつこし	*Mitsukoshi*	a chain of dept. stores
おしや	*oshiya*	pusher (onto trains)
パチンコ	*PACHINKO*	pinball game
さんぽ	*sanpo*	a walk
しずか	*shizuka (na)*	quiet, peaceful
しんごう	*shingoo*	signal/traffic lights
スキー	*SUKII*	ski/skiing

たき	*taki*	waterfall
とり	*tori*	bird

Topic Twelve

アイスクリーム	*AISUKURIIMU*	ice cream
あさごはん	*asagohan*	breakfast
ばんごはん	*bangohan*	dinner/evening meal
ごちそうさま でした。	*Gochisoo sama deshita*	Thank you (for the meal)
ごはん	*gohan*	meal/cooked rice
ごめん ください	*Gomen kudasai*	Anyone home?
はいります/はいる	*hairimasu (hairu)*	enter
はいって	*haitte*	*te* form of *hairimasu*
はし	*hashi*	chopsticks
へた	*heta*	not good yet/still unskillful at
ひるごはん	*hirugohan*	lunch
ひとつ	*hitotsu*	one
ふたつ	*futatsu*	two
みっつ	*mittsu*	three
よっつ	*yottsu*	four
いつつ	*itsutsu*	five
むっつ	*muttsu*	six
ななつ	*nanatsu*	seven
やっつ	*yattsu*	eight
ここのつ	*kokonotsu*	nine
とお	*too*	ten
いいえ、けっこう です	*Iie, kekkoo desu*	No, thank you.
いれます/いれる	*iremasu (ireru)*	put in
いれて	*irete*	*te* form of *iremasu*
いただきます	*itadakimasu*	said before eating
いや（な）	*iya (na)*	horrible, disgusting
ジュース	*JUUSU*	juice
からだ	*karada*	health, body
きっさてん	*kissaten*	coffee bar
こめ	*kome*	uncooked rice
コーヒー	*KOOHII*	coffee
コーヒー は いかが です か。	*KOOHII wa ikaga desu ka*	Will you have a cup of coffee?
まだ	*mada*	not yet
まずい	*mazui*	unpalatable/not nice
みず	*mizu*	water
モーニング セット	*MOONINGU SETTO*	morning set meal
むずかしい	*muzukashii*	difficult (adjective)
のみもの	*nomimono*	beverage/drink
おべんとう	*Obentoo*	lunch boxes
おちゃ	*Ocha*	tea (Japanese)
おあがり ください	*O agari kudasai*	Please step inside
おはいり ください	*O hairi kudasai*	Please come in
おはし	*Ohashi*	chopsticks
おいしい	*oishii*	delicious, tasty
おまたせ しました。	*Omatase shimashita*	Sorry to have kept you waiting
おんがく	*ongaku*	music

おしぼり	Oshibori	moist towels
おと	oto	sound
ポカリ　スエット	POKARI SUETTO	Pocari Sweat (drink)
しょくひん　サンプル	shokuhin SANPURU	window samples
しょうしょう　おまち　ください。	shooshoo omachi kudasai	Please wait a minute
そば	soba	buckwheat noodles
そう　では　ありません。	soo dewa arimasen	I don't agree (opposite of soo desu)
とけい	tokei	watch/clock
トースト	TOOSUTO	toast
つめたい	tsumetai	cold to touch
うるさい	urusai	noisy (adjective)
わしょく	washoku	Japanese food
ようしょく	yooshoku	foreign food
ゆうめい	yuumei (na)	famous (Qualitative Noun)

Interest

バナナ	BANANA	banana
バニラ	BANIRA	vanilla
チョコレート	CHOKOREETO	chocolate
ちょっと	chotto	a little bit
えきべん	ekiben	lunch boxes bought at a station
ふろしき	furoshiki	wrapping cloth
ガム	GAMU	chewing gum
ごみばこ	gomibako	waste basket
ハンバーガー	HANBAAGAA	hamburger
ひこうき	hikooki	airplane
ひま（な）	hima	free (time)
ホット　ドッグ	HOTTO DOGGU	hotdog
いちご	ichigo	strawberry
じゅく	juku	cram school
ケーキ	KEEKI	cake
けしゴム	keshigomu	eraser
コカコーラ	KOKAKOORA	Coca Cola
この　ごろ	kono goro	these days
この　まえ	kono mae	before this
マクドナルド	MAKUDONARUDO	McDonald's
ミルク　セーキ	MIRUKU SEEKI	milkshake
なま	nama	raw
なにも	nani mo	nothing
なりた　くうこう	Narita kuukoo	Narita airport
にぎりずし/まきずし	nigirizushi/makizushi	types of sushi
のど　が　かわきました　か。	nodo ga kawakimashita ka	Are you thirsty?
のり	nori	baked seaweed
ヌードル	NUUDORU	noodles
おいて	oite	te form of okimasu
おきます/おく	okimasu (oku)	put, place
おにぎり	Onigiri	rice cakes
オレンジ	ORENJI	orange
りんご	ringo	apple
さしみ	sashimi	Japanese dish

そばや	sobaya	soba noodle restaurant
すきやき	sukiyaki	Japanese dish
すし	sushi	Japanese dish
てんぷら	tenpura	Japanese dish
うどんや	udonya	udon noodle restaurant
いなぎや	unagiya	eel restaurant
わさび	wasabi	horseradish
やきとりや	yakitoriya	barbecue chicken shop

Topic Thirteen

あいきどう	aikidoo	martial art
あまり/あんまり	amari/anmari	not very/not many/ not much
あと	ato	after
ばん	ban	evening/night
ぼんさい	bonsai	miniature tree cultivation
ブラウス	BURAUSU	blouse
だめ　です	dame desu	It's no good
だめ　（な）	dame(na)	no good (Qualitative Noun)
できます/できる	dekimasu (dekiru)	able to do/can do
どんな	donna	what kind of (Qual. Noun)
どの　ぐらい　です　か。	dono gurai desu ka	How far/how long/how much is it?
えんか	enka	Japanese popular songs
ふで	fude	paintbrush
ごご	gogo	afternoon/pm
ごねんかん	gonenkan	five years' time/for five years
はいて	haite	te form of hakimasu
はきます/はく	hakimasu (haku)	wear on feet or legs
はんズボン	hanZUBON	short trousers/shorts
はやい	hayai	early/fast
はやく	hayaku	adverbial form of hayai
ひ	hi	day/sun
ひいて	hiite	te form of hikimasu
ひきます/ひく	hikimasu (hiku)	pluck/play a stringed instrument
ひま　（な）	hima (na)	free time
ひつよう　（な）	hitsuyoo (na)	necessary (Qual. Noun)
ほんとう　に	hontoo ni	truly/really/honestly
いけばな	ikebana	flower arranging
いきたい　です	ikitai desu	want to go
いなか	inaka	countryside
いろは　カルタ	iroha KARUTA	hiragana card game
いつ	itsu	when
いって　も　いい　です　か。	itte mo ii desu ka	May I go?
じゅうどう	juudoo	martial art
かいます/かう	kaimasu (kau)	buy
かいしゃ	kaisha	company/business
カラオケ	KARAOKE	sing along with tape
からだ	karada	health/body
からて	karate	martial art

かって	katte	te form of buy
けんどう	kendoo	martial art
きます/きる	kimasu (kiru)	wear on upper half of body
きて	kite	te form of kimasu
きもの	kimono	Japanese traditional dress
こおろぎ	koorogi	cricket (insect)
コート	KOOTO	coat
こたえます/こたえる	kotaemasu (kotaeru)	answer
こたえて	kotaete	te form of kotaemasu
こと	koto	Japanese harp
ことし	kotoshi	this year
クラシック おんがく	KURASHIKKU ongaku	classical music
クラス	KURASU	class
くろい	kuroi	black (adjective)
くつ	kutsu	shoes
キャンプ に いきます	KYANPU ni ikimasu	go to camp
きゅうどう	kyuudoo	archery
まだ です	mada desu	not yet
まえ	mae	before
まえ に	mae ni	before this
まいつき	maitsuki	every month
みどり いろ の	midori iro no	green
もちます/もつ	mochimasu (motsu)	have/hold
もちろん	mochiron	of course
もう	moo	already/more
もって	motte	te form of mochimasu
もって いきます/いく	motte ikimasu (iku)	take
もって いって	motte itte	te form of motte ikimasu
むし	mushi	insects/worms
むずかしい	muzukashii	difficult
なおります/なおる	naorimasu (naoru)	heal/get better
ならいます/ならう	naraimasu (narau)	learn
ならって	naratte	te form of naraimasu
なつ	natsu	summer
なぜ	naze	why?
ネクタイ	NEKUTAI	necktie
ねん	nen	year
にじ まで に	niji made ni	by two o'clock
にきび	nikibi	pimple
に きいて	ni kiite	te form of ni kikimasu
に ききます/に きく	ni kikimasu (ni kiku)	ask
のぼります/のぼる	noborimasu (noboru)	climb
のぼって	nobotte	te form of noborimasu
おんがく	ongaku	music
おりがみ	origami	paper folding
おしえます/おしえる	oshiemasu (oshieru)	teach/show how to do something
おしえて	oshiete	te form of oshiemasu
おそい	osoi	late/slow
おそく	osoku	adverbial form of osoi
おわります/おわる	owarimasu (owaru)	finish
おわって	owatte	te form of owarimasu
ペット を かって います	PETTO o katte imasu	keep a pet

ピクニック を します	PIKUNIKKU o shimasu	have a picnic
ピンク の	PINKU no	pink
ポップ	POPPU	pop music
ポピュラー おんがく	POPYURAA ongaku	pop music
らいねん	rainen	next year
らいしゅう	raishuu	next week
りか	rika	science
りょうり を します	ryoori o shimasu	do cooking
さんぽ	sanpo	a walk
セーター	SEETAA	sweater/jumper
せいふく	seifuku	uniform
しゃくはち	shakuhachi	vertical flute
しゃみせん	shamisen	three-stringed long lute
シャツ	SHATSU	shirt
しけん	shiken	examination
しります/しる	shirimasu (shiru)	know
しって	shitte	te form of shirimasu
したい です	shitai desu	want to do/have
しつもん	shitsumon	question
しょどう	shodoo	calligraphy
しゅくだい	shukudai	homework
しゅみ	shumi	hobby
しゅうまつ	shuumatsu	weekend
そして	soshite	and then
すぐ	sugu	soon
スカート	SUKAATO	skirt
すこし	sukoshi	a little/a little bit
ステレオ	SUTEREO	stereo
すわります/すわる	suwarimasu (suwaru)	sit
すわって	suwatte	te form of suwarimasu
たちます/たつ	tachimasu (tatsu)	stand
たいせつ （な）	taisetsu (na)	important (Qual. Noun)
たって	tatte	te form of tachimasu
ティーシャツ	TII-SHATSU	T-shirt
つかいます/つかう	tsukaimasu (tsukau)	use
つかれます/つかれる	tsukaremasu (tsukareru)	be tired
つかれて	tsukarete	te form of tsukaremasu
つかって	tsukatte	te form of tsukaimasu
つくります/つくる	tsukurimasu (tsukuru)	make
つくって	tsukutte	te form tsukurimasu
つまらない	tsumaranai	boring/worthless
つり を します/する	tsuri o shimasu (suru)	to fish
うんどう	undoo	exercise
うた	uta	song
うたいます/うたう	utaimasu (utau)	sing
うたって	utatte	te form of utaimasu
ワイシャツ	WAISHATSU	white shirt/business shirt
わかりました！	wakarimashita!	I know!
やぶさめ	yabusame	Japanese horseback archery
やまのぼり	yamanobori	mountain climbing
やすみ	yasumi	holiday/rest
よみます/よむ	yomimasu (yomu)	read
よんで	yonde	te form of yomimasu
ズボン	ZUBON	trousers

Interest

あぶない	*abunai*	dangerous
あつめます/あつめる	*atsumemasu (atsumeru)*	collect, gather
あつめて	*atsumete*	*te* form of *atsumemasu*
ベルト	*BERUTO*	belt
ぼうし	*booshi*	cap/hat
ちゃいろ　の	*chairo no*	brown
ちょうちょう	*choochoo*	butterfly
だいだい　いろ　の	*daidai iro no*	orange
だけ	*dake*	only
でんわ　ばんごう	*denwa bangoo*	telephone number
どくしょ	*dokusho*	reading
ドレス	*DORESU*	dress
ふきます/ふく	*fukimasu (fuku)*	blow (play flute, etc.)
ふいて	*fuite*	*te* form of *fukimasu*
イヤリング	*IYARINGU*	earrings
ジャケット	*JAKETTO*	jacket
ジーンズ	*JIINZU*	jeans
かぶります/かぶる	*kaburimasu (kaburu)*	wear on the head
かぶって	*kabutte*	*te* form of *kaburimasu*
かんがえ	*kangae*	idea
きみ	*kimi*	you (used only by males)
きって	*kitte*	postage stamps
コンピューター　ゲーム	*KONPYUUTAA GEEMU*	computer game
コンサート	*KONSAATO*	concert
めがね　を　かけます/ かける	*megane o kakemasu (kakeru)*	wear glasses
めがね　を　かけて	*megane o kakete*	*te* form of *megane o kakemasu*
もちろん	*mochiron*	of course
もも　いろ　の	*momo iro no*	peach pink
もしもし	*moshimoshi*	Hello (on phone only)
むらさき　いろ　の	*murasaki iro no*	purple
など	*nado*	etcetera
ねずみ　いろ　の	*nezumi iro no*	grey
おべんとう	*Obentoo*	packed lunch
プラモデル	*PURAMODERU*	plastic model
ショーツ	*SHOOTSU*	shorts
すばらしい	*subarashii*	wonderful
たこ	*tako*	kite
ゆかた	*yukata*	cotton kimono

Topic Fourteen

あるきます/あるく	*arukimasu (aruku)*	walk
あるいて	*aruite*	*te* form of *arukimasu*
バス	*BASU*	bus
バスのりば	*BASUnoriba*	bus stop
べんり(な)	*benri (na)*	convenient
ビル	*BIRU*	building
ちかてつ	*chikatetsu*	subway
ちょっと	*chotto*	a little bit
でぐち	*deguchi*	exit
でんしゃ	*densha*	train
どこ　の　へや　です　か。	*doko no heya desu ka*	which room is it?

どう です か。	*doo desu ka*	How is it?
どう します か。	*doo shimasu ka*	How will it be?/How will they get along?
ガレージ	*GAREEJI*	house garage
ごちそうさま でした	*Gochisoosama deshita*	Thanks for the meal
はじめ に	*hajime ni*	at first/in the beginning
ひだり に	*hidari ni*	to the left
ひくい	*hikui*	low (adj)/short in height
ひつよう（な）	*hitsuyoo (na)*	necessary (Qual. Noun)
いえ	*ie*	house
いれます/いれる	*iremasu (ireru)*	put in
いれて	*irete*	*te* form of *iremasu*
いりぐち	*iriguchi*	entrance
いそがしい	*isogashii*	busy (adj)
じんじゃ	*jinja*	shrine
じてんじゃ	*jitensha*	bicycle
ジュース	*JUUSU*	juice
かんこう バス	*kankoo BASU*	tourist bus
かお	*kao*	face
こみます/こむ	*komimasu (komu)*	be crowded
こんで います	*konde imasu*	is crowded
こんで いました	*konde imashita*	was crowded
こうそくどうろ	*koosokudooro*	expressway/freeway
こたえ	*kotae*	answer
くうこう	*kuukoo*	airport
まちます/まつ	*machimasu (matsu)*	wait
まがります/まがる	*magarimasu (magaru)*	turn/change direction
まがって	*magatte*	*te* form of *magarimasu*
まっすぐ	*massugu*	straight ahead
まって	*matte*	*te* form of *machimasu*
みぎ に	*migi ni*	to the right
ねます/ねる	*nemasu (neru)*	lie down/go to sleep
ねて	*nete*	*te* form of *nemasu*
にもつ	*nimotsu*	luggage
に のります/のる	*ni norimasu (noru)*	ride on
に のって	*ni notte*	*te* form of *ni norimasu*
ぬぎます/ぬぐ	*nugimasu (nugu)*	undress/take off clothing
ぬいで	*nuide*	*te* form of *nugimasu*
おぼえます/おぼえる	*oboemasu (oboeru)*	remember
おぼえて	*oboete*	*te* form of *oboemasu*
おふろ	*Ofuro*	bath
おふろば	*Ofuroba*	bathroom
おいて	*oite*	*te* form of *okimasu*
おじぎ	*Ojigi*	bow
おきます/おく	*okimasu (oku)*	put
おもい	*omoi*	heavy (adjective)
おもかった です	*omokatta desu*	was heavy
おります/おりる	*orimasu (oriru)*	get off/get out of
おりて	*orite*	*te* form of *orimasu*
おしえます/おしえる	*oshiemasu (oshieru)*	teach/show how
おしえて	*oshiete*	*te* form of *oshiemasu*
おてら	*Otera*	temple
りょこう します/する	*ryokoo shimasu (suru)*	travel
りょこう して	*ryokoo shite*	*te* form of *ryokoo shimasu*

さがします/さがす	*sagashimasu (sagasu)*	seek/look for
さがして	*sagashite*	*te* form of *sagashimasu*
さきます/さく	*sakimasu (saku)*	bloom/blossom
さいて	*saite*	*te* form of *sakimasu*
しんぱい します/する	*shinpai shimasu (suru)*	worry/be anxious
しんぱい して	*shinpai shite*	*te* form of *shinpai shimasu*
しゃしん	*shashin*	photo
シャワー を あびます	*SHAWAA o abimasu*	take a shower
たい です	*tai desu*	want to
たいへん です ね	*taihen desu ne*	It's serious, isn't it?
たかい	*takai*	high/tall/expensive
トースト	*TOOSUTO*	toast
つぎ	*tsugi*	next
うるさい	*urusai*	noisy (adj)
わすれます/わすれる	*wasuremasu (wasureru)*	forget
わすれて	*wasurete*	*te* form of *wasuremasu*
わたります/わたる	*watarimasu (wataru)*	cross over
わたって	*watatte*	*te* form of *watarimasu*
よく	*yoku*	well
よく しって います	*yoku shitte imasu*	know well
ようふく	*yoofuku*	Western style clothing
ゆうびんきょく	*yuubinkyoku*	post office
ざぶとん	*zabuton*	cushion
ぜんぜん	*zenzen*	nothing at all

Interest

だいぶつ	*daibutsu*	the great Buddha
だけ	*dake*	only
ディズニーランド	*DIZUNIIRANDO*	Disneyland
えはがき	*ehagaki*	picture postcard
ふつう	*futsuu*	usual
はたけ	*hatake*	field, vegetable garden
はずかしい	*hazukashii*	embarrassed/ashamed/ shy (adj.)
へび	*hebi*	snake
へいわ	*heiwa*	peace
いっかい	*ikkai*	ground floor
カーテン	*KAATEN*	curtains
カバー	*KABAA*	cover
かべ	*kabe*	wall
かいだん	*kaidan*	staircase
きって	*kitte*	postage stamp
こ/みずうみ	*ko/mizuumi*	lake
こくりつ	*kokuritsu*	national
コントロール	*KONTOROORU*	control
こと	*koto*	thing/matter/affair
もん	*mon*	gate
むし	*mushi*	insect
にかい	*nikai*	first floor/first story
にほんかい	*Nihonkai*	the Japan Sea
ニュース	*NYUUSU*	news
パンダ	*PANDA*	panda
パスポート	*PASUPOOTO*	passport
サイン	*SAIN*	sign

サラダ	*SARADA*	salad
さる	*saru*	monkey
せとないかい	*Setonaikai*	the Inland Sea
しゃしん	*shashin*	photograph
しぶや	*Shibuya*	district of Tokyo
シート　カバー	*SHIITO KABAA*	seat covers
そら	*sora*	sky
すぎ	*sugi*	cedar tree
すごい	*sugoi*	Great!
ターンテーブル	*TAANTEEBURU*	luggage carousel
たまご	*tamago*	egg
タワー	*TAWAA*	tower
と　いいました	*to iimashita*	he/she said
とじます/とじる	*tojimasu (tojiru)*	shut, close books
とじて	*tojite*	*te* form of *tojimasu*
トラック	*TORAKKU*	truck
トローリー	*TOROORII*	luggage trolley, cart
やね	*yane*	roof

Te form and verb list

To make the *te* form of any Japanese verb, it is necessary to know the dictionary or root form of the verb.

In the vocabulary list you will see that all the verbs you know have been offered with this form beside the *masu* form. There are irregular verbs for you to note especially:

kuru	*kimasu*	*kite*	come
suru	*shimasu*	*shite*	do
iku	*ikimasu*	*itte*	go

As you learn more verb forms, the way that these verbs change will always be explained to you.

All other verbs are divided into the two following groups with their subgroups.

GROUP ONE
Verbs that end in **eru** or **iru** take off the *masu* and add **te.**

taberu	*tabemasu*	*tabete*	eat
miru	*mimasu*	*mite*	see
ireru	*iremasu*	*irete*	put in
deru	*demasu*	*dete*	leave
neru	*nemasu*	*nete*	lie down/sleep
okiru	*okimasu*	*okite*	get up
shimeru	*shimemasu*	*shimete*	close
akeru	*akemasu*	*akete*	open

Mieru/miemasu is in this group but the *te* form is rarely used.

GROUP TWO: ALL OTHER REGULAR VERBS
Verbs that end in **bu, mu, nu,** all add **nde.**

yomu	*yomimasu*	*yonde*	read
nomu	*nomimasu*	*nonde*	drink
asobu	*asobimasu*	*asonde*	play
sumu	*sumimasu*	*sunde*	live (in a place)

Verbs that end in **gu** take **ide.**

oyogu	*oyogimasu*	*oyoide*	swim
nugu	*nugimasu*	*nuide*	take off clothes

Verbs that end in **ku** take **ite.**

kaku	*kakimasu*	*kaite*	write
aruku	*arukimasu*	*aruite*	walk
kiku	*kikimasu*	*kiite*	listen/hear
tsuku	*tsukimasu*	*tsuite*	arrive

Verbs that end in **su** take **shite.**

hanasu	*hanashimasu*	*hanashite*	speak

Verbs that end in **u** all take **tte.**

kau	*kaimasu*	*katte*	buy
au	*aimasu*	*atte*	meet

Verbs that end in **ru** also take **tte.**

wataru	*watarimasu*	*watatte*	cross over

magaru	magarimasu	magatte	turn
shiru	shirimasu	shitte	know
suwaru	suwarimasu	suwatte	sit

Verbs that end in **tsu** also take **tte.**

| matsu | machimasu | matte | wait |
| tatsu | tachimasu | tatte | stand |

Kanji Checklist

Here is a list of the *kanji* introduced for your interest only. The list will help you to recognize and remember them.

百	ひゃく	hyaku	hundred
千	せん	sen	thousand
万	まん	man	ten thousand
円	えん	en	yen
肉	にく	niku	meat
魚	さかな	sakana	fish
分	ふん/ぶん	fun/pun	minute
左	ひだり	hidari	left
右	みぎ	migi	right
出口	でぐち	deguchi	exit
入口	いりぐち	iriguchi	entrance
来ます	きます	kimasu	come
着ます	きます	kimasu	wear

カタカナ

ア	a	⁻	ア		タ	ta	ノ	ク	タ	マ	ma	⁻	マ	
イ	i	ノ	イ		チ	chi	⁻	ニ	チ	ミ	mi	`	ˎ	ミ
ウ	u	`	ˊ	ウ	ツ	tsu	`	˵	ツ	ム	mu	∠	ム	
エ	e	⁻	⊤	エ	テ	te	⁻	ニ	テ	メ	me	ノ	メ	
オ	o	⁻	寸	オ	ト	to	Ⅰ	ト		モ	mo	⁻	ニ	モ
カ	ka	⊐	カ		ナ	na	⁻	ナ		ヤ	ya	⁷	ヤ	
キ	ki	⁻	ニ	キ	ニ	ni	⁻	ニ		ユ	yu	⁷	ユ	
ク	ku	ノ	ク		ヌ	nu	フ	ヌ		ヨ	yo	⁷	ⁿ	ヨ
ケ	ke	ノ	⌐	ケ	ネ	ne	`	ネ	ネ	ラ	ra	⁻	ラ	
コ	ko	⊐	コ		ノ	no	ノ			リ	ri	Ⅰ	リ	
サ	sa	⁻	⁺	サ	ハ	ha	ノ	ハ		ル	ru	ノ	ル	
シ	shi	`	˵	シ	ヒ	hi	⁻	ヒ		レ	re	レ		
ス	su	フ	ス		フ	fu	フ			ロ	ro	ⁱ	冂	ロ
セ	se	⁷	セ		ヘ	he	ヘ			ワ	wa	ⁱ	ワ	
ソ	so	`	ソ		ホ	ho	⁻	十	ホ	ヲ	o	⁻	ニ	ヲ
										ン	n	`	ン	

カタカナ

ガ ga	ギ gi	グ gu	ゲ ge	ゴ go
ザ za	ジ ji	ズ zu	ゼ ze	ゾ zo
ダ da	ヂ ji	ヅ zu	デ de	ド do
バ ba	ビ bi	ブ bu	ベ be	ボ bo

パ pa	ピ pi	プ pu	ペ pe	ポ po

キャ kya	キュ kyu	キョ kyo
シャ sha	シュ shu	ショ sho
チャ cha	チュ chu	チョ cho
ニャ nya	ニュ nyu	ニョ nyo
ヒャ hya	ヒュ hyu	ヒョ hyo
ミャ mya	ミュ myu	ミョ myo
リャ rya	リュ ryu	リョ ryo

ギャ gya	ギュ gyu	ギョ gyo
ジャ ja	ジュ ju	ジョ jo
ビャ bya	ビュ byu	ビョ byo

ピャ pya	ピュ pyu	ピョ pyo

ひらがな

あ	a				た	ta				ま	ma		
い	i				ち	chi				み	mi		
う	u				つ	tsu				む	mu		
え	e				て	te				め	me		
お	o				と	to				も	mo		
か	ka				な	na				や	ya		
き	ki				に	ni				ゆ	yu		
く	ku				ぬ	nu				よ	yo		
け	ke				ね	ne				ら	ra		
こ	ko				の	no				り	ri		
さ	sa				は	ha				る	ru		
し	shi				ひ	hi				れ	re		
す	su				ふ	fu				ろ	ro		
せ	se				へ	he				わ	wa		
そ	so				ほ	ho				を	o		
										ん	n		

ひらがな

が ga	ぎ gi	ぐ gu	げ ge	ご go
ざ za	じ ji	ず zu	ぜ ze	ぞ zo
だ da	ぢ ji	づ zu	で de	ど do
ば ba	び bi	ぶ bu	べ be	ぼ bo

ぱ pa	ぴ pi	ぷ pu	ぺ pe	ぽ po

ぎゃ gya	ぎゅ gyu	ぎょ gyo
じゃ ja	じゅ ju	じょ jo
びゃ bya	びゅ byu	びょ byo

きゃ kya	きゅ kyu	きょ kyo
しゃ sha	しゅ shu	しょ sho
ちゃ cha	ちゅ chu	ちょ cho
にゃ nya	にゅ nyu	にょ nyo
ひゃ hya	ひゅ hyu	ひょ hyo
みゃ mya	みゅ myu	みょ myo
りゃ rya	りゅ ryu	りょ ryo

ぴゃ pya	ぴゅ pyu	ぴょ pyo

きゅう kyuu	きょう kyoo
しゅう shuu	しょう shoo
ちゅう chuu	ちょう choo
にゅう nyuu	にょう nyoo
ひゅう hyuu	ひょう hyoo
みゅう myuu	みょう myoo
りゅう ryuu	りょう ryoo